T0181976

Maker Innovations Series

Jump start your path to discovery with the Apress Maker Innovations series! From the basics of electricity and components through to the most advanced options in robotics and Machine Learning, you'll forge a path to building ingenious hardware and controlling it with cutting-edge software. All while gaining new skills and experience with common toolsets you can take to new projects or even into a whole new career.

The Apress Maker Innovations series offers projects-based learning, while keeping theory and best processes front and center. So you get hands-on experience while also learning the terms of the trade and how entrepreneurs, inventors, and engineers think through creating and executing hardware projects. You can learn to design circuits, program AI, create IoT systems for your home or even city, and so much more!

Whether you're a beginning hobbyist or a seasoned entrepreneur working out of your basement or garage, you'll scale up your skillset to become a hardware design and engineering pro. And often using low-cost and open-source software such as the Raspberry Pi, Arduino, PIC microcontroller, and Robot Operating System (ROS). Programmers and software engineers have great opportunities to learn, too, as many projects and control environments are based in popular languages and operating systems, such as Python and Linux.

If you want to build a robot, set up a smart home, tackle assembling a weather-ready meteorology system, or create a brand-new circuit using breadboards and circuit design software, this series has all that and more! Written by creative and seasoned Makers, every book in the series tackles both tested and leading-edge approaches and technologies for bringing your visions and projects to life.

More information about this series at `https://link.springer.com/bookseries/17311`.

Mastering Digitally Controlled Machines

Laser Cutters, 3D Printers, CNC Mills, and Vinyl Cutters to Make Almost Anything

Jean-michel Molenaar
Daniele Ingrassia

Apress®

Mastering Digitally Controlled Machines: Laser Cutters, 3D Printers, CNC Mills, and Vinyl Cutters to Make Almost Anything

Jean-michel Molenaar
Chapareillan, France

Daniele Ingrassia
Schwarzenbek, Germany

ISBN-13 (pbk): 978-1-4842-9848-0
ISBN-13 (electronic): 978-1-4842-9849-7
https://doi.org/10.1007/978-1-4842-9849-7

Managing Director, Apress Media LLC: Welmoed Spahr
Acquisitions Editor: Miriam Haidara
Development Editor: James Markham
Editorial Project Manager: Jessica Vakili

Distributed to the book trade worldwide by Springer Science+Business Media New York, 1 NY Plaza, New York, NY 10004. Phone 1-800-SPRINGER, fax (201) 348-4505, e-mail orders-ny@springer-sbm.com, or visit www.springeronline.com. Apress Media, LLC is a California LLC and the sole member (owner) is Springer Science + Business Media Finance Inc (SSBM Finance Inc). SSBM Finance Inc is a **Delaware** corporation.

For information on translations, please e-mail booktranslations@springernature.com; for reprint, paperback, or audio rights, please e-mail bookpermissions@springernature.com.

Apress titles may be purchased in bulk for academic, corporate, or promotional use. eBook versions and licenses are also available for most titles. For more information, reference our Print and eBook Bulk Sales web page at http://www.apress.com/bulk-sales.

Any source code or other supplementary material referenced by the author in this book is available to readers on the Github repository: https://github.com/Apress/Mastering-Digitally-Controlled-Machines. For more detailed information, please visit https://www.apress.com/gp/services/source-code.

Paper in this product is recyclable

Table of Contents

About the Authors

Jean-michel Molenaar helped create the first Fab Labs in the Netherlands, after which he moved on to other countries to do the same. He has managed a company in the UK selling tools internationally, implemented the use of digitally controlled machines at Tufts University as a Professor of the Practice, and started the Resilience Collective, a humanitarian effort to use digital technology for the most vulnerable populations. He has created makerspaces in over 12 countries and has spoken about education and digital tools during various conferences around the world. He currently works for the Fab Foundation and lives in the French Alps with his wife and their three sons.

Daniele Ingrassia has taught at Fab Academy for six years and served as a Fab Lab mentor since 2017. He is a Fab Lab Guru and founder of InMachines, a company focused on open source digital fabrication machines for makerspace and fab labs. With a background in computer science, he now implements local digital fabrication courses in official university programs and develops open source hardware. Leaving behind a long series of Fab Lab–made projects, Daniele managed to develop several open source machines, such as a dual-source laser cutter and the largest open source 3D printer. With projects being replicated in many other countries worldwide, Daniele has held several fabrication and machine building workshops around the world. He lives in Schleswig-Holstein, Germany.

About the Technical Reviewer

Wendy Neale, DipEd, is a word nerd and editor, maker, mender, and gleaner.

About This Book

The maker movement, Fab Labs, makerspaces, hackerspaces, 100K garages ...

There was a time when, if you needed a table, you went to see a woodworker and you would explain the size of your living room, the kind of wood you liked, and the shape of your desired table, and with chisels and blades, saws, and glue, the craftsman would build you a table.

You can still do this.

But not many people do.

Instead, they go to stores, the names of which we won't mention, where they get tables that are fabricated by the thousands and often contain more air per cubic centimeter than wood.

This is not a mistake we made as a society, but the progress we have gone through, thanks to, among many others, Henry Ford. If it wasn't for this model, not nearly as many people would have access to the kind of products they can now afford in their daily lives.

But perhaps this model is no longer the best model for the world we live in, nor has it developed in a way that is healthy for the planet.

In recent years, many different places have been created where (almost) anyone can access and use machines to make whatever they want. Some are more connected than others, but they are all spaces for turning ideas into objects, which places the power (and responsibility) to create back into partially everyone's hands and allows us to start making changes to how we consume and create.

One of these kinds of spaces, Fab Labs, came into being as a result of Neil Gershenfeld, an MIT[1] professor, teaching a class on "How to Make (Almost) Anything" and installing a digital fabrication space (or lab) for his students. The content of this space he shared freely with the world in conjunction with a vision of shared designs and open access to anyone interested. This, coming at the time where more and more people all over the globe started to call themselves "makers," came at the right moment, and the idea (and the spaces) spread quickly across the globe. The grand vision behind the class, which was at the birth of these spaces, is the eventual creation of the "*Star Trek* replicator" or a machine that makes anything, anywhere. This machine is still quite some years of research away, but it's something we are heading toward.

If we look at the progression of digital computation, we often forget how quickly we went from computers being very bulky and expensive tools accessible only to researchers and wealthy companies to being so ubiquitous that we don't even notice them anymore. Your house is filled with them, you carry them around, and we rely on them like it has always been like that.

Now imagine a similar progression in digital fabrication. Will we carry "personal fabricators" in our pockets in 30 years? Society will have to undergo a profound change if this becomes a reality, and we can hardly imagine how this is possible looking at the tools of today's makerspaces. But don't forget that Kenneth Harry Olsen from Digital (a company building computers) famously said, "No one needs a computer at home." The company closed its doors not long after, and chances are you are reading this on a tablet or phone.

Fab Labs, makerspaces – for us they are the start of a new socioeconomic era, the ramifications of which we cannot yet fully foresee. But their open nature and accessibility imply that this paradigm shift can come from not just the hands of the big companies building the

[1] Massachusetts Institute of Technology (Cambridge, USA).

matter of our lives, but YOU. You can go to any one of these spaces and learn how to make things, things you or others need in their lives, and learn how to become something other than a consumer in the world of Henry Ford. Look at these tools as the first computers, not that easy to use maybe, but already very powerful in the implications they carry. So appropriate yourself these tools, and become an actor in the changing field of fabrication and consumption, and perhaps in the future we'll see fewer trucks crossing each other when they drive across our countries full of silica, or products derived thereof.

So Why This Book?

This book is meant for people interested in learning more about the currently available tools and means of fabrication that are accessible today, but also for those who have been working in these kinds of spaces and looking to deepen their knowledge of the techniques or are looking for inspiration.

You can thus read it cover to back, but also treat it as a source of technical info, skipping directly to the part you need to know more about.

We have divided the book into chapters about individual machines (laser cutter, vinyl cutter, CNC [computer numerically controlled] mill, 3D printer) and a chapter about building machines yourself, and of course we also discuss computer-aided design (CAD), or how to design for digitally controlled tools. At the very end of the book, you'll find a section with only technical info, like recommended cutting speeds for CNC milling, general settings for laser cutters, and detailed information on materials you might use.

We hope you won't just enjoy reading all this but that it will inspire you to go into your garage or out of your door and to a makerspace, Fab Lab, or community workshop and *start building stuff* – for you, for your neighbors, for your family, for a better planet, for the fun of building, for your kids, for your company, your startup, your grandma, or just because you can.

Building the future with Fab Labs - Neil Gershenfeld

Prof. Neil Gershenfeld is the Director of MIT's Center for Bits and Atoms, where his unique laboratory is breaking down boundaries between the digital and physical worlds, from pioneering quantum computing to digital fabrication to the Internet of Things. He's the founder of a global network of over two thousand fab labs in 125 countries, chairs the Fab Foundation, and leads the Fab Academy.

After digital revolutions in communication and computation, we're now living through a digital revolution in fabrication. This one completes the other two, and is likely to be even more significant than them, because it brings the programmability of the world of bits out here to the world of atoms where we live.

The digital revolutions in communication and computation were forecast by Gordon Moore based on five data points, showing the doubling of the number of transistors in an integrated circuit. He projected that forward for ten years; the doubling actually continued for fifty.

The digital revolution in fabrication can now be seen in the doubling of fab labs, from one to over one thousand. These room-filling facilities for digital fabrication correspond to the minicomputer stage in computing. Those technologies eventually evolved to fit in your pocket, but that's the time when the Internet, email, video games, and word processing all evolved. And that's when the corresponding new kinds of businesses and institutions emerged along with them.

Likewise, it's not necessary to wait for the research roadmap to lead to Star Trek-style replicators. Programs like the Fab Academy, Fab Foundation, and Fab Cities are now doing the same for this digital revolution. Jean Michel Molenaar and Daniele Ingrassia have been leaders in the spread of fab labs, technically, organizationally, and pedagogically. Mastering the material in this book is the path to participating in this revolution today, and to shaping a future where anyone can make (almost) anything, anywhere.

Introduction

This book can be read and/or used in a few ways. Here we will take a quick look at the subjects discussed in this book, whom it is for, and how we have put it together.

When writing this book, we realized it's quite a challenge to create something that appeals to many (aspiring) makers of different skill and knowledge levels and to make sure there is enough, but not too much, information about all the possibilities digital tools give you.

We believe we have been able to create a great collection of information for you, the reader, but are also sure there is much more out there we did not speak about or explain. So take this book not as a final step, but either as an entry to learn more about the exciting possibilities of digital fabrication or to deepen your knowledge and widen your skill set!

You will need several parts to go from an idea to a running machine. First is the CAD (computer-assisted design) software, which as you will learn in Chapter 1 can be one of many. After that, you will need to generate a toolpath from that two- or three-dimensional (2D or 3D) design, so you need a CAM (computer-assisted manufacturing) program. Then, you'll need to decide on how you are going to control your machine and send it the G-code that has been generated in the CAM software.

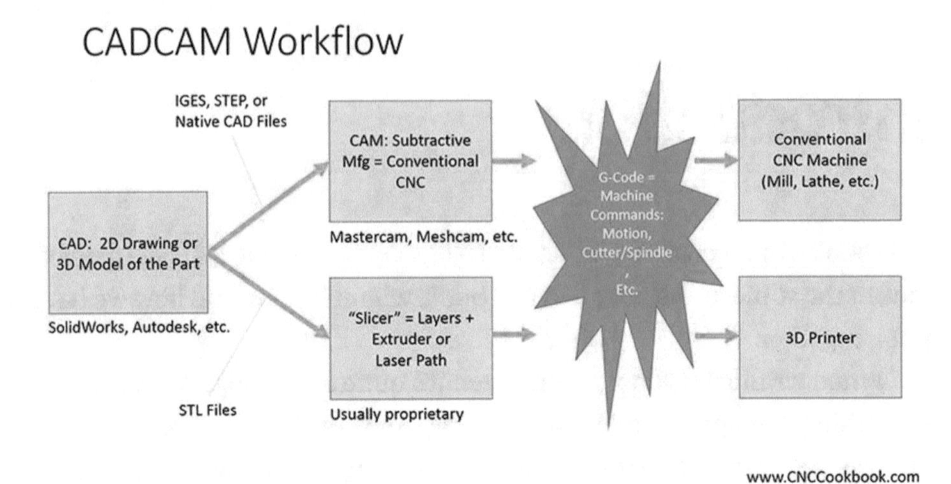

Figure 1. *CADCAM workflow (`www.cnccookbook.com/MTCNCSoftware.htm`)*

Each chapter of the book is either about a different digital fabrication machine type, software about how to make designs and operate machines, or how to build one. If you are interested in a specific type of machine, you can directly jump to the chapter and dive in to learn related information on how to use it, how it is made, or how to look for one to buy. Knowledge from chapters and parts made with different machines can be combined to achieve more advanced results, which can allow you to prototype your idea or even to build your own machine.

Let's start by taking a look at some history of numerically controlled machines and their impact over the years and then explore the capabilities.

History of Computer Numerical Control

The basis of the machines you'll read about in this book comes from NC – short for numerical control. But it could be traced back further to automated systems that were built in the 1820s or 1830s or even further to automata built long before that.

In 1818, Thomas Blanchard, an American inventor, created a machine for copying gun barrels. The lathe that he built basically copied an existing shape by following its contours with a roller and cutting a duplicate of the part using that movement. This obviously had no numerical control – the original shape had to be made by hand, and there was no possibility to truly program the machine.

***Figure 2.** A Blanchard lathe, with gun stock on the machine* (`https://commons.wikimedia.org/wiki/File:Harpers_Ferry_gun_smith_shop_-_Blanchard_lathe_-_01.jpg`)

By using cams (a mechanical linkage that allows you to translate rotational movement into linear motion or the other way around), systems were built that could be "programmed" in an abstract way. You could not directly encode the information about the part to be made into the system, but manually had to make the part that encoded the information. The Jacquard loom, invented by Joseph Marie Jacquard in 1804, used a series of punched cards that were "read" by the machine and translated into patterns of movement. This kind of information encoded on cards was also used by early computers and things like automata and self-playing pianos.

Before the birth of true numerical control, other systems were built that could copy shapes or that could be first moved by hand, where the moves were "saved" so they could be repeated without human intervention after.

The real start happened in 1942, when Parsons Corporation got the request to manufacture complex parts for helicopter rotor blades that were traditionally made of wood. To build these parts, Sikorsky Aircraft (the client) shared the shape with John Parsons by giving him a design made of 17 points that he had to connect using curves. This was used to make an outline and cut the final parts. But one of the wooden parts failed, and they started to look into other options, like making the parts out of metal. The tools they needed to make to use metal would have to be made out of tool steel, which was complex to shape.

Parsons went to visit Wright Field, an aircraft base, where he met Frank Stulen, who had such good ideas that he ended up working at Parsons Corp. Stulen's brother, who worked at Curtiss-Wright Propeller Division, gave him the idea of using punched card machines to calculate 200 instead of 17 points along the curves of the desired shape, which could then be used to drill on those locations and create the rough outline that could be shaped into its final form by hand. Basically the idea was to take a line and create points on that line that were spaced using the diameter of the tool to drill, thus creating enough holes to cut out the part wanted.

Once the calculations were done, they took them to the machine shop and manually moved a Swiss jig borer (a tool to drill holes, basically) to each of the positions before drilling down. This was a slow process, but it allowed them to reach high accuracy in the final product.

Having finished the process, Parsons realized the potential if the system they had developed would be further automated. In 1949, the Air Force provided him with funding to further develop his ideas, but they quickly ran into technical difficulties. The system they were using was not able to drive the motors with enough precision to make the wanted cuts. What they needed was a feedback loop from the motors, to make sure they moved the right distance. Since this was beyond the capabilities of Parsons himself, he got in contact with Gordon Brown, who was working on feedback systems at MIT.

The team at MIT that started working on the new system realized that Parson's idea could be further perfected. If the machine would not just drill down at the given points but follow the line between the points, it would produce products that would need less or no finishing after the automated process.

Initially the project at MIT would create a controller that could then be attached to a machine at Parson's workshop, but eventually MIT simply purchased a 28-inch Cincinnati Hydro-Tel vertical-spindle contour milling machine, which they modified significantly. Many original parts of the machine were removed or replaced, and controllers were fabricated for each of the axes. The numerical system that would control the machine was almost the same size as the machine itself, something hard to imagine today looking at a laptop or tablet computer that can control many different machines! The newly created system was able to move three axes with a precision of 0.0005" (0.0127 mm) by programming it using punched tape. The machine was also equipped with a feedback system – motors that would send electrical signals back to the controllers allowing them to assure the distance moved was correct.

***Figure 3.** The first numerically controlled machine at MIT (`www.joostrekveld.net/wp/wp-content/uploads/2016/11/MITnumericcontrol1.jpg`)*

In an electronic lab at MIT, engineers now are

Teaching Power Tools to Run Themselves

By Hartley E. Howe

SO JOE WORKSHOPPER figures he'd like to turn out a set of dining-room chairs—and at the same time break in his new Model 100 Super Tapemaster. Joe whips down to the hardware store and looks over photographs of different designs. He settles on a Swedish pattern popular 'way back in 1955—delicate and handsome, but full of difficult reverse curves.

That doesn't worry Joe. He plunks down $10 for a week's rental of a batch of tapes—one each for legs, arms, back and seat.

That night, he clamps a nice piece of birch into his Tapemaster, slips the tape into the control box, flips the switch, and sits back with his pipe and the new issue of *Outdoor Life*.

Forty minutes later, the rumble of the Tapemaster stops and Joe takes a look. One leg is finished. So he clamps on another piece of birch . . .

Sure it's a dream—in 1955. But the engineering basis for Joe's Tapemaster exists right now. Sitting up in the Servomechanisms Laboratory of the Massachusetts Institute of Technology in Cambridge, Mass., is a milling machine that will turn out any metal part at the command of a little roll of tape. Originally a standard, vertical 28" Cincinnati Hydro-Tel, it now has hitched to it $50,000 worth of electronics.

To conceive, design and build the MIT machine took some quarter-million

Punches in tape code size and time of each cut.

Tape is fed into computer where code is converted to electric signals.

Too big yet for home shop, this MIT milling machine is run by computer-control at left.

Signals control three-dimensional movement of cutter head, time each cut.

***Figure 4.** Article on the first CNC mill, as published in Popular Science, August 1955 (`www.turkcadcam.net/rapor/CADCAM-tarihcesi/MITcnc1.jpg`)*

While the project was a great success looking at the new technological advances that were made, the machine was extremely complex and expensive to build.

While various efforts were made to develop similar but cheaper systems, the idea of automating fabrication did not immediately take off, probably also because of the fact that the time needed to produce parts was not significantly reduced, but simply shifted to a different task, that of translating the designs to punched cards for the controllers.

The step toward CNC (instead of just NC) was taken when MIT researchers created a program that would create the punched cards automatically instead of making them by hand. This led to the creation of teams working on a standardized language to program machines and several groups joining together to combine this into the world's first computer-controlled NC system.

***Figure 5.** The first CNC mill, with the computer/controller on the right (www.cncmanufacturing.com.au/wp-content/uploads/2016/06/The-CNC-Story.jpg)*

From 1959 on, parallel to the advancement of machines, different organizations were working on CAD, and it was the combination of that with CNC and the drastic decrease in the cost of computers that led to the systems we have today.

In 1968, John Parsons got recognition for the work he had done and the revolution he started when he was given the Numerical Control Society's inaugural Joseph Marie Jacquard Memorial Award. Next to that, the Society of Manufacturing Engineers named Parsons "The Father of the Second Industrial Revolution" in 1975.

Today, you can go out and buy a machine yourself that is better than some of the first machines, or you could even choose to build it yourself! While the initial CNC machines were mills and drills, today you can buy or build laser cutters, vinyl cutters, 3D printers, and more, which are all controlled from your laptop or even your phone.

If you want to know more about how CNC mills further developed over the years, just go to the beginning of Chapter 4.

Overview of Capabilities

If you learn how to use all the machines described in this book, you'll be able to make (almost) anything, provided you also know how to design parts and electronics. Some materials are harder to work with than others, and machines that are able to work with materials such as metal or glass are less often found in makerspaces, but are still within reach. Similarly, learning how to weld or blow glass can often be done with professionals in dedicated spaces and is a rewarding hobby to take up, even if you don't yet know what to make!

This general overview will give you an idea of the capabilities of the different tools, but is absolutely not exhaustive.

Machines	Capabilities	Materials	Additional Needs
Laser cutter	2D	**Cutting:** Wood and derivatives, (some) plastics, cardboard, paper **Engraving:** Same as the preceding ones + glass, ceramics, stone, some metals (depending on the laser)	Compressed air, filter, and/or fan for extraction of fumes
CNC mill	2D and 3D	**Cutting:** Wood and derivatives, plastics, soft metals, composites, printed circuit boards (PCBs) **Engraving:** Glass, ceramics, stone, PCBs	Dust collection
Vinyl cutter	2D	**Cutting:** Vinyl, paper, copper tape	None
3D printer	3D	**Printing:** Nylon, PLA (polylactic acid), ABS (acrylonitrile butadiene styrene), resin, gypsum, gold, silver, stainless steel, titanium, paper	Proper ventilation and in some cases additional systems

Now that you know how we arrived at the point in time where almost anyone can use these tools and machines (so that includes you), it's time to look at the machines that you will be able to find close to you and what you can do with them.

One of the best ways to really understand and learn how to make the things in your head is to try and experiment, check the results, and go try again adjusting parameters. While you are reading this book, try and locate a makerspace, tech shop, or Fab Lab close to you, and find out how you can use their machines. You can start with cheap materials, and if you don't yet know what to make yourself, you can duplicate some projects of others, which is a great way to understand the machines and techniques better.

Are you ready? Let's start by diving into CAD and then look at a machine that is both easy to use and gives you many different possibilities – the laser cutter.

CHAPTER 1

Computer-Aided Design

Introduction

Before you can make anything with a computer-controlled machine, you'll have to "tell" the machine what you'd like to fabricate. Any object you like to fabricate needs a 2D and/or 3D design file to start from, which you can either make by yourself or grab online. Before being usable by machines, data in the file is converted to a toolpath, telling the machine what to do to fabricate the desired object. It's like converting bits (of the model file) to atoms (of the fabricated object).

There are a myriad of ways you can go about this, and if you are a beginner at this point, we recommend trying different programs until you find the ones that fit your way of thinking and your needs. There usually isn't a single solution to make everything, but rather different ways or combinations, depending on the object you'd like to make. Before starting to use any of the machines in this book, a good grasp of CAD programs will prepare you to design parts for them.

You could also start designing something without a computer at all and then digitize the drawing or image and use it with a machine. We sometimes do this in workshops with kids (especially if they are numerous) where everyone makes a drawing with a pencil, which we then scan (with

J-m. Molenaar and D. Ingrassia, *Mastering Digitally Controlled Machines*, Maker Innovations Series, https://doi.org/10.1007/978-1-4842-9849-7_1

a flatbed scanner) and engrave onto a material with a laser cutter. This way everyone gets a laser cut object they designed to take home, without the need to know how to use a computer!

In general you can design in 2D or 3D using GUIs (graphical user interfaces) where you use the mouse or a stylus to design by dragging around objects and parts, or you can use code, describing the object as formulas and mathematical equations. Modern CAD software often offers functions beyond the creation of shapes, like simulation, rendering, animations, virtual reality, and more.

The programs that we will discuss in this chapter all belong to what is known as CAD – computer-aided design. This works together with CAM (computer-aided manufacturing) to create parts. You'll learn more about CAM in each chapter, as toolpathing is specific for each machine.

Because there are so many different software solutions out there, we cannot discuss all of them in this chapter. At the end of this book, you will find a list of software available at the time this book was written, both open source and commercial, so that you can try and find one that is a perfect fit for your needs.

History

All CAD programs are based on Euclidean geometry, so in a way we could say computer-aided design could not exist if it weren't for Euclid of Alexandria who laid down the ground rules in 350 BC. But let's look at the more recent history.

In 1957, Dr. Patrick J. Hanratty created PRONTO (Program for Numerical Tooling Operations), which was CAM software. It was built to control machines, rather than design parts. Even so, he is mostly referred to as the "father of CAD/CAM."

It was in the early 1960s that the first program was developed that allowed a user to design lines on a computer. Ivan Sutherland developed his program "Sketchpad" as part of his study at MIT, which made use of a light pen to draw directly onto the screen of a computer. This of course only allowed for two-dimensional designs, and the software was used by engineers for technical drawings.

Between 1966 and 1968, Frenchman Pierre Bézier created UNISURF as part of his work for Renault to make it easier to design tools and parts for the automotive industry. This was the first system capable of three-dimensional design.

In the early years of CAD, it was really only used by the aerospace and automotive industries, as they were the only ones who could afford the then very expensive computer systems capable of running that kind of software. As the use was limited to these industries, internal teams would use these systems exclusively for their company.

One of the first commercially available CAD packages was called ADAM (automated drafting and machining) and was released in 1972 by MCS, who were already providing software to companies individually. In 1977, CATIA (Computer-Aided Three-Dimensional Interactive Application) was created by "Société des Avions Marcel Dassault," a French manufacturer of airplanes, which became one of industry's standards. It was ported to UNIX systems in 1988, making it available for computers like the ones we find in homes today.

In 1979 the IGES (Initial Graphics Exchange Specification) file format was developed by Boeing, General Electric, and the NBS (National Bureau of Standards), and it was implemented the year after. This was the first standardized file format for sharing CAD information across platforms.

Many different programs were developed during that period, but still mostly for large companies with money to spend. The arrival of AutoCAD changed that, in conjunction with the arrival of the IBM PC in 1981. The first version of AutoCAD released in 1983 was still mostly 2D, but it was only a fraction of the price of the other systems. In 1990 standard computers became powerful enough to handle 3D geometry and made the arrival of many of the programs that are still around today possible.

Where CAD/CAM started out as a tool for large industries, it has become available for anyone to use at home and is no longer only for designing machines and airplanes. Let's take a look at some basic concepts that are good to understand before designing your first piece.

Some Basic Concepts and Notions

If you are getting into designing objects using software, you'll quickly discover that there are not only many different programs and techniques to choose from but also a host of concepts and principles you need to understand to work with them. If you do not yet understand the difference between vector and raster (pixelized) images or between NURBS (Non-Uniform Rational Basis Spline) and meshes or if you don't have a clue what a Boolean operation is, keep reading. If all this is as clear as day, you can probably skip this part and go to the part about the software packages.

Let's start with the difference between raster and vector. **Raster** images are made out of pixels and are easy to understand. You can simply think of them as little squared dots that together make up an image. This means, for example, that a line drawing made up of pixels is basically a collection of very small blocks that provide you with the image of the line. When pixels are many, and very small, you cannot see the squared edges allowing the display of smooth curves (to the human eye) and to draw complex details such as in photos. If you would draw the same line as a **vector**, instead of using pixels, the line is defined by a mathematical formula drawing from point A to point B. Using formulas to draw shapes makes it possible for them to be changed and makes them infinitely zoomable. A vectorized line operates independently of resolution, meaning you can scale the drawing up or down, without losing quality or changing the shape of the line. If you would scale up a raster drawing, one would start to see the squares (pixels) it is made out of. Even though you can scale or zoom in vectors indefinitely, they would become too complex when functions are needed to draw images full of details, such as photos.

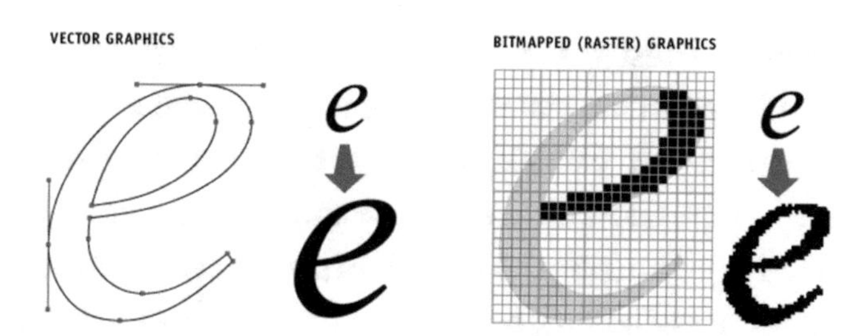

Figure 1-1. *The same image designed using vector (left) and raster (right) (https://signalizenj.files.wordpress.com/2015/01/vector_raster.gif)*

Both in 2D and 3D modeling, you will encounter something called **Boolean operations**. These are, simply put, ways to add or subtract parts of shapes from others. If you have done some programming, you will know the words AND, OR, NOT, and XOR, representing logical operations. If you apply this to shapes, you get what's explained in Figure 1-2, the option to create new shapes by using two existing ones – keeping either both, one minus the other, only the part where they overlap, etc.

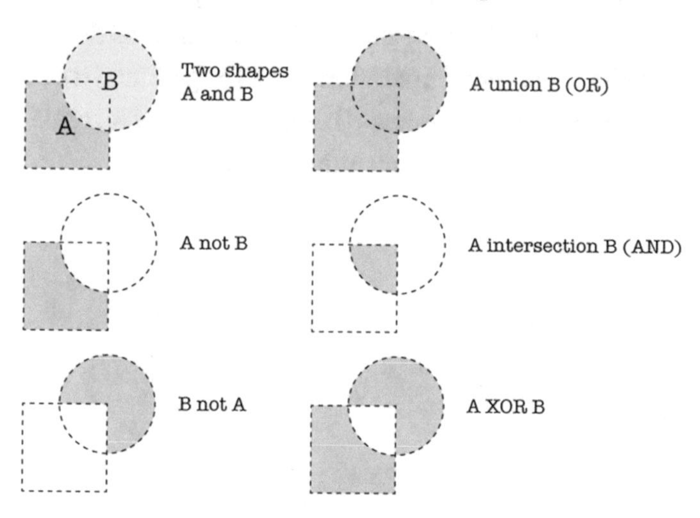

Figure 1-2. *Boolean operations for 2D drawings (https://en.wikipedia.org/wiki/Boolean_operations_on_polygons#/media/File:Boolean_operations_on_shapes.png)*

Working with 3D design, you will often use Constructive Solid Geometry (CSG), which means you will be working with solid shapes (spheres, cubes, etc.) and using Boolean operations to create the desired object. Then there are a few different techniques to represent objects. We won't go too deep into the details, but in general you can distinguish between meshes (tessellation), b-rep (boundary representation), and f-rep (function representation).

The way **meshes** represent objects is by using triangles to form the three-dimensional object. You can compare this to pixels, in the sense that scaling the object will diminish the precision. If you have a small CSG sphere and scale it up, you will end up with an approximation of a sphere made of lots of triangles.

If meshes are pixels in 3D, then **b-rep** (boundary representation) is the equivalent of vectors. B-rep uses mathematical formulas to create lines that dictate the object surface or limits, like NURBS (Non-Uniform Rational Basis Spline), so they are similar to vectors in 2D design. Another way to represent shapes is using **f-rep** (function representation), which means your object is represented as a mathematical formula describing the volume. If you do Boolean operations on a f-rep object, it's not rebuilt using triangles (mesh) or vector lines (b-rep), but a new formula is created that represents the volume of the resulting space.

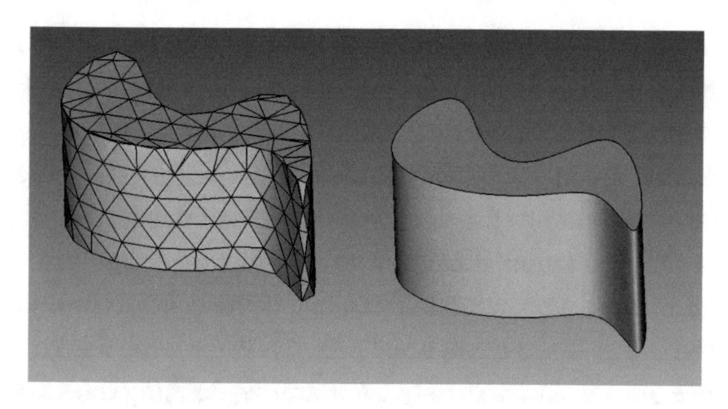

***Figure 1-3.** The same 3D model is made as a mesh (left) and as a b-rep (right) (`www.freecadweb.org/wiki/images/1/1a/Mesh_vs_brep.jpg`)*

Parametric Design

Whether you are new to CAD or an experienced user, it's a good idea to use parametric design, unless you are certain your models or parts of them are never ever going to be changed or reused (if you do everything right the first time, skip this part ...but hey, be honest ...).

CAD programs that are parametric basically allow you to define parameters to design parts and to define relationships between them. If you change one or more parameters, a part automatically adapts to the change and also the other parts depending on it. Often, parametric design software also allows you to apply design constraints. Constraints are geometrical rules to be applied to your design that will be automatically kept when your design changes. Examples are to constrain lines to be perpendicular, equal, vertical, horizontal, coincident, etc.

Let's start with a simple example. Imagine you are designing a chair, where the legs need to fit into slots that are part of the seat. The size of the slots is obviously[1] dependent on the thickness of your material, so if you change materials, you would need to change the design. With a parametric system, you could change the thickness of the material; all the parts that need to be changed automatically do so too. Another simple example is designing a nut and a bolt and defining that if you change the thickness of the bolt, the nut needs to change accordingly. Parametric design can also add/remove objects automatically, for example, defining rules saying how many screws are needed according to the length of an object.

All this is possible with parametric design, which then leads to very different ways of creating products and architectural structures. Because you can define relationships, you can start creating more complex and organic shapes that would be almost impossible to create without this technique – especially if they need to be changed by hand one by one. Look at the roof of Shenzhen Bao'an Airport in China in Figure 1-4. Its roof is designed using parametric technique, yielding very organic-looking shapes.

[1] If this is not obvious, consider taking a bar of 10mm-thick material and fitting it into a square hole – the hole needs to be 10mm in at least one of the directions, right?

***Figure 1-4.** Roof of Shenzhen Bao'an Airport in China (`www.fuksas.it/files/styles/full/adaptive-image/public/media-images/projects/shenzhen-baoan-international-airport-terminal-3-1-691.jpg?itok=KhLx1tpp`)*

File Formats

There are different file formats that you can work with, and it will depend on the program you use what file type you end up with. It's useful to understand the limitations and possibilities of some of these formats as they don't all handle the same precision and information.

Some file formats can store your BOM (bill of materials),[2] include color, and contain multiple parts. Some allow for high precision (b-rep or f-rep), some allow for fast rendering[3] (meshes), and some contain both. Next to that, we can distinguish between "neutral" formats (not tied to a program) and proprietary formats that are part of a software package.

[2] A list of the raw materials, sub- and intermediate assemblies and components, parts, and quantities of each needed to manufacture an end product.

[3] The process of generating an image from a 2D or 3D model.

Many people using 3D printers will use the STereoLithography (STL) file format, which is lightweight but does not allow for color or any additional information and uses a tessellated mesh to represent the object. In comparison, IGES (the first standard) can contain a BOM and color, but only allows for single parts. The STEP format allows for the most flexibility - you can include a BOM, multiple parts, and color information, and it's high precision because it uses b-rep. If you want to look at the file (specifically online), it will need more computing power though. VRML is a nice format if you'd like to show your 3D design online - it's a mesh (so less precise), but can contain a BOM and color.

Where IGES, STL, STEP, and VRML are formats shared between programs, software packages will have their own format with their individual specifications, but almost all of them will always allow for maximum precision and inclusion of information.

Look at the end of the book for a list of file formats and their options.

Open Source, Free, and Commercial Software

Now that we have explored some of the basic concepts behind computer-aided design, let's take a look at the software.

There are many different packages you can use to design your desired piece, and much depends on your way of working. Next to that, we can distinguish three different kinds of software (not only for design but in all fields): open source, free, and commercial.

Open Source

You can obtain and use open source software for free, you can use it to commercialize anything you design with it, and sometimes you can sell the software itself. Open source software also gives you, as the name implies, access to the source code of the software, allowing you to change and modify the original program.

Some very useful open source software are discussed briefly in the following.

GIMP

If you do not need 3D functionality and mainly want to focus on image and photo manipulation, take a look at GIMP (GNU Image Manipulation Program), which is used for things like photo retouching, image composition, and more. This program is designed to mainly work with pixels, not vectors. It's comparable to Photoshop (which we'll discuss later in the "Commercial Software" section) but completely free and runs on GNU/Linux, Windows, and MacOS X.

Inkscape

If you want to design using vectors, try Inkscape, which we can compare with Illustrator (again, more in the "Commercial Software" section on that). Inkscape is used for artistic and technical illustrations such as cartoons, clip art, logos, typography, and much more and runs on GNU/ Linux, Windows, and MacOS X.

Blender

Perhaps the most well-known 3D software in the open source category is Blender, a 3D modeling and animation package made by the Blender Foundation.

Blender is a 3D modeling software with the mission to give artists 3D tools. The possibilities of Blender are quite stunning (ranging from simple 3D objects to full-blown animated movies and games), mainly focusing on animations and visual effects, but the interface itself can be quite a challenge, especially for people who are already used to some of the more traditional design interfaces. Blender does offer some parametric features, also in the definition of the object's primitives.

Figure 1-5. *Blender interface (*`www.blender.org/wp-content/uploads/2013/05/rendered_object_mode_with_wire-1024x646.png?x71180`*)*

Figure 1-6. *Still from an animation movie made with Blender (`https://i.ytimg.com/vi/mmFR3DxsQFs/maxresdefault.jpg`)*

FreeCAD

Developed and supported since 2001, FreeCAD has grown in stability and functionalities in recent years, becoming the main alternative as open source parametric 3D CAD software with a GUI. FreeCAD natively implements parametric design and a set of constraints to manage relations between 2D elements. The software is divided in workbenches, each implementing a subset of functionalities, with more and more workbenches being independently developed and added to the main program. By default, more than 20 workbenches are available in FreeCAD, offering functionalities such as part design, sketching, drafting, simulation, computer-aided manufacturing, rendering, inspection, and mesh reworking.

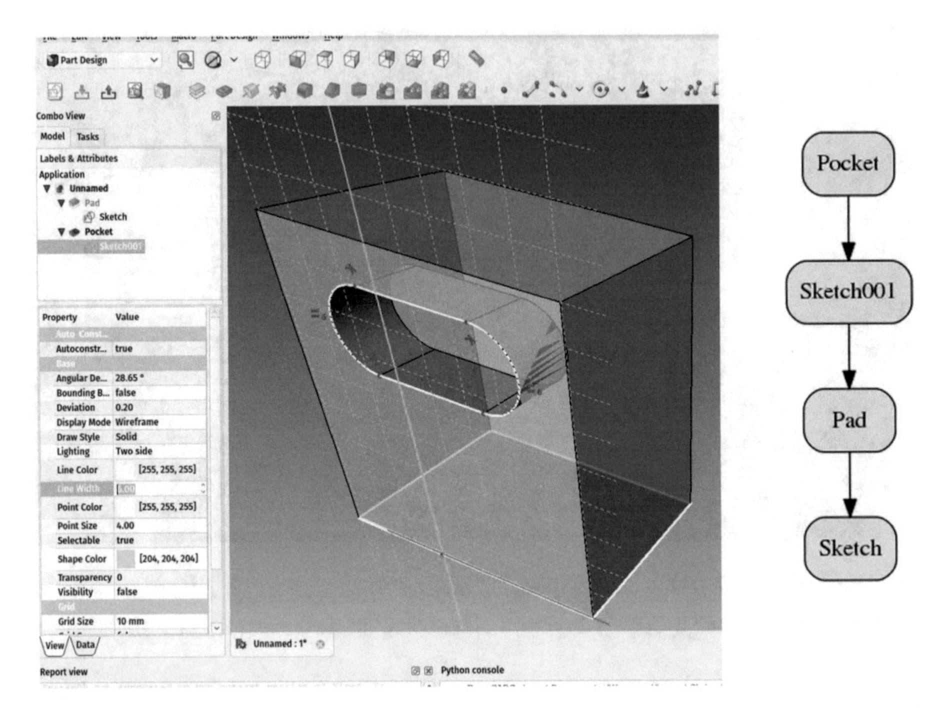

Figure 1-7. *FreeCAD parametric design (`https://wiki.freecadweb.org/About_FreeCAD`)*

OpenSCAD

A different open source solution is OpenSCAD, which allows users to "code" objects by using a script language. The code defines the desired object, which OpenSCAD can then render and save as a 3D file. If one would, for instance, like to create a cube of 20 units in either direction, simply typing "cube(20);" and rendering will do the trick. Parametric design is implicit in OpenSCAD, because functions to create 3D objects have parameters to change them according to any of the logic defined in the code.

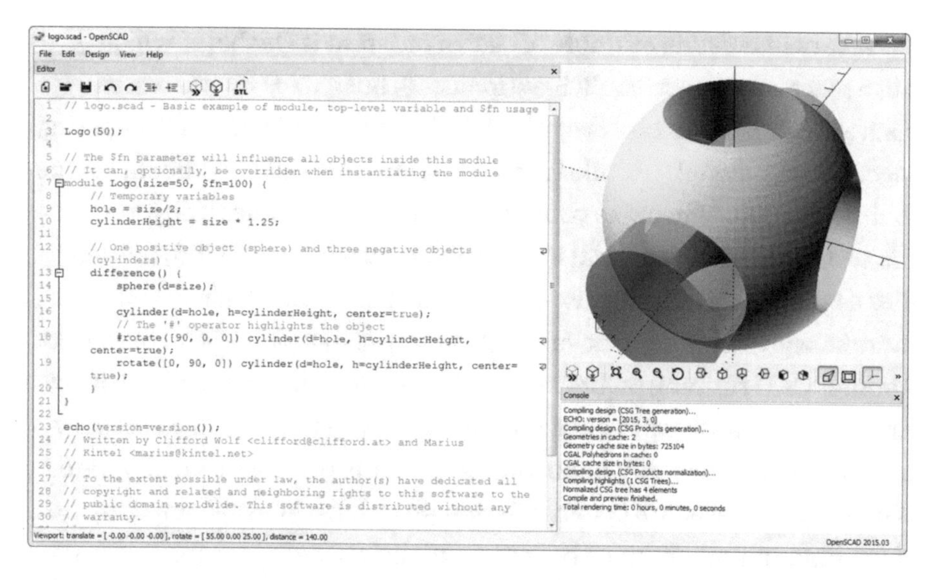

Figure 1-8. *OpenSCAD, with the interface for coding (left) and the output rendered in a window (right)*

Other open source programs using a graphical interface are (among others) LibreCAD and BRL-CAD. LibreCAD is a 2D CAD that has a similar workflow to AutoCAD to create 2D technical drawings. BRL-CAD uses optional parametric 3D modeling often referred to as belonging in the mechanical computer-aided design software category (like SolidWorks and Inventor; see in the following).

Free Software

There is a whole bunch of software that you can use to design your pieces that are not open source, but are free to use. This means you don't have access to the code that makes up the software (and you are thus not able to modify it), but you don't have to pay to use it. Often you will have to sign in or create an account and share your designs freely on the Web.

A very interesting example of such a program is Onshape, which is not a piece of software you'll have to install, but a CAD interface that runs entirely on your browser, which has as an added bonus that working together on a digital CAD file is as easy as sharing a text document via the Web. If you decide to make your designs freely accessible to anyone on the Web, you can create (and if you want, download and build) as many files as you'd like, but they also propose licenses if you'd like to work on more sensitive projects that you do not (yet) wish to share with the world. Another CAD running on browsers is Tinkercad, who on their website even say that "no design experience is required." It will not let you create very complex objects or verify them, but as a starting point it's a great option. With browser-based CAD software, you don't have to install anything on your computer other than a browser, and the software is accessible from any operating system.

There are more and more platforms dedicated to sharing digital design files (2D and 3D) and the creation of communities around this. Once you have many objects online in an easily searchable repository, there are many business models to make some money out of that, and offering online design space helps those models.

Commercial Software

If you are willing to spend some money, there are great pieces of CAD software out there for you. We'll go over a few of them here, but if you are interested in doing a lot of work and you want a stable program that works for you, most of them offer trial versions that you can use for free for a while. If you are in school, many of these packages also offer educational licenses or even a free student version.

We won't talk about commercial software that's mainly used for animation (making films and short videos) like Maya, Cinema 4D, and LightWave, since this book focuses on making tangible objects, but if you already work with a package like that, you can either export to other software or probably use it directly. A recent alternative to model 3D animation, and even virtual reality environments, are game engines such as the Unreal and Unity engines.

In terms of 2D software, Adobe has two programs that are relevant to our type of projects – Photoshop is an extremely versatile and powerful tool for photo editing and manipulation (talking pixels here), whereas Illustrator is made for vector design. Both are only available via a subscription model where you pay a monthly fee, which is not cheap, but they are extremely powerful packages that smoothly work together.

Perhaps the most well-known commercial CAD package is SolidWorks, used in many (engineering) schools and universities as well as in companies doing engineering work. Different projects call for different tools though, and there is a range of professional CAD programs that all have their specific uses. Some examples are CATIA, made by the same company as SolidWorks, which is known for its extensive complexity and can be used for anything up to complete airplanes, including simulation of the engines and other moving parts. Rhinoceros is more focused on architectural applications, but can be used for almost anything. It comes together with Grasshopper, which allows you to create parametric designs. There are many more of these tools, and we cannot go over each one individually. Check the list at the end of this book for more of these.

Next to allowing for models with high complexity, all these packages feature many additional options such as finite element analysis (a way of analyzing the effect of applying different forces to the object or combination of objects) and simulating movement and interaction of parts. If you are planning on doing very complex projects involving moving parts and the interplay thereof, as well as things that need computer simulation or testing of strength, you might want to try some of these packages to see which one fits your need.

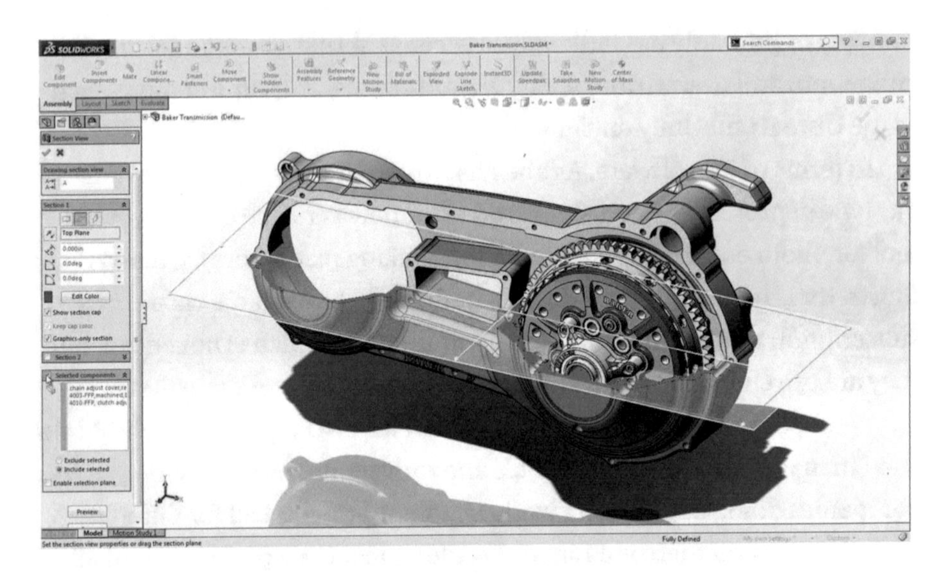

Figure 1-9. *The interface of Solidworks, showing a complex assembly of parts (`https://i.ytimg.com/vi/nB5O3P7jnfo/maxresdefault.jpg`)*

In 2016, Autodesk Fusion 360 CAD made a big entrance into maker communities and Fab Labs because of its intuitive and easy way to make advanced designs. As the name of the software indicates, Fusion integrates not only 3D parametric design but several additional functionalities, making it an all-round solution for many scenarios. For example, it offers complete functionalities to design printed circuit boards (PCBs) and to prepare files for manufacturing for many standard machines (mills, lathes, laser cutters, and 3D printers), along with more traditional rendering and simulation capabilities. Fusion 360 is cloud based, meaning it requires an Internet connection and it saves all your work in the cloud. It supports cooperation to work simultaneously on the same file, while it saves the design history, allowing the user to go back to any previously saved version. There are limited free plans for personal use, educators, and students.

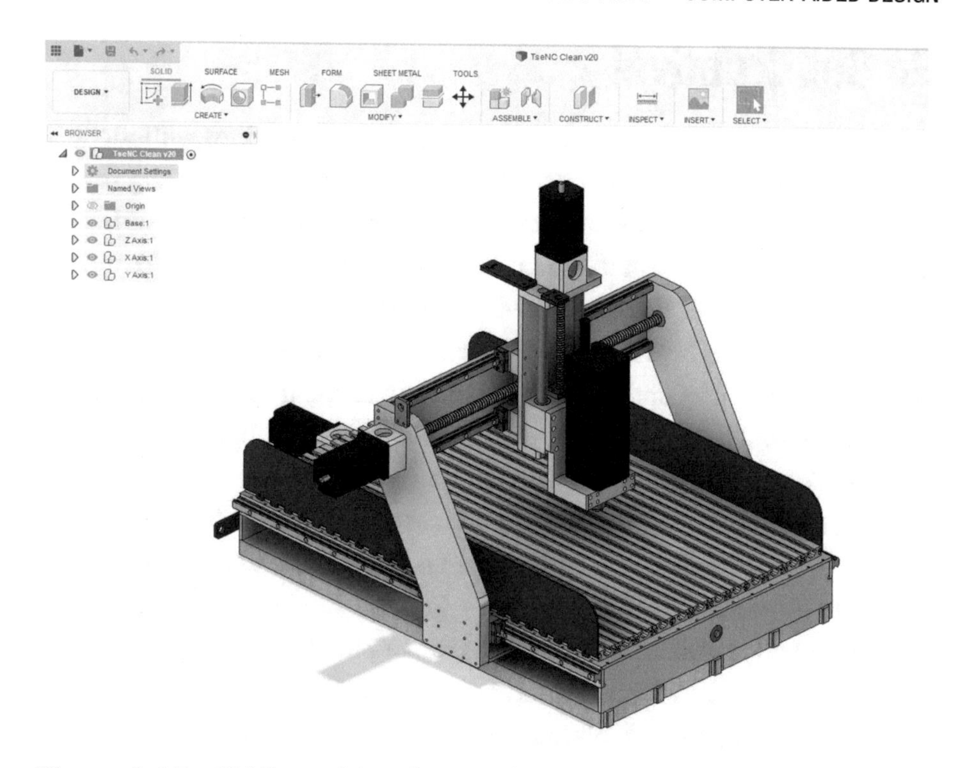

Figure 1-10. *CNC machine designed in Fusion 360*

Not everyone thinks and works the same way, and not all projects need the same precision or type of operations. Our advice is to try some different CAD programs to see what style you like. Perhaps you are more graphically oriented or you really like programming. The end result should be an enjoyable experience allowing you to create what you have in your mind. Give some programs like Blender some more time in the beginning, and you will be amazed at what you can create. It's not always easy, but mastering CAD is a great step to being able to make anything you can think of!

So Get Creative!

You can definitely start using computer-controlled machines without any CAD knowledge, whether it's 3D printing, laser cutting, milling, or something else – there are a myriad of websites offering free (or paid) files to download allowing you to fire up your machines fast. But if you want to make something unique or something that needs a specific size or shape, you'll need to learn how to use CAD software. There are easy packages allowing you to make basic shapes, which you can learn to use fast, but you'll be limited in what you can design, and they won't have additional features like rendering, toolpath generation, and more. If you spend time learning one of the more advanced packages out there, you'll need more time in the beginning, but eventually be faster and able to work on more advanced projects.

You can choose from open source, free, or paid software – our advice is to try out several packages to find out what works for you (graphical interfaces, coding, a combination, etc.), and once you find one you like, follow some tutorials to ramp up your knowledge.

And if you need ideas, think about other things you might enjoy. Like cooking? Design some unique cookie molds! Love running? How about a shirt with integrated lights for safety at night? Or maybe your fridge can use a new handle. Or that old lamp might look better with a new shade! The possibilities are endless.

But first, let's move on to the first machine, the laser cutter.

CHAPTER 2

Laser Cutters

History

As we spoke about the history of CNC machining earlier in the book, we will only focus on the beginnings of laser cutting technology here. If you did not read the general history of CNC in the Introduction, you might miss some information.

The word *laser* is an acronym meaning "light amplification by stimulated emission of radiation" and is essentially defined as a light having spatial and temporal coherence. In contrast to normal light, where photons (particles of light) are scattered in many directions and light color can vary, laser photons are equally distributed in space (spatial coherence), and the coloring of the light is very precise (temporal coherence). Those characteristics allow laser light to transport a high amount of energy in a narrow space, meaning in this case that we can precisely cut through various materials. The generation of a laser involves the usage of a light pump, filled with an excited medium. A light pump consists of two parallel mirrors, with one mirror being only partially reflective, corresponding to where the laser is output. See Figures 2-1 and 2-2 for an exposed version and a schematic of such a system.

J-m. Molenaar and D. Ingrassia, *Mastering Digitally Controlled Machines*, Maker Innovations Series, https://doi.org/10.1007/978-1-4842-9849-7_2

Figure 2-1. *An exposed CO_2 laser tube*

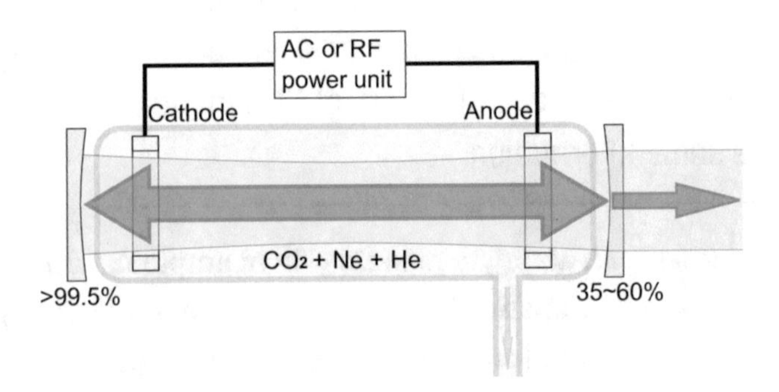

Figure 2-2. *Light pump schematic*

The laser was invented by Theodore H. Maiman in 1960 – you can see the system in Figure 2-3. The first use of a laser to cut materials appears in 1965 for the fabrication of diamond dies (used in industry to cut, shape, or stamp other materials). The birth of laser cutting as you'll encounter it in Fab Labs can be traced back to Cambridge where in 1967, Peter Houldcroft experimented with a 300-watt slow-flow CO_2 laser, so this technique is older than you probably expected! The system used to generate the laser beam was about 10m long, but the laser was powerful enough to cut through a 1mm-thick steel sheet. It wasn't the same machine as you'll find in makerspaces today, even though they both use CO_2 to generate the laser beam. The first systems were oxygen jet cutters that were combined with a laser, rather than machines using "just" a laser beam. Jetting a gas stream to the point where the laser is cutting often helps the material combustion and energy absorption while also removing possible generated flames.

Figure 2-3. *The world's first laser*

When the technique was proven to work, more people started to experiment and further advance the development of what is now known as laser cutting. In 1969, three Boeing engineers released a paper on the cutting of materials such as ceramic and even titanium using gas-assisted lasers. They did not actually build the machine they imagined, but tools built later on look similar to the technical drawing they added in their paper (see Figure 2-4).

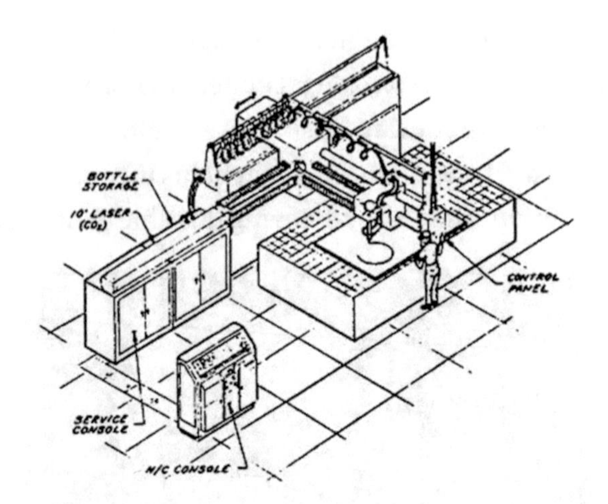

Figure 2-4. *1969 concept for a laser cutting machine tool (`www.twi-global.com/technical-knowledge/published-papers/in-the-beginning-the-history-of-laser-cutting-october-2002/`)*

From 1967 on, CO_2 laser systems were also developed to cut non-metals, such as wood, plastics, and textiles, because the laser beams were strong enough to cut through these materials without the oxygen jet. The first system using moving optics to direct a beam generated by a CO_2 laser was probably sold by Laser-Work AG of Switzerland in 1975. Since then, these systems have evolved into the systems you see today, with improvements in both the generation of the beam, the optics, and the axial systems. You can see an early Laser-Work AG machine in Figure 2-5.

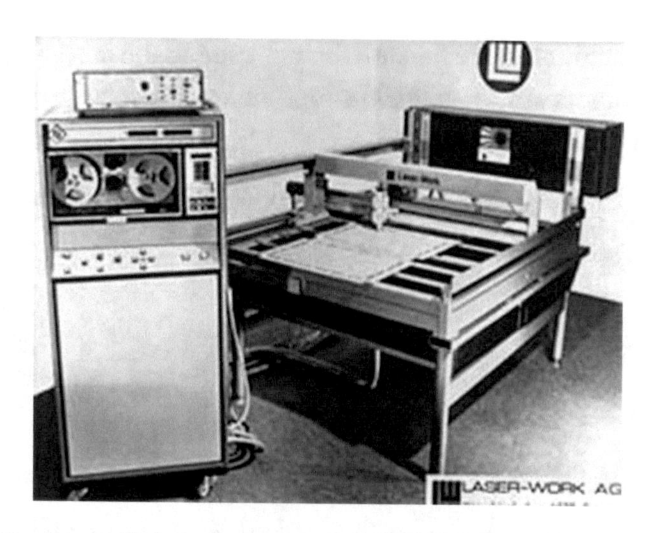

Figure 2-5. *An early laser cutter made by Laser-Work AG in Switzerland*

How They Function

Once it had been shown that different materials could successfully be cut using lasers, different systems and techniques were developed that are still in use today. The laser cutter you'll use in your Fab Lab will either use vaporization cutting or the melt and blow technique. Vaporization cutting transforms the material in the beam path into gas and dust. This technique works great for materials that do not melt, such as wood and cardboard. Melt and blow is required for all materials that melt instead of burning by absorbing the laser beam energy, which, for example, happens with plastics such as acrylic. Metal is also cut using the addition of a gas jet, blowing the molten material out of the cut. Lasers can also be used to cut glass, where a technique called thermal stress cracking is used. Basically, the material is heated up until it fractures, and the fracture is directed along the surface using the laser beam. Other techniques (that you most likely won't encounter) are "stealth dicing" used in the fabrication process of semiconductors and "reactive cutting," which is similar to oxygen torch cutting but uses a laser to ignite the gas.

Figure 2-6. *Picture of comparison of melt and blow (left) vs. burn and dust (right)*

Laser cutters are used to work with flat sheets of material, using a focused high-energy light beam. The laser beam is directed onto the material using a combination of mirrors and lenses, and your laser will very precisely burn or melt through the material you put in the machine. The head of the laser is moved over the cutting bed using motors and has a lens through which the laser beam is focused on the material. This way, the machines can move from one coordinate to another while manipulating the laser to achieve the wanted result. You can see an exposed schematic of this setup in Figure 2-7.

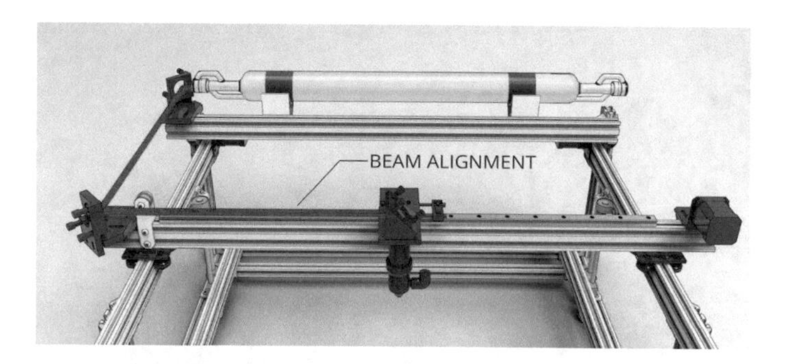

Figure 2-7. *Exposed laser tube and optics of a laser cutter*

By adjusting the movement speed and the laser beam properties, a laser cutter is able to either mark, engrave, or cut through the material.

Laser marking, also called laser etching, uses a low-power laser beam in combination with high-speed movements to only discolor the material surface or to remove a thin layer of it. Laser engraving works in a similar way to laser marking, but uses a more powerful laser beam and slower movements resulting in deeper removal of the top surface of the material.

What happens when you engrave with a laser is simple to understand by looking at the way we print with ink: small pixels (dots) are being placed on the material (this is why we speak about DPI, dots per inch, when we discuss the resolution of images) to form the image. Engraving with a laser works similarly, but instead of dropping ink, it will burn little dots in the material. More power means deeper burns, and by placing more or less dots, we can obtain grayscale images.

And finally, using most of the laser power and slow movements, a laser is able to completely cut through the material. In general, a laser cutter consists of the following main parts: a laser source, a set of laser optics, and a numerically controlled motion system. Having a look at those can help you better understand what a laser cutter is and can help you decide when buying one. Figure 2-8 shows you how the beam moves from the source to the final workpiece.

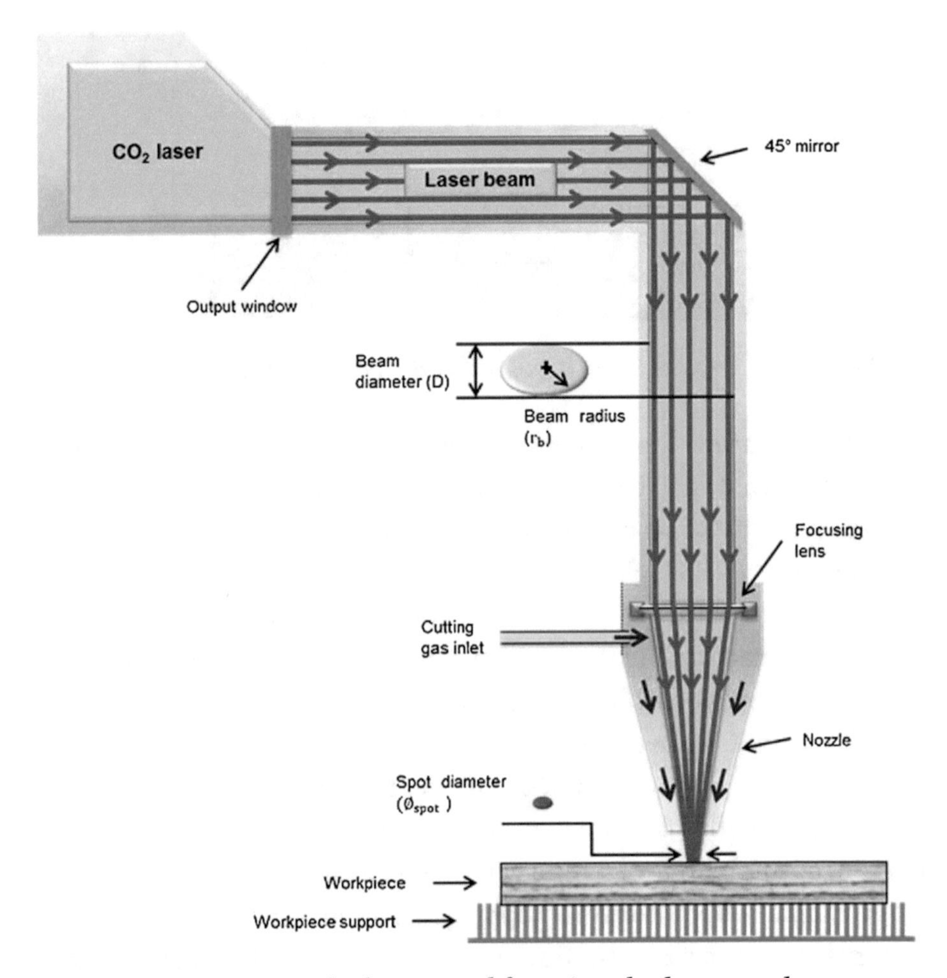

Figure 2-8. *Directing the beam and focusing the laser on the workpiece*

Examples of additional accessories are an exhaust filtering system to expel the smoke coming from lasering the materials, an air compressor for air assist, and a water chiller to cool down the laser source.

Laser optics are required to manipulate the laser beam. The laser optics used are usually the following: mirrors, lenses, beam expanders/ reducers, and beam collimator. Mirrors are used to redirect the beam, while the rest of the optics are employed to change the beam diameter.

Some optics are stationary and others move (called flying optics). Depending on the laser source and its position, a certain number of mirrors are needed to redirect the laser beam from the source to the machine head. In the path of the beam, any of the beam expander/reducer/collimator optics may be placed. The function of those is to increase/reduce/straighten the beam.

A change of diameter can be useful, and depending on the lens, you can achieve a differently focused spot diameter. Straightening the beam avoids power losses for long beam paths. The lens is usually in the machine head, and it is used to focus the beam. Having a cylindrical shape, the beam going through the lens will get focused (to a very small diameter, normally 0.3 to 0.1 mm) at the focal distance. See Figure 2-9 for the different focal lengths of lenses. It is important to note that, because of the required energy concentration, the beam is able to cut through materials only when in focus. The focal range defines a distance range from the lens where the beam is in focus. On many machines it is possible to change the lens for one with a different focal length. The focal length influences the spot diameter and the focal range, resulting in a larger spot diameter and focal range with a long focal distance and vice versa with a short focal distance. Smaller spot diameter means higher engraving precision and energy concentration and therefore higher cutting power; larger spot diameter results in less powerful cut but easier-to-focus laser and also allows engraving on surfaces that are not completely flat.

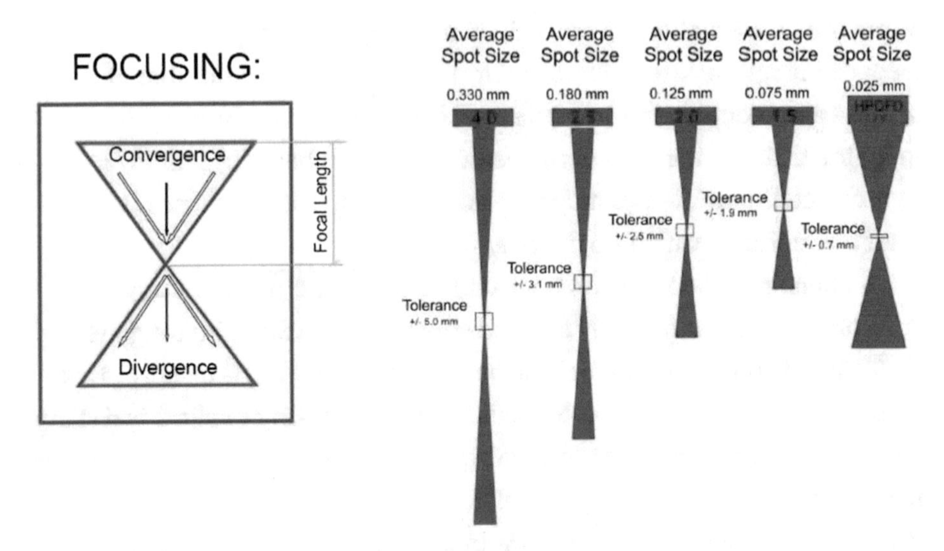

Figure 2-9. *The resulting spot size with different lenses*

Because the "tool" we use is made out of light, the laser cutter does not apply much force to the machine mechanics. For this reason, and due to the amount and length of movements required to laser cut a piece, light and fast mechanics are used. Given the limited focal range, which allows the laser to cut through materials, a laser cutter mainly works with flat sheets. Cheap laser systems only have X and Y axes, allowing the focus to be set manually with an adjustable head, while more expensive ones also offer a bed that is able to move up and down along the Z axis. With a movable bed, it is possible to fit taller objects and engrave or cut on top of them. The movement of the bed can be actuated in different ways depending on the machine, with the simplest way being done manually with a rotating lever or using a motor, which can either move the bed with buttons or be digitally controlled. If the Z axis is digitally controlled, the machine is also likely to offer autofocus functionality.

Some laser cutters are equipped to use a rotary axis. The rotary axis is attached on top of the laser cutter bed and allows cylindrical-shaped objects to be engraved or marked. The object is fixed at the sides and rotates while the X axis moves back and forth to engrave the object line by line.

The power and precision of the mechanics moving the X and Y axes influence cutting speed and quality. The horizontal movements of the laser head (X axis) are generally much faster than the vertical ones (Y axis), because you want high engraving speed and the amount of weight to move is low. Advanced systems use fast servo motors with encoders, quickly accelerating while keeping precise positioning. Cheaper systems use open-loop stepper motors. Almost all the laser cutters use belts and pulleys to implement fast movements. The movement ranges of the X and Y axes define the maximum area the laser can cut, usually called cutting area. The finest movement possible from the combination of the different mechanics used, together with the spot size, defines the laser cutter resolution, usually expressed in DPI (dot per inch).

Accessories

Laser accessories are usually provided or recommended by the manufacturer or the reseller of the laser cutter.

Filters

A laser cutter filter consists of one or more air pumps and a layered set of filtering materials. The air pump ensures a continuous stream of air coming into the laser cutter, pushing the generated gases and smoke through the different filters. The filtering system size and air flow are directly proportional to the laser cutter cutting area. A laser filter can be controlled through the machine itself, or it can be provided as a separate device. An automatically controlled filter offers several advantages, avoiding any user error (e.g., the user forgets to switch the filter on when cutting) and improving efficiency by automatically regulating the flow. Some brands have integrated filter systems that use proprietary filter formats (which can be expensive), while with separate systems standard filter materials can be found, making them cheaper and easier to replace. Laser filters can output the filtered air directly into the room or can be adapted to output outside. If a filter is used completely indoors, it is required to have fresh airflow in that space. If a window is available, it is always recommended to connect the filter output to the outside. Usually laser filters can be regulated in flow intensity, being quieter when at a low level.

Air Assist

Nowadays, offered in almost all the laser cutters, the air assist pushes a thin jet of air from the laser head to where the laser is cutting. Mainly used to avoid small flames, it also minimizes the combustion and leaves cleaner edges. Similarly to the laser filter, the air assist can be automatically controlled or manually operated.

Cutting Beds

Some laser cutter brands also offer different cutting beds as additional accessories to help cutting specific materials or speed up the setup time. A vacuum bed, for instance, is used to flatten and quickly secure soft and wavy materials, a highly spaced aluminum lamella bed is used to reduce laser backfire to improve the cut quality, and a magnetic bed can help position thin materials with magnets.

Figure 2-10. *Laser cutting medium-density fiberboard (MDF). The beam arrives from the right into the opening. Photo by Marion Sabourdy*

Types of Lasers

Laser cutters may differ in shape and features, but the most important specification is the type of laser source used. A laser source is always defined by the medium it uses – for example, CO_2 lasers are so called because CO_2 gas is used to generate the laser beam. Depending on the laser source, the laser cutter will require different parts and accessories, with substantial differences in terms of price. The **laser wavelength**, expressed in nm or μm, defines the range of materials the laser cutter is able to work with, with some materials not being compatible with any laser. The core principle of laser cutting is how efficiently the energy from the light is being absorbed by the material.

The wavelength of a laser depends on the medium used – in Fab Labs we usually find lasers that are CO_2 based (10.6μm) and sometimes fiber based (1024nm). Both CO_2 and fiber laser wavelengths are invisible, so the machine must be fully enclosed for safety.

The **laser power** defines the energy intensity of the laser light. It is generally directly proportional to the maximum cutting thickness and to the maximum speed at which the laser can cut through materials. The **laser frequency** refers to the possibility of having a "pulsed" or "continuous" laser beam. A pulsed laser beam consists of an intermittent laser light (think of switching on and off a torch) at a frequency, while a continuous beam (also referred as continuous wave, or CW) is continuous output. Changing the laser frequency, commonly expressed in Hz or pulse per inch (PPI), allows you to regulate the amount of heat transmitted to the material. Continuous wave lasers are the cheapest available, while pulsed lasers are found in professional laser cutters.

Each laser source has a different time it needs to reach the wanted output power, called response time. This time, preferably as short as possible, is an important factor for positioning in fast movements and making quality engravings at high speeds.

Laser sources can be air or water cooled. Air-cooled sources are cooled using automatically controlled fans. Water-cooled sources require an external cooling system usually consisting of a water chiller. Usually air-cooled sources have a longer lifespan and are of higher quality than water-cooled ones.

Within the same laser source type, for example, CO_2, different subcategories of laser sources can be found with different features, but they'll all work with the same set of materials. It is important to note that laser cutters with multiple laser sources exist, with the goal of combining the features of the different sources. Some laser cutters are even more focused, like machines specifically designed to only cut tubes, serving tube manufacturing industries.

Because most laser cutters are completely enclosed and precision must be high even when the beam travels long distances, the size of the cutting area is the second specification influencing the laser cutter price, with large lasers usually being more than double the price of smaller ones. Some machines will give you the option of opening the front and the back, to put in bigger materials. This allows you to engrave doors or pieces of material that are too long to normally put in the machine. (This often sounds great to people, but in reality is used very rarely.)

The choice of laser cutter depends on different factors, such as the materials you need to work with, whether it is for serial production or for making prototypes, and the space and budget available. We would advise you to not get the biggest cutting platform, but spend a little bit more on laser quality. You rarely need to cut very large things (and you can find a CNC mill if you need to), and the extra power will save you quite some time. Laser tubes are consumables (the CO_2 gets depleted), and you'll have to replace them from time to time, depending on how much they are used. Laser sources are not cheap!

In the following table is an overview of the most common laser cutter types available on the market.

Recently, new diode laser cutters have entered the market, making them highly attractive for those in need of more affordable and compact machines. Nowadays, it is possible to purchase a 20W or even 40W blue laser diode, enabling the cutting of nearly all materials similar to a CO2 laser but without the need for laser beam calibration and corresponding laser mirrors within the machine. In fact, the laser source is housed inside the module that attaches directly to the head.

Laser diode machines are typically much more budget-friendly than CO2 lasers, making them an excellent choice for those who are just starting with laser cutting. One notable exception is that a blue diode laser cannot cut transparent acrylic. However, they can directly engrave on metals without the need for additional paint or coatings.

Several compact CO2 laser cutters have emerged in the market, reducing the required space and cost for accessing CO2 laser cutting technology. Typically designed to fit on household tables, these machines integrate a camera and offer standard accessories such as a rotary table. They commonly employ a CO2 glass laser tube as the laser source with an integrated chiller and air assist within the machine itself to save space. Examples of brands include Glowforge, Gweike, Beambox, and XTool. Two exceptions in terms of features are the Gweike Cloud RF, which uses an RF CO2 laser source, and the XTool P2, which has the functionality to engrave on curved surfaces.

Fabulaser Mini is an open-source desktop laser cutter that can be easily replicated using makerspace or Fab Lab equipment. As one of the few available open-source laser cutters, the machine is intentionally designed to be easily assembled from a kit to educate users about how a laser cutter functions. With complete design files and an assembly manual provided, after assembling the Fabulaser Mini, you will be able to repair and even modify the machine yourself later on. The Fabulaser Mini is well-suited for schools, where students can build it together with their teachers.

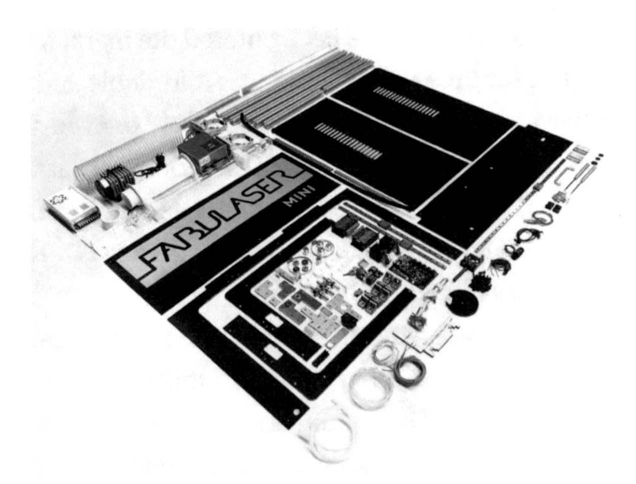

Figure 2-11. *A Fabulaser Mini assembly kit from InMachines. (`https://www.inmachines.net/`)*

Machine Type	Laser Source	Typical Power	Working Area	Used For	Used From	Visible Laser?	Cost
DIY laser engraver	Diode 400–450nm	0.5–40W	From 100 × 100mm to 800 × 500mm	Light engraving, cutting of thin soft materials (few mm)	Hobbyists, Fab Labs, makerspaces	Yes	$
CO_2 laser cutter and engraver	DC CO_2 10.6μm (continuous wave)	40–150W	From 300 x 200mm to 2500 × 1250mm, typically 1000 × 700mm	Cutting and engraving mostly organic and plastic materials, producing small batches of prototypes	Fab Labs, makerspaces, architects, small and medium shops	No	$$
	RF CO_2 10.6μm (pulsed laser)	25–130W		Cutting and engraving mostly organic and plastic materials, producing small batches of high-quality prototypes			$$$

(*continued*)

Machine Type	Laser Source	Typical Power	Working Area	Used For	Used From	Visible Laser?	Cost
CO_2 + fiber laser cutter and engraver	RF CO_2 10.6μm and fiber 1064nm	CO_2: 25–130W Fiber: 30–60W		Cutting and engraving mostly organic and plastic materials, engraving metals, producing small batches of high-quality prototypes			$$$
YAG laser engraver	YAG 1064nm	20–70W	From 100 × 100mm to 400 × 400mm	Fast marking and engraving of metals; product branding, labeling, and writing	Metal shops, small industries		$
Fiber laser engraver	Fiber 1064nm						$$
Fiber laser cutter	Fiber 1064nm	500W–10KW	Usually large, 2500 × 1250mm or more	Fast and precise cutting of sheet metals, metal parts production	Metalworking industries, production		$$$$

YAG laser machines are becoming obsolete in favor of the more reliable fiber laser. We would only recommend getting a YAG laser if it's substantially cheaper than the fiber laser alternatives, like a used machine for a low price.

Materials

As described in the "How They Function" section, the type of material that can be processed with a laser cutter mainly depends on the kind of laser source used. The wavelength influences how efficiently the energy (in this case heat) is being absorbed by the materials, while the laser power gives an indication of how fast and how deep it is possible to cut. Because of the working principle of burning or melting, some materials may release toxic fumes or dust and/or damage your laser cutter. It is therefore super important to check with the manufacturer for approved and safe materials that can be used. For more information have a look at the materials annex on page.

In Fab Labs and makerspaces, the most common materials for CO_2 lasers are solid wood, plywood, MDF, acrylic, paper, cardboard, and textiles. Generally speaking materials over a certain thickness, about 12mm or about half an inch, can be quite hard to cut, not only because of the laser power needed but also because the surface quality on the side of the cut will be influenced by the burning and/or melting of the material, potentially resulting in less precise and angled cuts. Cutting metals is not possible with CO_2 lasers, while engraving metals is possible with a special marking spray.

Plywood consists of wood layers that are glued together, with each layer being rotated up to 90 degrees one to another. There are different types of plywood, which depend on the kind of wood used. The weight of plywood and the type of glue used between the layers define how hard it is for the laser to cut through it. For example, poplar plywood can easily be cut in thicknesses of more than 10mm, while birch plywood is usually limited to a maximum of 6mm. Engraving on bright plywood is well visible and quickly done. Plywood is one of the most used and easy-to-find materials for laser cutting and offers nice rigidity to make solid prototypes.

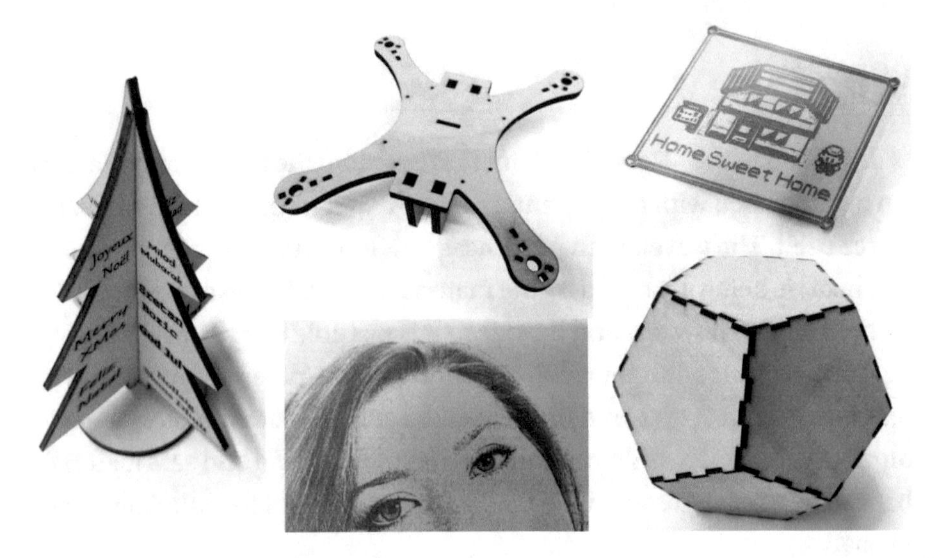

Figure 2-12. *Cut and engraved plywood*

Medium-density fiberboard, or MDF, is usually denser than plywood and therefore harder to cut. Consisting of wood residuals glued and compressed to form sheets, it is usually cheaper than plywood, but on the other hand, weaker and less flexible. Because of the high amount of glue used to make it, MDF usually generates much smoke, quickly filling the filtering system.

Figure 2-13. *Press-fit kit with colored MDF*

Poly(methyl methacrylate), or PMMA, sometimes known as acrylic or plexiglass, is a kind of thermoplastic typically produced in transparent sheets. Being laser cut with the melt and blow technique, acrylic can be precisely laser cut to create transparent models. Usually much more expensive than plywood and MDF, acrylic can also be found in colored sheets either semi-transparent or opaque. Acrylic is usually produced by casting or by extruding it. Cast acrylic, named as "acrylic GS," offers higher weathering and aging resistance and better surface quality. Extruded acrylic, indicated with "acrylic XT," on the other hand offers lower prices and lower thickness tolerance. CO_2 lasers easily cut acrylic up to 6mm thickness, with stronger lasers able to cut 12mm or more.

Cardboard and paper are the fastest materials to be laser cut, because of the low power required. Cardboard is used to create light and cheap prototypes, but also to preview laser jobs, allowing you to check dimensions and make sure you didn't make any mistakes, before risking using more expensive materials. Because cardboard can easily burn, you should make sure to get your setting right before cutting. **Good cardboard bends round; bad cardboard kinks.**

Figure 2-14. *3D objects made from 2D parts, designed in Slicer for Fusion 360*

A bare CO_2 laser beam is not able to cut through metals nor engrave them. Historically some CO_2 laser cutters used a stream of pure oxygen to be able to be absorbed by metals, but this process has been discouraged because of the fire danger and because it requires higher power than Fab Lab machines (150–300W). What can be done instead is called light metal marking, through the use of a special marking spray. When this spray is applied and dried on a metal surface, you can then mark it using a CO_2 laser. Most products that let you mark aluminum or other metals are quite toxic and should be handled with care. If the laser cutter has a fiber laser or it has a dual-source laser including the fiber laser, then it is possible to directly mark metals. Heat-dissipating materials like copper and aluminum are the most difficult to work with, often requiring multiple passes to have recognizable material marks. A special application of marking fiber laser machines is to engrave printed circuit boards, offering an alternative production technique to CNC milling or chemical etching.

Considering the preceding discussion as a general overview about the most common materials to laser cut in Fab Labs and makerspaces, several more materials can be precisely shaped with laser cutting. Acetal, also known as POM, is a very strong plastic that can be used to make mechanical parts. Thin sheets (0.8mm) of polypropylene, or PP, are great for folding designs. Many textiles can be cut or engraved to form customized clothes. And much more!

If you are new to lasers, start out with thin and cheap materials. Paper and cardboard are easy to find and cheap and will let you make tons of great projects. As with all materials, you'll have to adjust your settings according to the power of the laser, the speed with which it moves, and the thickness of your material.

For a list of laserable materials, please refer to the materials annex.

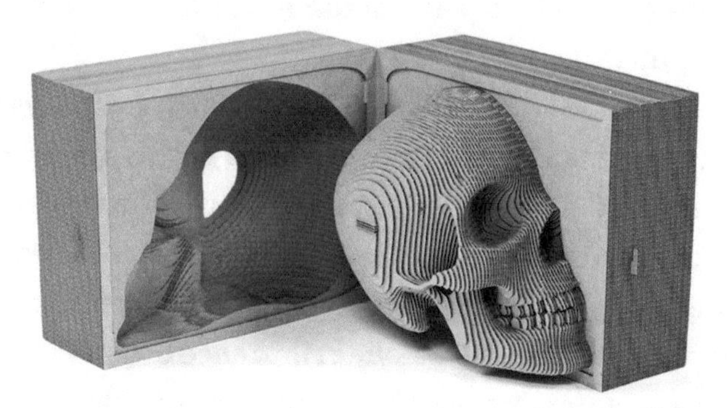

Figure 2-15. *Cardboard skull created by stacking lasercut layers (`http://theawesomer.com/photos/2014/12/cardboard_safari_vince_skull_3.jpg`)*

Running the Machine

Designing Objects

Designing for laser cutting is the first step in producing your parts. There are some important considerations to keep in mind for your design.

Remembering the laser cutter burns or melts through the material, you will realize the laser cut parts are always smaller than your dimensions in CAD. The amount of material being burned or melted away is removed from the final piece, resulting in a little offset from your design. Similarly to other cutting processes where the width of the cut is considered (e.g., sawing), **kerf** is defined as the width of material that is removed by the laser beam. Kerf must be considered in your design whenever precise dimensions are needed or tight joints have to be made. If a joint is cut without considering the kerf, it will result in a loose coupling. Because kerf depends on many factors such as laser power, material type, and thickness, it is always recommended to perform some tests to calculate its value, before laser cutting your job.

Once the kerf value is known, it can be applied to your design by, for example, making the holes and joints smaller so that by removing the kerf they will end up the desired size. For complex designs where many sections require to be changed because of the kerf, we would recommend using parametric functionalities that automatically add constraints to efficiently apply the modifications. Kerf is usually in the range of tenths of a millimeter.

Because laser cutters are mainly able to work with flat materials, the design to be laser cut is always 2D. But even if lasers need a 2D design, this does not exclude the possibility to create 3D objects. By using joints and folding and bending techniques, it is possible to create press-fit kits that can be assembled like puzzles. To make sure your design will fit and have the wanted result, it is recommended to extrude and assemble your design in a 3D CAD software. Or vice versa, first design the 3D object and then export the single faces in a 2D design.

When it comes to engraving images, it is usually preferable to pre-process images for better-quality results. In most laser cutters, this involves converting the image to grayscale, sharpening it, removing the background, and reducing the grayscale colors.

In some of your designs, you might need to control the order of the different cuts and/or engravings. Consider, for example, laser cutting a wheel. If the outer cut is done first, the piece could detach from the material sheet and move a bit. If the hole in the center of the wheel is done after that, it may not be properly centered. To avoid this, you should cut the inside circle first. Some other sections of your design may be cut or engraved. Depending on the laser software, the cut and/or engraving order can be selected in different ways. The most common way is by using different colors, with the software allowing to define per-color settings and order (usually called color mapping). Similarly to colors, another way is to use different design layers. It is important to note that, for different colors or layers, not only the order and the kind of operation can be defined, for example, cutting/engraving/marking, but also that the same operation can be done with different settings, for example, two cuts with a different speed or power. This functionality is quite useful when testing the settings for a new material.

In most laser cutters, thin vector lines are considered cuts, while filled-in areas and raster pictures are considered as engravings. The final format of the design will depend on the laser cutter software capabilities and compatibilities.

Sending Files to the Machine

Most commercial laser manufacturers have proprietary software packages that allow you to use the machine. Some laser cutters are seen as printers by the computer, and therefore the design can be sent and previewed directly from a design software. In that case the workflow is similar to previewing and printing a paper document, with the printing settings being the laser settings and the job properties. Other manufacturers offer dedicated job centers that can import specific file formats. Common vector formats for laser cutting are DXF, SVG, and PDF, and when it comes to raster, JPG, PNG, and BMP are often used. In both of the preceding cases, the laser cutting software and drivers have a dedicated interface to input the laser cutting settings and the job properties. Once everything is set, the laser software transforms the given design into the machine code (usually G-code or similar code), and the job is sent to the machine. The job can either be sent to the machine memory, so that multiple jobs can be memorized and sent when needed, or it is streamed to the machine controller. If the job is streamed to the machine for cutting, it is important to keep the computer on and free from other running applications.

Finding the Right Settings

The laser cutting settings define the main properties of your laser cut job. There can be settings available only to some laser cutter type or manufacturer. The ones considered in this book are the most common for CO_2 laser cutters typically found in Fab Labs and makerspaces. Settings are fundamental for best laser cut results and sometimes also safety. To determine the optimal settings, it is always recommended to run tests before cutting your job. Because of the variability of the material consistency, even within the same type but, for example, from a different manufacturer, it is not possible to determine the settings with high accuracy when using a new material. Manufacturers often give some generic indications that can be used as a starting point for a type of material and offer the possibility to create materials libraries with user-defined settings.

The following is a table that summarizes the most common laser settings for CO_2 lasers.

	What Does It Do?	What Is the Effect?	Important Notes
Laser power	Changes the laser beam intensity. More power means a stronger laser beam.	High power makes deep cuts and is suitable to cut thicker materials. Low power makes thin cuts, and it is used to cut thin materials.	Too much power can burn the materials; too little power may not cut through completely. Optimal is when the material requires a little push to be detached and there are no burned edges. Low power is also used for engravings.
Cutting speed	Changes the movement speed during a cut.	The slower the laser moves during a cut, the deeper it cuts and vice versa. Similar to power considerations but inverted.	Similar to the power notes but inverted, high speeds are also suitable for engravings. Usually if at 100% speed, the laser is not able to cut; it is recommended to reduce the cutting speed.

(*continued*)

	What Does It Do?	What Is the Effect?	Important Notes
Laser frequency/pulses per inch	Changes the frequency the laser beam is being output.	Low frequency results in low heat being applied to the material and vice versa.	Only available with RF laser sources. Low frequencies are suitable for materials that can burn if cut with too much heat, such as wood and cardboard. High frequencies are needed for materials that need to be melted to be cut, such as acrylic.
Number of passes	Defines how many times to repeat the same job.	Runs the same cut and/or engraving multiple times.	Needed in some specific cases, for example, when the laser is not able to cut with minimum speed and maximum power and so the job can be repeated, when the material is not cut completely because it is not flat, etc.

(*continued*)

	What Does It Do?	What Is the Effect?	Important Notes
Resolution	Changes the approximation of the machine movements to the design details.	Higher resolution results in slower, but more precise cut lines and engravings. Lower-resolution jobs are faster but less precise.	To be adjusted according to the design type. Cuts with not so small details are optimal at 600DPI, while pictures with engraving and fine details may require higher resolution.

When cutting certain materials, such as acrylic, it's normal to see a small flame, which even helps create a smooth finish on the cut. If the acrylic has a protective foil on the top surface, it's best to remove it to reduce the flames and to avoid it melting when engraving.

With certain materials, the air assist is shut off to create a better finish. This is usually done in engravings that may generate some sticky smoke that can change the color of the surrounding area if pushed against the material surface from the air assist blow. Similar scenarios may occur if the exhaust suction is too fast, making the smoke stick to the area on top of your engraving. Not much smoke and flames are generated from engravings; therefore, exhaust speed and air assists may be adjusted accordingly. It's a good idea to do some tests and create an overview of the result of different settings to keep next to your machine, like that shown in Figures 2-16 and 2-17.

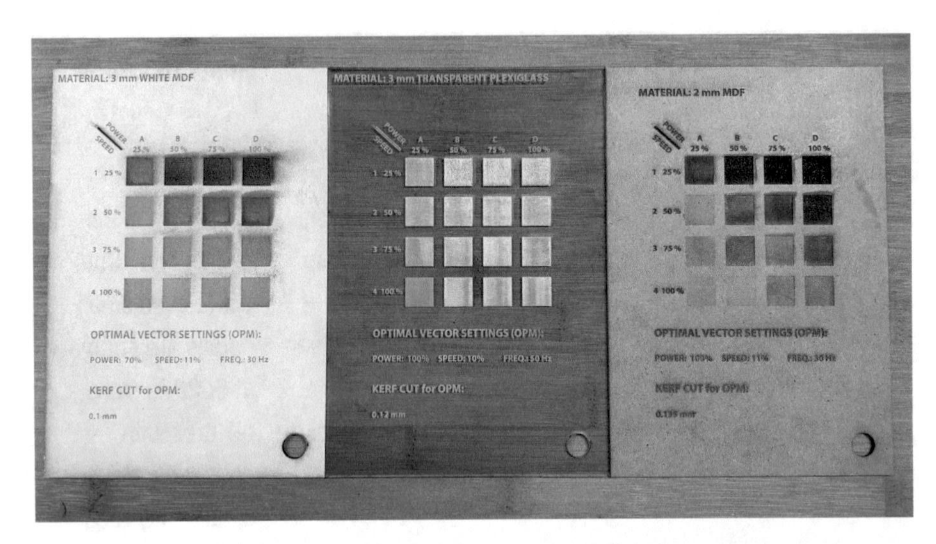

Figure 2-16. *Different settings and the result on MDF and plexiglass*

For picture engraving jobs, most laser software have a different image dithering available. Dithering defines how the dot patterns will be engraved giving different results in the definition and style of the final result. Default dithering is usually preferable for engravings using a single color, while Jarvis, Stucki, and Floyd-Steinberg are best for pictures. If you do a lot of engraving, we would recommend experimenting with the dithering settings to find the right one for you – the point being that it all comes down to personal preference.

Figure 2-17. *The result of different speed and power combinations*

For the laser to function well, the focus needs to be correct. Most lasers are able to focus automatically, but all can be focused by hand. The lens will focus the laser into a cone, and the further away or the closer you get from or to the lens, the larger or smaller this cone becomes. To cut correctly, you'll want the focal point to be at the center of your material. The hand-focused lasers use specific focusing tools to determine the right distance, while autofocus works by setting the material thickness in the laser software.

Laser source power influences the settings a lot, especially related to how fast you can cut thick materials. A 35-watt laser will need to move slowly to cut 5mm-thick wood, where a 120-watt laser will move much faster to do the same cut.

Some interfaces also will have the option to run files using special settings to create stamps (using rubber) or to apply some simple image transformations to mirror your images or change the scale. If you are in a space where multiple people use the machine, check these settings well; perhaps the users before you changed them, and your files will be mirrored or cut two times as big as you planned!

Next to those, some laser software allows you to assign different settings (power, speed, pulse rate) to different colors (often RGB) or layers so you can send a single job with many different settings to the machine. You can engrave different depths, engrave using the cutting mode (but with too little power to actually cut) and cut all the way through, define the order of the different operations, etc.

Never, Ever, Launch a Long Job Without a Test

Lenses get dirty, lasers can be badly aligned, and tables can be "not-exactly-perfectly-flat." There are many reasons to always do a little test to see if your settings cut your material like you want to (clean cut, but not too much burn marks) before launching a long cutting or engraving job. We have seen many people send a file to the laser that took an hour or more to cut, only to find when the machine was done that they did not get the settings right and they'd have to run the file again or finish the work by hand. And that's exactly what you don't want to do if you have an awesome laser.

***Figure 2-18.** Check your settings before launching a cut*

Maintenance

When it comes to laser cutters, all of the commercial vendors will provide you with a maintenance manual, in your own language. Try to follow the manufacturer's advice closely, as different techniques and cleaning products might have different results and you could even damage your machine. The advice on maintenance we give here is general, and we cannot take any responsibility if you handle the machine incorrectly!

Signs that your machine needs maintenance appear when it is performing less well than it should or when something is not working at all. Because of the many parts involved and the precise laser beam calibration, analyze the situation before rushing in doing something, especially because lasers can be quite dangerous and the calibration may require time to be done. Usually in commercial lasers, problems are easier to solve than DIY or self-built machines, with some of the recurring problems described in the machine manual. As with other machines, laser cutters require regular maintenance to function well. Many parts are consumable and deteriorate with time and use.

Most of the problems with laser cutters are about the tool not cutting or not cutting well. The root of those can vary and depend on many factors. The following is a table with the most common problems and solutions.

Problem/ Possible Solutions	1	2	3	4
No laser is output.	Check if the power setting is correct and that the job is not a simulation. Check the G-code when possible.	Check if the laser window is well closed and the interlocks are working properly or if they are dirty.	Check that mirrors and the lens are in place and are not substantially shifted.	Check if the laser source is working well.
Laser is not cutting.	Check the material used, it could be very hard to cut.	Check that focus is taken correctly.	Check if the mirror or the lenses are dirty.	Check the laser source age; if very old, it may have lost much of its power. Some lasers may lose power after working continuously for some time.
Laser is not cutting everywhere.	Check if the material is flat. Some materials may have a different consistency in different areas.	Check that the bed is leveled and that the focus is the same in the four corners.	Check if the laser path is well calibrated.	
Laser cuts with a bevel/ slanted angle.	Check if the laser head has been hitting something.	Check if the lens is loose.	Check if the mirror or the lenses are dirty.	

We once spent a long time looking why one of our laser cutters would not fire the laser (but moved the head around happily), and after replacing the tube, checking mirror alignment, reconnecting all the cables, and countless cups of coffee, we eventually found out the top door did not shut properly (one of the hinges was loose) and because of that the safety switch did not engage, causing the laser to not turn on at all. We discovered this by slowly moving into a state of total despair and leaning down heavily on the door - which caused the safety to engage and the laser to fire.

Cleaning Your Optics and Encoders

So one of the most important things with lasers is keeping the optics clean. Especially if you use materials that create a lot of fumes and residue (like MDF), you'll often need to remove the deposits of these from the mirrors and lens. Dirty lenses and optics may be the cause of many of the cutting and quality problems. The optics in a laser are delicate and should always be treated and handled with extreme care. Do check them at least twice a week. The difference between a well-cleaned lens and a dirty one can mean hours of difference in cutting time!

To clean the mirrors and lens of your machine, you can use cotton swabs, optical cleaning paper, and either a professional lens cleaner, isopropyl alcohol, distilled white vinegar (ten parts water, one part white vinegar), or pure grain alcohol. Never use anything else on optics, or you could completely destroy them and end up having to buy replacements. Whenever possible, clean the mirrors in place to prevent misalignments in the laser beam. The laser lens can be removed and placed back, because it usually stays in a fixed position.

Certain brands of lasers have an encoder strip that you'll also regularly have to clean. If the strip becomes too dirty, the machine can "lose" its position during engraving or cutting, and you'll end up with deformed engravings or shapes. If you see your image is deforming while engraving, stop the machine and clean the encoder strip before continuing. If you are hesitating between buying two machines and one has an open encoder strip, go for the other one.

To clean the encoder strip, you can use cotton swabs and distilled water or a window cleaner. You never want to use too aggressive products, because you might end up removing the markings on the strip, in which case your only option is to completely replace it with a new one.

After optics, it's always a good idea to keep your laser cutter clean of cuttings underneath the cutting bed (cuttings that have fallen through the cutting bed are prone to catch fire) and to generally keep the machine (glass doors, rulers on the side of the laser bed) cleaned well. The longer you leave the dust and deposits on the machine, the harder it'll be to get it off. Trust us, we tried.

Alignment of Mirrors and Lens

If you need to use more and more power to cut the same material (which might also mean your tube is close to the end of its life) or if it seems your laser is not focused well or the cuts are quite angled or if you replace the laser tube, you might need to (re-)align your optics. If the laser is not passing through the center of the lens, you lose power, and your cuts will be slanted. It is important to note the laser must be centered on the lens in any of the reachable positions of the head. Most lasers will allow you to slightly change the position of the mirrors directing the beam into the lens with precision knobs and preload springs, to ensure a correct focus.

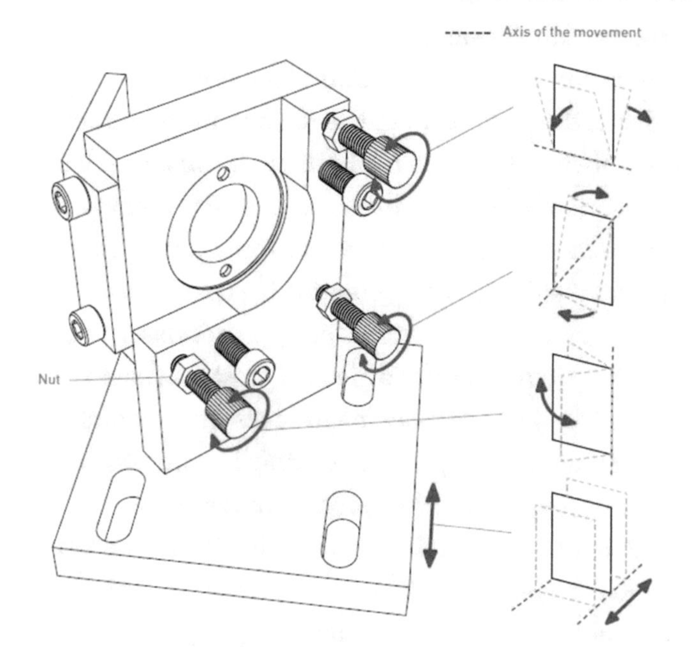

***Figure 2-19.** Possible movements for the calibration*

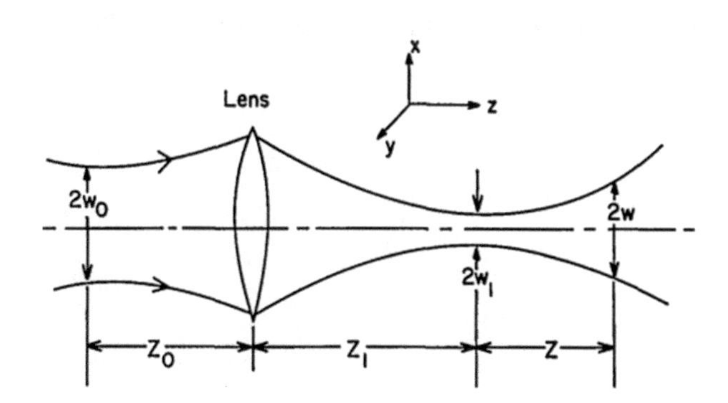

***Figure 2-20.** Lens, with deformation of the laser beam shown (`http://imagebank.osa.org/getImage.xqy?img=OG0kcC5sYXJnZSxhby0yNS0xNC0yNDIxLWcwMDE`)*

Start by checking the mirror in the laser head (the easiest to get misaligned) and then gradually follow back the laser path checking the other mirrors up to the laser tube. Lasers with a "red dot" or a secondary/coaxial laser to indicate the position of the head have an alignment procedure that's less obvious than you might think. If you align all the mirrors using this secondary laser and there is a bad alignment between the actual laser (doing the cutting) and the visible one, you might think you did your work well, but it still won't cut properly. If a coaxial laser pointer is not available, the process usually involves firing a short laser pulse and detecting the position by letting it burn a piece of masking (paper) tape. Because you may need to open the machine to access the mirrors, it is very important to not have anybody around during this process and to use proper safety protection, especially laser-protective glasses.

First, you have to figure out what the first location is that the laser beam passes through – usually optic holders have holes for that. You then put a piece of tape over this hole and fire your laser (very briefly). You'll see a tiny burn mark that should line up perfectly with the center of the optic holes. A misalignment of half a millimeter at the start can mean an enormous difference at the end! Make sure they are PERFECTLY aligned.

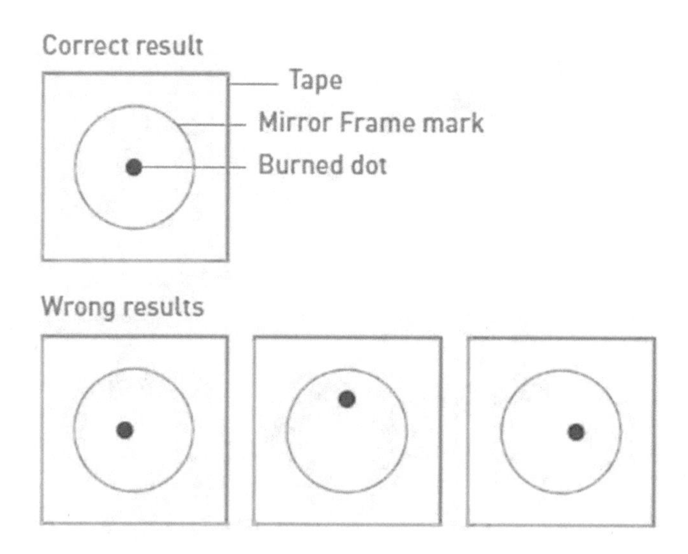

Figure 2-21. *Optic holes*

Then, move on gradually through your machine, and repeat this process until you are at the cutting zone. It is important to note that the center must be hit at all the possible positions of the optics you are aligning. First, check and align the laser beam to the closest position to the previous mirror or laser tube, and then gradually move the optics further away and align the mark made into the closest position to the one that is the furthest away. This process does not apply to the fixed optics, usually used for the first mirror holder.

Once, after we spent two hours fine-tuning our laser, we could use 20% higher speeds when cutting! This saves lots of time, but it's a delicate process, and don't hesitate to start over if you did not get it just right. If you spend one more hour on fine-tuning your machine, it might cut cleaner, faster, and better!

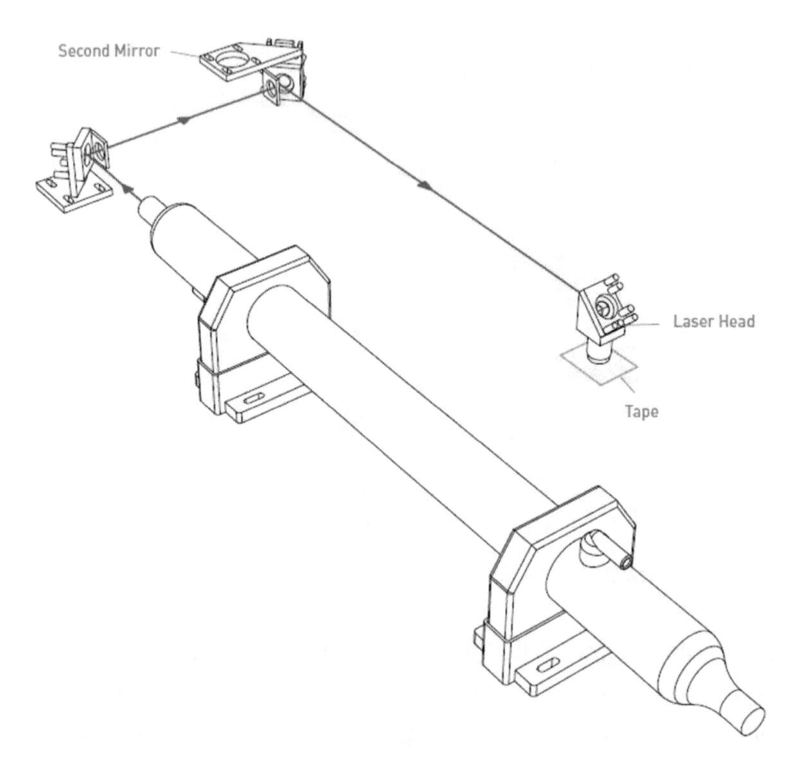

Figure 2-22. *Laser*

Placement, Power

Laser tubes need to be cooled to function with either air or water. If you install a laser in your space, make sure it's not against a radiator or in full sun during the summer and that the laser is not close to something that obstructs the air vents. If you keep the tube cool, it will last much longer. For water-cooled laser tubes, it is important temperatures stay under 30 °C/86 °F, and for air-cooled laser sources, make sure the fans are functioning well and that the system is clean of dust. Next to that, many lasers are sensitive to power fluctuations. If you have many machines in your space, try and give the laser its own power supply, free of fluctuations and power cuts. Again, this will save you money in the end!

Safety

Laser cutters use high-energy light to burn material. It's possible, and even quite easy, to start a fire with them! Although we have seen it happen multiple times, if you react fast and correctly most of the time, there is little danger and the laser can be saved. Make sure you have fire extinguishers next to your machine (we would recommend a powder-based one) and make sure there is someone in the space with proper training on how to use them. If the material in your machine starts to burn, open the door of the machine and immediately remove the material if this is still possible without burning yourself. Turn the compressor and exhaust off, so they don't add extra oxygen to the space.

If a fire occurs in a machine, it's usually due to human error. If someone cut thick wood and set the speed very low and the power very high and the next user forgets to change these settings but cuts cardboard, it will surely catch fire. Teach your users to be responsible and to check the settings every single time before they start the machine. Check out Figure 2-23, and let it serve as a warning.

Figure 2-23. *Laser cutters can catch on fire. Safety always comes first! (https://hackadaycom.files.wordpress.com/2016/05/burnt-laser-arcbotics-com.jpg?w=400&h=267)*

Most important: You should never cut any material that produces chlorine when heated. PVC and some other plastics like Lexan should never be cut, even if you have a good air filter. The chlorine gas produced by cutting these materials is bad for you and will also eat away at your optics. So if you'd like to keep your lungs and the lenses in your machine in good health, check all materials before they are put in the machine.

The laser beam produced inside a laser cutter is very dangerous for your eyes, your skin, and your body. In fact it can make you blind, burn your skin, and penetrate inside your body. Laser cutters are made safe by different mechanisms and precautions implemented by the manufacturer. Those are usually window switches/interlocks, a completely closed machine body, water flow sensors, etc. Lasers are classified depending on the risk they pose. Every laser cutter should have a sticker identifying the laser class of the machine, usually class 1 or 2 because of the precautions taken. An open laser tube, or an open laser cutter (e.g., when making the calibration), corresponds to laser class 4. To reiterate, when your laser cutter has a "class 1" sticker, but you open the sides of the machine, you change it into a class 4. The following is a brief description of the classes.

Class 1	Safe to be used in all operating conditions.
Class 1M	Safe to use without optical instruments.
Class 2	Possible damage with accidental direct viewing longer than 0.25 seconds. Visible laser.
Class 2M	Possible damage with accidental direct viewing (> 0.25 s) without optical instruments. Visible laser.
Class 3R	No damage if handled carefully, low risk of injury. Max power of 5mW.

(continued)

Class 3B	Hazardous if exposed directly. Reflections are not dangerous. Max power is 500mW.
Class 4	Direct viewing and the diffuse reflections can be very dangerous. Capable of setting fire to materials onto which they are projected.

Laser cutters are wonderful machines to use, but safety comes first, every time.

Applications of Laser Cutters

What Are the Professionals Making?

Figure 2-24. *A lamp made by laser cutting paper*

Let's start by looking at some industrial applications of this tool. Look around. Are you at home? You might have some kitchen utensils that are laser cut or perhaps some stainless steel coasters your glass is resting on. At work? Your pen holder might very well be laser cut or that little wooden table your laptop sits on.

Laser cutting might have been used for any architectural models you've seen, small pieces of scale models, or a flyswatter you have lying around. The engraving possibilities of this tool you'll see in any prizes you've won (good job!), rubber stamps, barcodes, displays, signs, and much more. Since lasers "cut" by burning or melting material, some materials might have undergone a finishing process, in which case you'll have trouble distinguishing cuts made by a laser and, for instance, a waterjet cutter (see Chapter 6). New uses of lasers are constantly being developed, like cutting glass for phones and drilling components for turbines.

Commercial laser cutting is widely used by small and medium companies who offer personalization of objects and tools and cutting of relatively simple shapes like signs and nameplates. Many of these companies will also own a vinyl cutter (see Chapter 3) and will offer services like signage and decoration as well as customized prizes and awards.

Bigger and more powerful fiber laser systems are used in industry to cut steel, aluminum, stainless steel, and titanium, while CO_2 lasers are employed to process paper, plastics, wood, and fabrics. CO_2 systems with large areas and fast movement are widely used in the textile industry to quickly cut textiles. You'll find laser cutting systems almost anywhere, from very technical aerospace applications to everyday consumer products.

Machines used in industry are expensive, because of the continuous production capabilities, and you probably won't have access to them, so let's take a look at what you can do with the machines that use low-power CO_2 or fiber lasers that are slightly smaller and need less maintenance (something to think about when you choose one for your makerspace).

What Can YOU Make?

Laser cutters differ from other Fab Lab machines in the fact that they use a very small tool (the laser beam) and also because they can produce large prototypes much faster than 3D printers and CNC machines. They are usually easier to learn and to use than other machines, being usually defined as "the most used machine in a Fab Lab." It is common to use a laser cutter to quickly fabricate a prototype that can later on be manufactured with other machines.

Snap-Fit, Just Assemble, and Go!

The precision laser cutters offer (in the order of 25 microns and up) allows for great snap-fit applications. This means you cut several pieces in a 2D plane and then assemble them into a 3D structure. Take a look at Figure 2-25 of a laser cut Hoberman sphere, named after Chuck Hoberman (an artist, engineer, architect, and inventor of folding toys and structures), folded and unfolded. This shape consists of about 1600 laser cut pieces of wood, held together by friction only, no glue involved. They are simply pressed together, but the shape can still move without them falling apart. While the sphere is a complicated example, you might start with less complex shapes to make lamps, stands, tables, boxes, cupboards, and bowls.

***Figure 2-25.** A friend inside a wooden Hoberman sphere. Photo: Nicolas Dartiailh*

When you want to do snap-fit (or press-fit) projects, most of the time you'll have to use the thickness of your material in your designs; don't forget this if you are not using a parametric system! The nice thing about this kind of assembly is that you can easily scale up your design and use it on a large-scale CNC mill to make the same object, but bigger.

Figure 2-26. *"To be or not to be" – skull made of laser cut wood. Photo: Marion Sabourdy*

Figure 2-27. *Laser cut wooden lamps. Photos: Marion Sabourdy*

Folding Wood and Plastics, Snijlab, and Hasso Plattner

Another fun thing that we see more and more is a technique invented by the "Snijlab" in Rotterdam, the Netherlands. If you cut parallel lines close to each other in wood or other not too rigid material, it becomes flexible (see Figure 2-28). The trick is to space the lines in such a way that none of them separate the piece completely and have them be close enough to each other to make the material bend. This can also be done with a CNC mill (see Chapter 4), but it is a little harder since you can't make a cut as thin as with a laser.

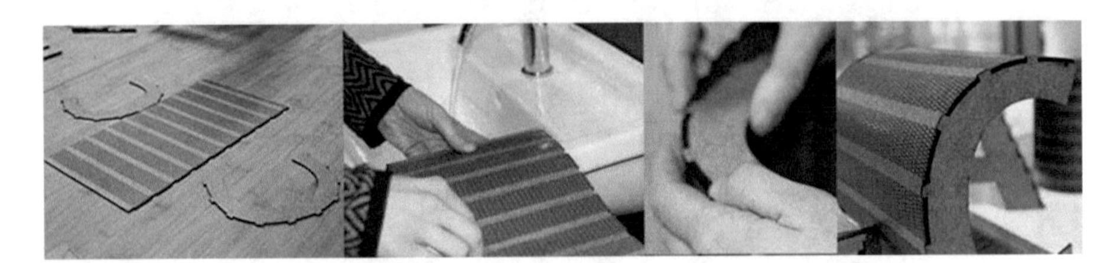

Figure 2-28. *Bending wood by partially cutting through it*

Another cool thing similar to the Snijlab technique is not only cutting the material you are working with but also using the heat of the laser to fold it. The people at the Hasso Plattner Institute came up with the idea to unfocus the laser after using it to cut through plexiglass, thus heating the material just enough to get soft and bend down because of gravity. This means you'll have to suspend the material you are cutting in your laser, but then you'll be able to create penholders, plant suspension, and phone add-ons in a matter of minutes, no finishing or assembly required! Check out Figure 2-29 for an example of their work, and visit their website if you'd like to try the same.

Figure 2-29. *Hasso Plattner Institute's laser origami*

Thin polypropylene folds really well if engraved or partially cut along lines. From a single sheet, if calculated correctly with folding features of CAD software, it is possible to create fully 3D shapes. Some shapes can be folded by using snap-fit joints, and others may require additional clip closing mechanisms.

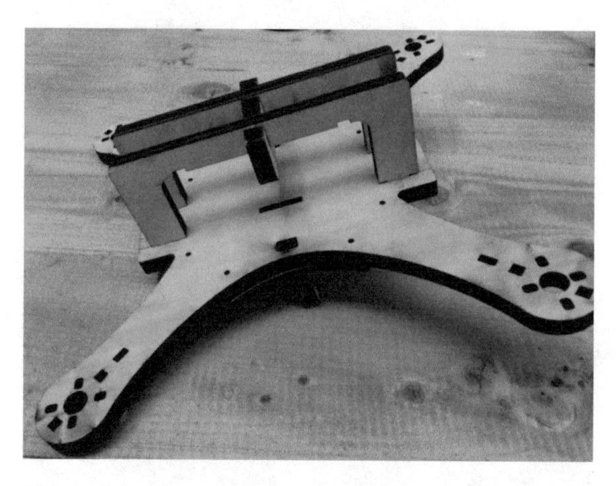

Figure 2-30. *The frame of a drone built by laser cutting 8mm plywood*

Stacking Layers

If you are trying to create 3D structures with a laser, another option would be stacking your material horizontally or vertically to create the desired shape (see Figure 2-31). This is a technique that is often used by architects to create beautiful scale models, but it can easily be employed for many other applications, like containers, bowls, lamps, and even furniture.

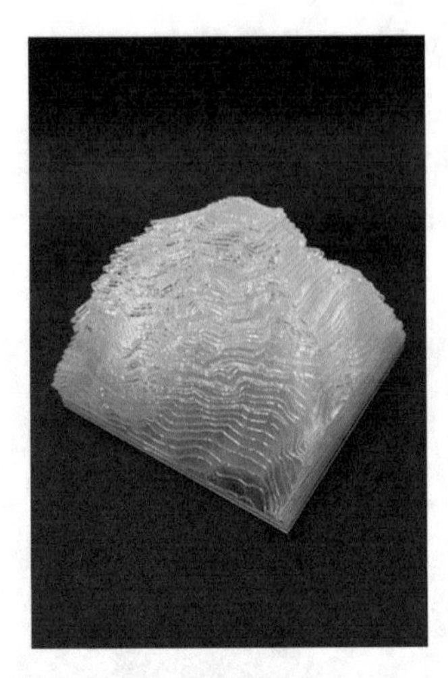

Figure 2-31. *Topographic map created by stacking laser cut pieces. Photo: Marion Sabourdy*

Figure 2-32. *Scale model of a part of the planet Mars made with a laser cutter (`www.ponoko.com/blog/wp-content/uploads/2011/04/tlc23f.jpg`)*

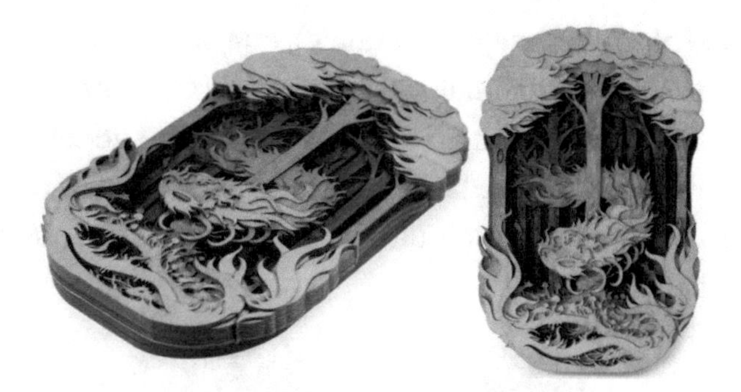

Figure 2-33. *Example of stacked cutouts forming intricate imagery (www.woodworkingnetwork.com/sites/woodworking/files/styles/large_landscape_desktop/public/itcamefromthewood2.jpg?itok=3wKRK7SO)*

The thinner your material, the higher the precision of the final object, but thinner material means more pieces and more time assembling. Often it's a better idea to use quite thick material and finish by hand with some sandpaper or a saw. Digitally controlled tools are great, but sometimes finishing by hand is the best (and fastest) option!

Engraving and Decoration

When engraving, color is not an option, but there are materials on the market that have multiple layers with different colors, so by burning away one or more layers, we can create images that consist of multiple colors.

Generally, the lighter the material is, the better it will look when you engrave it. Since the laser burns, it will blacken the material you are engraving, thus creating a nice contrast with the non-engraved parts. You can also engrave things like tiles, mirrors, and stone, but in those materials it's not the burn marks of the laser you'll see, but the impact of the dissipating energy provided by the beam. It's like hitting the material with an extremely small and pointy hammer. Here it's rather the darker your material, the more detail you'll discern after engraving.

In the Fab Lab of La Casemate (France), one of the applications for engraving is making personalized skateboards and longboards (see Figure 2-34). We'll first laser engrave images, designs, and texts onto the wood, then cut the shapes, and assemble the layers together using epoxy and fiberglass. This can of course also be applied to making tables, chairs, or other big objects.

Figure 2-34. *Longboard engraved with a laser cutter, design by MAGO. Photo: Marion*

If the laser cutter has a rotary axis, many of the engraving jobs can be replicated onto cylindrical objects. It's common to see personalized glasses or bottles with a personal or a company name on them. If a long focus lens is used, it is possible to engrave also on non-perfectly cylindrical objects, obtaining different kinds of engraving effects.

Printed Circuit Boards

If your machine has both CO_2 and fiber lasers available, then you can use them to produce printed circuit boards (PCBs). The integration of the two lasers is usually automatically managed in a way that is possible to use both in the same job, with the machine adjusting the focus when using one or the other. The fiber laser is used here to engrave normal copper boards, normally used to manufacture PCBs. Many of the common copper boards will work, ranging from FR1 to FR4. Even if the thickness of the copper is just 34 micrometers, because of the high heat dissipation copper has, multiple passes are often necessary to completely remove it. The engraving removes the unwanted copper, in order to isolate the circuit traces. After the PCBs have been engraved, it is then possible to use the CO_2 laser to cut out the underneath layer, consisting in a mixture of paper and resin on FR1 and FR2 and in a fiberglass board on FR4.

Figure 2-35. *PCB with copper traces left after engraving with a fiber laser*

Making More Machines

Many other machines can be built from laser cut material (mostly wood, for it has a good combination of rigidity and flexibility).

MakerBot, the American company making 3D printers, made one of their first versions (the Cupcake) with laser cut wood. UltiMaker, a company from the Netherlands, uses laser cutters to make the frames for their first version of 3D printers. Their designs are completely open source, so you could build their machine yourself by laser cutting the parts and putting them together (see Figure 2-36).

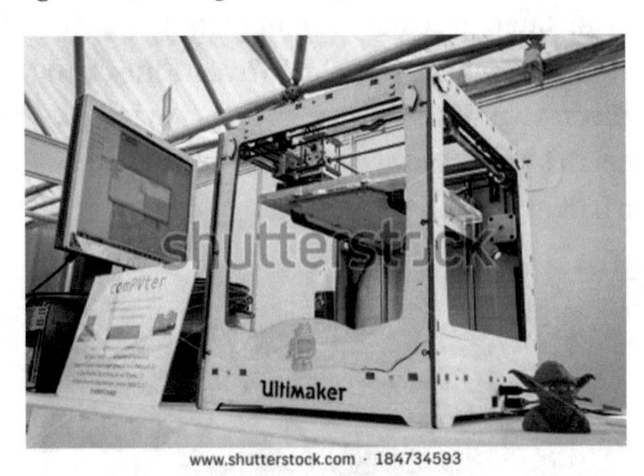

***Figure 2-36.** UltiMaker 1 – assembled from laser cut parts*

There are many more machines that can be built this way, from drawing bots (Figure 2-37) to little CNC mills to more laser cutters.

Figure 2-37. *Laser cut drawing system using wires (`https://tinkerlog1.files.wordpress.com/2011/09/b_img-1956.jpg`)*

So Get Creative!

There are of course many more cool things you can do with a laser cutter. The trick is to start with a simple project and then get creative! In one lab people have lasered pig skin (for an art project) and cheese (as a personalized gift – this was in France), and we even worked with a food designer who hosts workshops in which people personalize their food with the laser cutter before having a DIY lunch in the lab.

Figure 2-38. *Aubergine engraved with the laser cutter. Source:* `www.figurasfondo.fr/?p=775`

If you are completely new to laser cutting, I'd suggest starting with a simple project like making a laser cut lamp or penholder.

Figure 2-39. *Example of a lamp shade, made with a laser cutter. Photo: Marion Sabourdy*

A good technique to learn is making snap-fit pieces, and in the Fab Academy, one of the first assignments is to make a snap-fit construction kit (like that in Figure 2-40), which is both fun to design and great to use with kids and even grown-ups.

Figure 2-40. *Construction kit made from laser cut plywood. Photo: @utopikphoto*

Summary

Laser cutters are awesome tools for many reasons – they can work with a large variety of materials, are pretty easy to use, and can nowadays be found in many Fab Labs and makerspaces around the world. So whether you want to make architectural models, construction kits, circuit boards, signs, skateboards, or much more, the laser cutter is your tool.

If you plan on buying one, make sure you know what you'd like to use it for and do your homework. There are many commercially available machines and kits you can assemble yourself, but not all lasers are created equal ... Some are super-fast in engraving metal (great for PCBs); others are best for cutting wood and plastics. Additionally, make sure you have the proper space for such a machine, be it in your garage or in your company shop – you need good ventilation, a space that doesn't become too hot in the summer or too cold in the winter, and your electrical installation should not only be able to handle the power draw but also be stable. Small interruptions of power decrease the laser's lifespan.

Lasers also need proper safety precautions, so train all the people who are allowed to use the tool well, and never EVER leave a laser cutter running without supervision.

In the next chapter, we are going to take a look at vinyl cutters - much cheaper tools, but also offering many possibilities and great projects!

CHAPTER 3

Vinyl Cutting

History

Vinyl cutters evolved from (pen) plotters, which were built as early as 1959 by CalComp (a USA-based company, founded the same year). The first variants had paper on a drum (like a roll) that a pen could move across in the Y axis. By rotating the drum with the paper on it, the tool could make drawings with a simple ballpoint pen. The next variant of plotters moved to a system we now see in CNC mills, where the pen would move in the Y axis, which would be mounted on a bar that moved along the X axis. The material that you wanted to draw on would be lying flat underneath this system, thus limiting the size you could work on and limiting the speed. Hewlett-Packard created the first machines in the 1980s that look like the vinyl cutters you'll see today. Wheels grip a sheet (or roll) of material and move it back and forth while a pen (or cutter) moves laterally over it. This heralded the possibility to create designs (and cut parts) using rolls of material you loaded in the machine, which can be as long as you want.

How They Work

Vinyl cutters take their name from the material they work with, even though there are other materials that you can use with this type of machine. The principle is that all materials cut with these machines are on

J-m. Molenaar and D. Ingrassia, *Mastering Digitally Controlled Machines*, Maker Innovations Series, https://doi.org/10.1007/978-1-4842-9849-7_3

a backing or transfer material. On most machines you will never cut all the way through, because if you do you'll damage the part of the machine the material rests on, which must be smooth to create proper counterforce to the knife or pen.

Vinyl cutters have a small knife that sits in a system allowing it to rotate freely, which is fixed to a head that can move in two directions (laterally and up and down). Underneath, a flexible material is fixed between rollers that moves the material back and forth. This allows you to send the machine commands that move the head and the material to cut shapes you've designed with a computer. The knife moves down when cuts are needed and is dragged through the material and up to move the head and material if no cutting is needed. You can change the cutting speed and the force the knife pushes down with, so you can cut different materials.

Figure 3-1. *Roll of red vinyl loaded into the back of the vinyl cutter. Photo: @utopikphoto for La Casemate*

Figure 3-2. *Roll of red vinyl coming out at the front of the machine. Photo: @utopikphoto for La Casemate*

Types

The simplest machines you'll encounter will do only one thing, which is cutting. They will cut different materials though, for which you might need different blades. More advanced vinyl cutters have indexing systems that allow you to load special materials or materials on which you printed first, which have special marks that are recognized by the machine. The machine is thus able to cut on or around prints or other prepared materials.

Even more advanced machines not only cut but also print on your materials, allowing even more complexity. With the right kind of ink, this allows you to print images that you can then transfer to another object with a special press, to make custom cups, caps, shirts, and more.

These machines are obviously more expensive, but if you often need to print big posters and signage, it might be a good idea to look into those options.

You'll find different brands of machines in makerspaces. If you want to buy a machine for yours, your choice will depend on size, speed, and additional features you want or need. Most brands make a range of sizes, and you can get a machine that not only cuts but also prints and in many cases has indexing systems allowing it to do both operations with very high precision and repeatability. Roland, Summa, and Graphtec are some brands you can check out when shopping for a vinyl cutter.

Figure 3-3. *Simple Roland vinyl cutter on the Maker Faire Grenoble. Photo: @utopikphoto*

Materials

In makerspaces, you'll mostly find two kinds of materials being used with these machines, vinyl and heat transfer vinyl (which is sometimes called flock or flex).

Vinyl is used to create stickers, signage, stencils, and masks. You can find many different kinds of vinyl, in many price ranges. Some of them are specially made for outdoor use and will, when applied correctly, stay in place many years; others are created for sandblasting or stencils.

Other kinds of vinyl can be heated up slightly to become more flexible, so they can be stretched over curved surfaces.

Figure 3-4. *Rolls of flex in different colors. Photo: Marion Sabourdy*

There are several different ways of making vinyl, and the type and brand you get will have an impact on the lifetime and kind of application you can use the material for. The difference is in the manufacturing process. There is vinyl that is "cast" and vinyl that is "extruded." Cast vinyl basically means it has been created by pouring the resin (the liquid material) onto a very flat surface and then curing it in ovens. This means there is less "stress" on the material during the fabrication process, and cast vinyl generally has better dimensional stability, color pigmentation, UV stability and higher gloss levels (shiny!).

Extruded or "calendered" vinyl is created by using rollers, a process that gives it less dimensional stability in the direction it was rolled. Extruded vinyl is easier to make though and a lot cheaper.

Vinyl can also be monomeric or polymeric. Polymeric vinyl has bigger molecules and longer chains, resulting in better longevity, flexibility, and additional film stability with less shrinkage.

To sum up, if you want the best stuff there is, to stick onto your shop window or car, and you want it to still be there (and look good) when you sell your car (or shop) many years later, go for polymeric cast vinyl. But remember, this is also the most expensive stuff on the market.

Monomeric calendered vinyl is often the best choice for makerspaces, where people are not necessarily looking for very long stability, as it's used for decoration and simple stickers. You could always have some more expensive material in your lab, for people who want to create products that will withstand the test of time. There are many different brands of vinyl, but we'll refrain from giving you advice on which one to go for. Our advice is to ask a supplier for some samples and just try them out (adhesion on different surfaces, leaving it in the sun for a week, etc.) and find the one that gives you the best combination of price and quality.

Since vinyl has little or no adhesion to (most) fabrics, heat transfer vinyl is used to add text and images onto tissues and to make personalized T-shirts (look, e.g., at Figure 3-5). It has an adhesive on the bottom surface that will only activate when heated and when pressure is applied to it. Using a heated press, you can add logos, text, and images to clothing or other products made out of tissue.

***Figure 3-5.** Heat transfer vinyl pressed into a T-shirt*

A material less used, but very interesting, is copper tape. Since the tape is conductive, it is possible to create flexible electronic circuits using a vinyl cutter or even multilayered circuits by stacking the cut copper traces with non-conductive material in between the circuit layers. Should you wish to use this, understand that the sticky side of the tape also is conductive! So you need an insulating layer if you want to use it for a circuit. To do this, you'll need the right kind of material and to get the settings just right, but if you do you can add sensors to a round object with ease (see Figure 3-6).

Figure 3-6. *Example of a flexible circuit made with the vinyl cutter*

Along with the materials you'll cut with the machine, there are special kinds of transfer tape that will help you put your final product in place. You'll find more on this in the following section.

Software: How to Run the Machine

Commercially available vinyl cutters will come with a driver, making them behave as a printer when it comes to sending them jobs. You'll open the files you wish to cut, which will contain vector lines, and send them to the machine. Some machines will have a separate interface where the files get sent first, so you can position your job on the material available and adjust settings.

When it comes to cutting, remember the knife rotates freely allowing it to follow the lines that it is supposed to cut. This means that in tight corners, when the direction of cut is changed rapidly, the knife must turn many degrees rapidly. To make sure it does not drag or damage the material because it rotates at the wrong speed, some systems will slow down on sudden change of direction (a technique called ramping, also seen in CNC milling), or you will have to adjust the speed manually.

Since the knife is supposed to cut only the top material, there is only a very small part sticking out of the head, which in some machines needs to be adjusted manually to cut materials of different thickness.

Settings

There aren't many settings to consider when using a vinyl cutter, and because of this the machine is relatively easy to use, but there are some very important things to get right if you want your product to come out well and you want your machine to last. Knives are consumables, so it's good to have some extra ones ready for when you need to change one, but if you get the settings right, you won't need to change them often.

Most machines will let you change settings both in the software and on the machine. The main setting is the force with which the knife will be dragged through the material you are cutting. Too much force will have it cut all the way through the backing and damage your machine. Too little force means your material won't be cut well, and weeding out the waste (see in the following) will be difficult or even impossible. If you get the settings right and you have good material, you can take off the cut pieces by just peeling them away slowly from the backing.

Next, you'll want to set the speed at which the machine will cut so that tight angles come out correctly as well. This depends on the complexity and size of the lines you are cutting: if you cut very big letters, for instance, your speed can be much higher than when cutting tiny lettering. Don't hesitate to test this; as long as you don't use too much force, you can crank up the speed till your results deteriorate. Lower your speed a bit, and you know you have optimized your time and quality.

Most machines can measure the width and optionally the length of your material automatically, which allows for easy positioning of the parts you'd like to cut.

Weeding

When the shapes are cut into the material, the next step is to remove it from the machine and take away all the pieces that are not part of the final product (see Figure 3-7). We call this process weeding, and this is best done by keeping the parts you'd like to remove as flat as possible and peeling them off slowly. For small parts it's possible to use a handheld precision knife or even some tweezers. If your machine is set correctly, this part is easy, but can still take quite some time! Vinyl cutters are fast, but complex designs can take ages to finish by hand.

Figure 3-7. *Weeding vinyl after cutting – note the material is held flat for easy removal (`http://metalguruschool.com/wp-content/uploads/2013/07/weeding-vinyl-masks-2.jpg`)*

For some applications (e.g., copper tape), it's often easier to do the weeding on the final surface. You stick transfer tape to the whole part that is cut with the machine, including the parts you want to remove, stick all of it onto the final surface you want it to stay on, remove the transfer tape, and then remove the unwanted parts. Specifically when making flexible circuits, this saves time and frustration.

Finishing Your Product

The idea behind the combination of materials (vinyl, backing, transfer) is to allow this process: The backing the vinyl is on will have slightly less adherence to the vinyl than the transfer tape, so when putting the transfer tape on top, you can peel away the backing. Then, when you place the vinyl where you want it to be and apply pressure, the vinyl will have more adherence to that surface than the transfer tape, so you can peel that one off. Now your product is in place!

This means that you can only apply vinyl to certain materials, and some products will have no adherence at all. Check if your vinyl sticks well where you'd like to put it before preparing complex shapes!

Safety and Maintenance

Safety

Vinyl cutters are perhaps the safest machines in a Fab Lab, but you'll need to use them correctly to make sure they will have a long life.

The knife sticks out very little, so it's not really possible to cut yourself, but while the machine is working, it is possible to pinch your fingers or hair in between the rollers holding down the material or the cutting head. As with all CNC machines, when it's on, never put your hands close to the tool, and if you have long hair, please tie it well behind your head or put on a cap!

Maintenance

The piece of a vinyl cutter you'll have to change from time to time is the knife. If the machine is used correctly, you'll need to do this perhaps two or three times per year, if it's used regularly. When lines become ragged or the knife starts to drag the material, it's time to check. Take the blade out of the machine, and check it with a microscope (if you have one) or with the naked eye. If the side seems uneven, not smooth, it's time for a new one.

If you (or your users) put too much force on the knife while cutting, it might cut all the way through the material, and even cut the backing, into the surface (often a plastic strip) underneath. If this happens, that normally smooth surface will become damaged and must be replaced. You'll notice this when the machine cuts well, except in a certain location. Check the strip with your fingers (while the machine is off!) for any irregularities. If you feel small cutlines in the surface, take it off and replace it with a new one. If you use the machine well, this normally never has to be done!

Since knives will wear with time, the force you'll need to use to cut will increase over its lifespan. This is normal, but if cuts become ragged or uneven, replace your knife immediately!

Normally machines will never need to be greased, but you should obviously keep them clean and dry.

Applications

Most people will use the vinyl cutter to create stickers, both in a professional setting and in makerspaces. The letters you'll see on the window of a shop or restaurant and the text and graphics on a car will be cut with a vinyl cutter.

Signage really is what vinyl cutting is mostly used for – directing your visitors to the right spaces, telling them to remember to turn on the compressor before laser cutting, showing what cupboards contain dangerous stuff and which ones are filled with food. It's great having one in your makerspace even just for annotating the space itself. I cut many explanatory stickers when installing machines, because even the most experienced users will forget things and can use a reminder right on the machine.

Figure 3-8. *Warning signs – more or less useful*

Figure 3-9. *Signage directly applied to the floor. Photo: Marion Sabourdy*

Figure 3-10. *Stickers made with kids in a Fab Lab. Photo: Marion Sabourdy*

Multicolored, Complex Designs

Vinyl comes in many colors, but it is not possible to create gradients, meaning, directional change in image intensity except when you use them in combination with a printer. Some systems allow you to use white vinyl, print on the material, and then cut it. So when you see stickers with a special shape and multiple colors, they were probably printed and then cut.

If you'd like multiple colors in your design without a printer, it's possible to cut multiple layers and assemble them where you want the final product, like that shown in Figure 3-11. This is quite easy to do, thanks to the transfer material. You cut all the different colors and put on the transfer tape; then you create a mark (or preferably two or three) somewhere on the surface you'd like the product on and align all the different colors with those markers, applying them one by one. Of course, this is also possible for flex, when making T-shirts.

Figure 3-11. *A complex multi color mural made with vinyl*

Wrapping

As explained before, some vinyl is made to stretch and allows for what we call "wrapping." Using a heat gun, the material can be made even more flexible and stretched around curved surfaces before sticking it on. This allows you to change the color of a car or any kind of curved surface rapidly. This is not easy to do though. You'll need many hours of training to become proficient if you'd like to master this technique, but once you know how to use your tools well, you can change the color of your motorbike helmet whenever you feel like it.

Stencils, Sandblasting

It's also possible to cut shapes with the vinyl cutter to use as a stencil. You'll cut the shapes you want to paint on a surface, apply the sticker, and use it as a mask to apply paint. Make sure you apply it well before painting, so no paint can get under the mask, and wait until the paint is dry to the touch before removing the stencil. If you are making a stencil and you are using text, the vinyl cutter is often a better option than the laser cutter, because it's easier to transfer the letters into the correct position (without losing, e.g., the triangle in the letter "A"), but your masks will most likely be single use.

There are also special materials that can easily be cut using a vinyl cutter, but that will resist the impact of sand projected at it with high speed. This allows for the creation of masks on glass or other materials for which sandblasting is used, to create images too complex to obtain otherwise with this technique. This is a wonderful way of marking glass and semi-transparent plexiglass, but you'll need a sandblasting tool.

Multilayered Circuits

Using special copper tape, you can use the vinyl cutter to make flexible electronic circuits or multilayered ones. You'll want to use a good blade to cut this, which won't last long, because the material is tougher than vinyl, but, since it's flexible, you can stick it onto curved objects, like a cup, and solder SMD (surface-mount device) components on there to, for instance, measure the temperature of your coffee. If you want to do more complex multilayered circuits, you can cut the layers separately and then stick them together with non-conductive layers in between. We have also seen people use the copper tape to make small antennas or reflective parabolic surfaces to direct light.

Another fun use for the copper tape is using it to make simple circuits, for instance, on folding postcards, where, once the card is folded, a circuit is closed and a little LED lights up. Great for short workshops with kids, but adults love this too! See Figure 3-12 for a nice example from the Exploratorium (San Francisco).

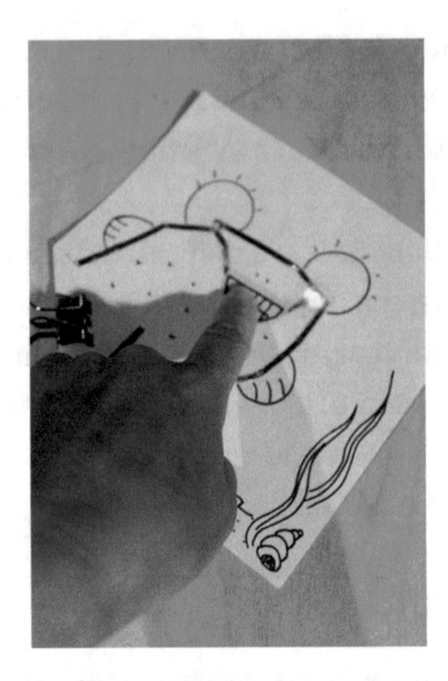

Figure 3-12. *Example of a circuit made with vinyl cut copper tape*

Screenprinting (Silk Screen)

This is a simple way to design and make your own T-shirts, bags, etc. Vinyl positioned as a resist on silk screens can stay in place for a small number of prints before deteriorating, so limited runs of branded garments or wearables are possible. You can also do an analog-looking poster using the same technique. Conductive ink can be screened onto fabrics (though you have to be careful which fabrics you use) for wearable electronics and more.

Summary

To sum up, vinyl cutters are perhaps the easiest machines to use in a makerspace, but allow you to create diverse interesting and useful objects. From personalized clothing to signage to antennas and flexible circuits, vinyl cutters are fun and versatile and a great way of getting into digital design, because all the items you make with them only need 2D designs. If you want to get a machine or find one somewhere to use, realize they come in different sizes and do not all have the same functionality – some only cut, while other more sophisticated tools also print or are able to scan the material and cut in and around designs already present.

They are great machines to use in workshops, but can also be used for commercial applications, especially if you have a more sophisticated machine that can also print (which might help sustain part of your lab financially).

Since simple vinyl cutters are relatively small, not too heavy and quite sturdy, they are also perfect for workshops and demonstration on location or for use in a mobile makerspace!

CHAPTER 4

CNC Milling

Any machine digitally controlled by a computer is by definition a "computer numerically controlled" (CNC) machine. Machines connected to a computer have computer numerical control and are therefore CNC machines. However, when people refer to a CNC milling machine, they often say a CNC machine, as though they were the same. Including the word "milling" identifies the process that involves the cutting of material with a rotating tool. Using the correct term helps you sound knowledgeable and professional. In this chapter we will be discussing CNC milling machines.

History

Looking at the collection of machines in this book, what unites them is the CNC part. They have computer numerical control or, simply said, are controlled by a computer. The machines in this chapter, CNC milling machines, were actually the first to be so controlled. In 1955 researchers at MIT[1] connected a (then very bulky) computer to a milling machine and created the first pieces without piloting the machine by hand, by sending the machine coordinates and controlling its movements digitally. This was a big thing for a few reasons: you could attain extremely high precision and

[1] Massachusetts Institute of Technology, Cambridge, USA.

J-m. Molenaar and D. Ingrassia, *Mastering Digitally Controlled Machines*, Maker Innovations Series, https://doi.org/10.1007/978-1-4842-9849-7_4

repeatability; you could run machines for much longer periods of time; and you could be at a distance when the machine performed its duties, resulting in lower risks and higher accessibility.

The Introduction of this book covers the general history of CNC, so we will not dive into that again, but let's take a closer look at CNC milling specifically.

There are many different types of mills, and most of them can be found in a computer-controlled version. What really made it possible for CNC milling to become so commonplace in manufacturing and even in makerspaces was not the development of the machines itself, but the lower cost of computing and the arrival of mini computers.

The introduction of microcontrollers in the 1970s made it possible to create machines that had a small dedicated computer system. The arrival of CAM (computer-aided manufacturing) allowed companies to build machines able to create parts with higher complexity using not only three but five or even more axes (see Figure 4-1). Programming machines with so many degrees of freedom (like robotic arms) is only possible using dedicated software that can create the toolpath while optimizing the movement of all axes simultaneously.

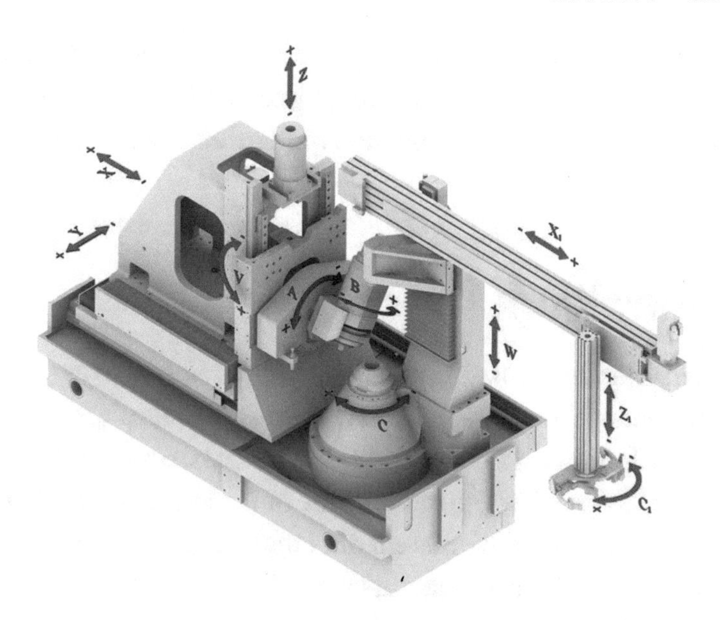

Figure 4-1. *Motion of a multiple-axis CNC milling machine (`www.wordsun.com/assets/press/num-2-13431193162.jpg`)*

Different companies started to fabricate NC and later CNC machines, and though the invention of CNC machines happened in the United States, in the beginning the market was mostly controlled by Germany and Japan who were fabricating machines for a lower cost than their American counterparts.

Small-scale CNC machines (like the ones you will find in Fab Labs) were made possible in part thanks to the Enhanced Machine Controller project, run by the National Institute for Standards and Technology in the United States. The program developed an open source operating system for the control of machines up to nine axes, making it possible for smaller-scale manufacturers to create machines for a lower price. The project was later renamed into EMC2 and finally into LinuxCNC (about which you can read more in Chapter 7, which focuses on open source hardware).

This meant that hobbyists could build their own machines and tools, eventually making this technology available to everyone.

Today machines are available with up to nine axes of freedom (and even more if you consider tool changers as axes), which can produce very complex parts with minimum intervention, also called "single-setup machining."

How They Work

Milling machines use a rotating mill (sometimes referred to as cutter, or end mill) to remove material and create the desired piece. (To find out the difference between a mill bit and a drill bit, please see the "Tooling" section of this chapter.) While rotating, the mill cuts the material to the desired shape by moving in different directions. The end shape is created by cutting out "chips" (small material pieces) out of a solid block of material, called "stock." Because of the way this works, it is often referred to as one of the main subtractive technologies. The number of degrees of freedom the machine has is the number of axes. The most common machines have three axes (X, Y, and Z), while more advanced ones have five axes (X, Y, Z, B, and C), and there are machines with nine axes or more. The number of axes defines how complex the final piece can be, with the machines having five or more axes able to produce shapes resembling 3D printing capabilities. Three-axis machines are the most common, but they cannot do undercuts or anything that involves tilting the end mill. Undercuts are spaces the tool cannot reach, like the gray areas in Figure 4-2.

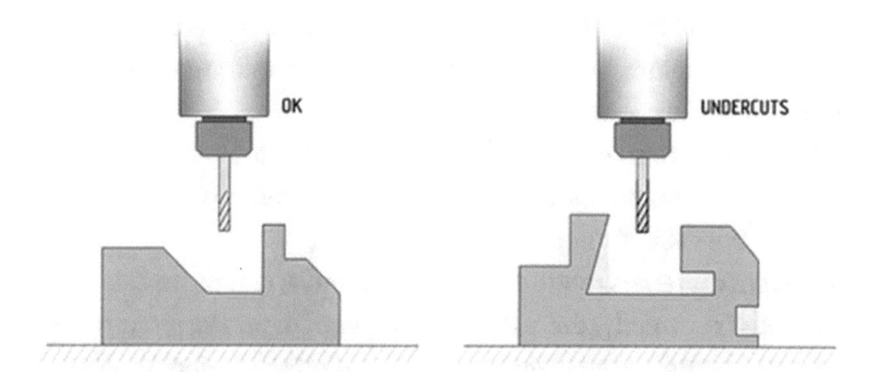

Figure 4-2. *Undercuts are spaces the tool cannot reach, like the gray areas shown (`https://prototechasia.com/wp-content/uploads/CNC-Contre-depouille.png`)*

In order to be milled successfully, a piece of stock material is firmly fixed to the machine bed, while the rotating mill is moved around by powerful motorized axes. A key part to understanding CNC milling is learning about the forces involved. Whenever the mill is cutting the material, the stock material applies a certain force to the mill. The force applied to the mill goes through the machine frame arriving back to the bed where the piece is attached. The structure of a CNC machine is made in such a way that avoids any distortion, which could lead to loose tolerances (i.e., pieces not fitting together correctly). In comparison with other machines, where there are no forces coming from the material that are applied during operation (e.g., laser cutters, 3D printers, etc.), CNC machines are made to be as heavy and as rigid as possible. Because of this, they often move slower than other kinds of machines.

The cutter needs to rotate at a certain speed and with certain torque to cut chips away from the stock. The rotation is created by a powerful motor attached to the machine head, usually a spindle or a router. These motors are able to rotate at the required RPMs (rotations per minute) and will consume kilowatts of power to output the required torque.

The CNC mill in your Fab Lab gives you a host of different options and techniques to explore, but is perhaps the most complex machine to use, especially if you are new to the principle.

The software used to generate the CNC milling toolpath, called computer-aided manufacturing (CAM), involves many parameters, which depend on the desired shape and material used.

Different materials require different end mills, and if you calculate your speeds incorrectly, there is a real danger of damaging your machine and space, but most importantly yourself and others. Before you get started with this machine, make sure you are well trained and know how to handle it!

If you are opening a makerspace or Fab Lab, you'll most likely install a three-axis machine, so let us take you through an overview of the different machines available, but then focus mainly on three-axis milling.

Types

There are different types of CNC milling machines, from very small and high-precision desktop machines (often used for jewelry and dental applications) to extremely big machines able to machine mold the size of a ship or windmill blade.

Many Fab Labs will have two different mills, a small one for projects needing high precision and for printed circuit board (PCB) fabrication and a large one for press-fit objects like furniture or even small house structures.

When choosing a CNC mill, you should start by asking yourself what you and your users would like to do with it.

The main parameters to take into consideration when choosing a CNC milling machine are the working area and the materials it can work with. The working area defines the size of the parts that can be produced, while the materials it can work on define the machine stiffness, structure, and accessories.

Price and overall machine size vary greatly depending on the working area and usable materials. Machines able to work with soft materials usually have a lighter structure than the machines able to work with metals, and they are often offered at a lower price. Machines able to CNC mill metals are very heavy and quite expensive and also offer a quite small working area relative to the machine size.

To give an example, let's look at larger format machines. Are you going to make a lot of guitars, but probably not much furniture? Then you could get a machine with a smaller footprint, but perhaps five axes instead of three. Close to the sea? Perhaps people will want to make surfboards, which needs a certain-size machine to comfortably fit material on. Or maybe you want to machine metals as well? Then you should ensure the machine you choose is able to handle that and comes with adequate dust collection and cooling systems.

Visiting other spaces and asking for their experience with the machine(s) they have, for both the large format machines and the smaller ones, is a great way of understanding the differences in machines, sizes, possibilities, and more. And even once you have found a brand you like, they probably have the same machine in different sizes, and you can choose to either get a router or a spindle that rotates the cutter. On this we can say that in general, spindles are more stable and more silent and they last longer. On the other hand, they are also more expensive.

If you do not have a lot of money to spend, you could also build your own machine, knowing that CNC milling machines encounter a lot of force during their normal operations and need to be well built and robust.

The following is a comparison of the most common types of CNC milling machines available on the market.

Machine Type	Description	Typical Working Area	Typical Machinable Materials	Cost	Found In	Used For	Examples Machines	Notes
Gantry	Machines using an overhead bridge-like structure (gantry)	From 600 × 400 × 100mm to 3000 × 1500 × 300mm	Wood, plastics, PCB, machinable wax, aluminum, brass	$–$$$	Wood shops, Fab Labs, garages, and the advertising industry	Furniture, sign making, woodworking, PCBs, mold making	ShopBot Alpha, CNC6040, CNC3020, Jens's Humphrey	Some specialized machines are made to mill marble or glass.
Desktop	Compact machines usable in small environments without special requirements	From 100 × 100 × 50mm to 400 × 300 × 100mm	Wood, plastics, PCB, machinable wax. Some also aluminum and brass	$–$$	Dental and jewelry industries, Fab Labs, homes, garages	Precise small machining such as PCBs and molds. Teaching purposes	Roland: SRM-20, MDX-20, MDX-40 ShopBot Desktop, Bantam Desktop, LPKF ProtoMat	The most affordable CNC milling machines on the market, great to start learning or try out the technology. Also used in jewelry and mold making

C-frame	Machines having a fixed head moving horizontally	300 × 150 × 200 mm to 1200 × 600 × 500 mm	Mostly hard metals	$$–$$$$	Metalworking shops, metal industry, garages	Professional production of metal parts	Haas VF series, EMCOMILL E, Mazak FJV	Also called vertical milling machines
Five-axis				$$–$$$$				There are machines with more axes
Other	Machines with configurations different from the preceding ones or having special configurations	Depends on the machine, from micromachining (about 100 × 100 × 50mm) to meters-range machines	Depends on the machine	$–$$$$	Homes, garages, metal industry	Small machines are mainly for hobbyists. Five-axis is for the advanced metal industry	Shaper Origin, Maslow CNC, five-axis milling	Often proposing an innovative way of working or dedicated to special industrial purposes

An alternative and innovative approach to CNC milling wood (or soft sheets in general) involves the technique used by Shaper Origin. Typically, the material stock is placed on top of a bed and surrounded by the CNC milling machine structure, which moves the head accordingly to make the cut. With the Shaper, if the sheet is larger than the machine itself, the milling head is moved by hand while the spindle precisely follows the design to cut. Shaper uses special stickers placed onto the sheet to orient itself according to the cut. This way, you can cut large sheets without the need for a large-format CNC milling machine, and especially without moving the sheet if it is already in place (e.g., an installed wooden wall).

SainSmart is a Chinese brand that introduced a very small and affordable CNC milling machine line called Genmitsu. Currently priced at around $150, the 3018-Pro represents the most economical and straightforward means to own your personal CNC milling machine. While it is limited to working with relatively soft materials due to its lack of stiffness, it certainly serves as a valuable learning tool before transitioning to larger and more expensive machines. Additionally, if you are delving into electronics and want to test your electronic designs, the 3018-Pro is capable of engraving simple PCBs.

Materials

Many different materials can successfully be machined with a mill, but you will most likely be limited when it comes to material choice in your makerspace, because denser and harder materials (like metals) require more professional (and expensive) dust collection systems and tools.

In Fab Labs, we mostly machine wood, some plastics (like PVC, acrylic, HDPE (high-density polyethylene), POM, etc.), and occasionally plastic composites and light metals (like aluminum or brass).

Wood and Derived Materials

Wood is a wonderful material to work with and easy to come by in most places of the world. It's solid enough to make beautiful furniture and even houses, but soft enough to be machined easily. There are many different kinds of wood to choose from, ranging from composites such as MDF and plywood to a plethora of hardwoods and products like bamboo.

MDF is easy to machine and relatively cheap, but not great when it comes to waste. It's made by compressing a mix of glue and wood scraps, and there are often toxic chemicals in this product. Unless you really optimize your layout, you will add quite some waste to this world if you use it without thinking. It has also a limited plasticity, irremediably bending if too much force is applied to it.

Figure 4-3. *MDF sheets (`https://andrewsdiy.co.uk/product/mdf-6mm/`)*

Plywood is a little better and (depending on the quality) more stable and structurally sound. It gives your product more of a "real wood" look, if you like such a thing. It is the main material used to make CNC-milled furniture and such.

Figure 4-4. *Plywood sheets (`www.slecuk.com/index.php?route=product/category&path=145`)*

Hardwoods (such as hickory, maple, oak, and birch) are often used for things like furniture and kitchen tops, which give beautiful results when done correctly, but this material is not cheap.

Figure 4-5. *Hardwood sheets (`https://908ltd.co.uk/shop/wood-sheets-and-backing-boards/solid-cherry-sheets`)*

Bamboo is a nice product to use when you are making composites, such as skateboards, and it's relatively good for the environment to use this, as it is a material that grows extremely fast.

Figure 4-6. *Bamboo sheets (`https://m.made-in-china.com/product/Bamboo-Solid-Panel-3mm-Caramelized-Vertical-for-Laser-Cutting-Furniture-1938069705.html`)*

Plastics and Composites

You can machine all kinds of plastics with a CNC mill, but you'll need to get suitable tools that will make sure the plastic is cut (into nice chips) and not heated up, which causes it to melt. If plastic melts, it can easily stick to your tool, to the point of breaking it and/or pushing the working piece out of the clamps holding it down.

You can use cheap foam, like polystyrene or polyurethane, which machines super-fast and gives nice results. Denser plastics like HDPE are also machined easily and are great for building rigid structures and other machines, like the MTM snap in the following image.

You can also machine carbon plates, which are super-strong but lightweight and often used in model making.

Acrylic (also known as plexiglass) is a strong thermoplastic often used as an alternative to glass. It's great to use with laser cutters, but acrylic can also be CNC milled, which is more common for thicker sheets, which cannot easily be cut with a laser (usually above 10mm). Next to using it for windows and transparent builds, acrylic can be used as structural material for maker projects. It is important to know that acrylic is quite brittle, and once it cracks it loses its strength. Among the different plastics, acrylic is one of those that easily sticks to your tool, requiring extra care in observing the job and finding the right settings. Single-flute end mills are recommended.

Figure 4-7. *Acrylic sheets (`www.ravellilaser.com/en/product/extruded-transparent-plexiglass-4mm/`)*

HDPE (high-density polyethylene) has a good balance between strength and elasticity. It has relatively low price and widespread availability, and the fact it's easy to machine makes HDPE one of the first plastics you should try to cut with a CNC machine. In Fab Labs it can be used to build snap-fit parts (using its plasticity) and other structural elements.

Figure 4-8. *HDPE sheets (`www.tapplastics.com/product/plastics/cut_to_size_plastic/hdpe_cutting_boards/346`)*

Being a little elastic and partially self-lubricating, **POM** is a commonly machined plastic mostly used to make mechanical parts or parts required to have high strength. In makerspaces it is often used for machine building. POM is easy to machine, with very good dimensional accuracy. It can be machined with dedicated end mills for plastics or end mills made for aluminum.

Figure 4-9. *POM sheets (`www.desertcart.cr/products/54586551-plate-pom-c-black-1000-x-1000-x-3-mm-sheet-acetal-alt-intech`)*

Foam is one of the easiest materials to machine. Even with wrong settings, it might still result in a strong and precise shape. Note that, as many other plastics, some foam can melt and stick to the end mill; therefore, it is recommended to avoid using very high RPMs.

Figure 4-10. *High-density foam sheets (`www.frieser-muenchen.de/index.php/frieser-40b-xps-daemmplatten-aus-extrudiertem-polystyrol-hartschaum-styrodur.html`)*

Aluminum composites or sandwich panels are composed of two thin aluminum sheets with a layer of polyethylene or polyurethane in the middle. Being widely used in construction work, this material offers good rigidity and low weight while also being cheap and weatherproof. Because of the composition, it is quite easy to mill and to rework manually. Milling tools are similar to the ones used for wood and plastics. Example usages in Fab Labs are housings (for electronics), light structures, signs, and more.

Figure 4-11. *Aluminum composite sheets (`https://bauzuschnitt.de/Aluverbund-Platte-ALUCOM-Blau-3mm`)*

Tougher Stuff

Softer metals like aluminum and brass can be machined even with low-cost machines, and higher-powered professional machines chip away the most tough steel and glass without a hitch.

If you'd like to try your hand at machining metals, you'll need to make sure you have an adapted dust collector, because metal is more abrasive than wood dust. Also, mixing wood and metal chips can lead to fire caused by the heat the metal chips retain. Thus, a separate exhaust system or a dedicated shop vac is recommended. Also, you'll probably need a cooling system for the tool and workpieces. For occasional jobs it is possible to cool the system by hand spraying some coolant, like WD-40, cutting oil, or similar, onto the spaces being machined. A good option is to find a local machine shop and speak to them about what they use and recommend.

Aluminum

Available in different alloys and shapes, aluminum is a light metal that you can usually mill with CNC machines found in makerspaces (excluding the very small ones usually used for PCBs). This material is particularly suited for machine building (see Chapter 7) and parts that are required to be strong and lightweight. End mills having one to three flutes are recommended, together with step-downs from 0.5 to 1mm. It's a common problem to have aluminum sticking to the end mills. 5754 aluminum alloy (also known as EN AW-AlMg3) is what we would recommend for makerspaces.

For a complete list of materials you can use with CNC milling machines, with their density and some examples of use, check out the appendix in the back of the book (`https://docs.google.com/spreadsheets/d/1BOYzpdWmH21ZGEqBtH4ilasU-54bzSsLeyPG9WPOpDw/edit#gid=660704295`).

Figure 4-12. *Aluminum sheets/blocks (`www.heck-sevdic-gbr.de/index.php`)*

Tooling

Different Kinds of Cutters and Tools

Most of the things you'll be cutting will be done with an end mill – either a flat one or a ball nose, that is, a spherical end. A mill bit cuts materials using the edge of the flute, whereas a drill bit cuts materials using the tip and thus is only able to make holes. Make sure to check it, but most mill bits are also "center cutting," meaning you can plunge (i.e., decent straight down) into materials with them. You have end mills (sometimes also called cutters) for all different kinds of materials, and even though some cutters can be used for multiple materials (e.g., both plastics and wood), make sure you have the right cutter! Using a cutter made for hardwood on aluminum will lead to horrible results, and you will have to buy a new cutter, and good ones are not cheap. Check the following table for images and more details.

There are many different types of cutters, but you will likely at least find these three varieties: up-cut, down-cut, and compression bits. Up-cut bits will eject the chips upward, making it easy to extract them further with a dust collector. This type of cutter will create a nice and smooth finish at the bottom of your material, but might create ragged edges and chips on the top. It also might pull the material you are machining up, especially if it's not fixed well, and this might result in damaged pieces or other disasters.

Down-cut bits eject the chips downward, pushing them onto the material. This conveniently pushes your material down onto your machining bed and creates a nice finish at the top, but not the bottom.

Compression bits are a little bit more technical and expensive tools to use but, if used well, provide a great finish both on the top and the bottom of your material. They are machined to have a double spiral, one in each direction. This means you have to cut through your material in one go (to fully utilize the effect of the cutter), and it limits the thickness of the material you can cut to get the desired effect. Simply put, the part at the bottom of the cutter will eject the chips upward, creating a smooth finish at the bottom part of the material, and the top part of the cutter will eject them downward, creating a nice finishing on the top. It "compresses" the chips, hence "compression bit." On top of their usefulness, they look really beautiful.

Figure 4-13. *Compression bit (`www.woodcraft.com/products/freud-77-510-mortise-compression-spiral-router-bit-1-2-shank-1-2-d-1-3-8-cl`)*

In the following overview of different end mill types and their typical applications and settings, you might find some technical language you are unfamiliar with (like "step-down" or "feed rate"). Not to worry, these terms are explained later in this chapter. Come back to this overview if you need to buy a tool or are getting ready to machine something. Note that most manufacturers of end mills offer precise settings for all of their tools per material type, which you should rely on if available. The settings in the following table are a good starting point.

Material to Machine	End Mill Types	Sample Image	Typical Settings	Recommendations	Notes
Wood and derivatives	Single flutes, up-cut or down-cut, HSS, or carbide		Step-down 2–10mm, step-over from half to the full diameter of the end mill, feed rate 1000–4000mm/min, RPM 15000–20000	Wear protective glasses and a protective mask in case the machine is open and without an extraction system. Carefully observe the job (wood can catch fire easily). Avoid mixing wood chips with metal ones.	Recommended settings are for Fab Lab machines and single-flute end mills.
Plastics	Single, double, or triple flutes, up-cut, HSS, or carbide		Step-down 1–4mm, step-over from half to the full diameter of the end mill, feed rate 500–1000mm/min, RPM 8000–14000	Wear protective glasses if the machine is open. Watch out that plastic isn't melting while milling.	Recommended settings are for Fab Lab machines and two- or three-flute end mills.

(continued)

Material to Machine	End Mill Types	Sample Image	Typical Settings	Recommendations	Notes
Composites	Diamond toothed, up-cut, carbide, or special coating		Step-down 0.5–1mm, step-over half the diameter of the end mill, feed rate 200–700mm/min, RPM 8000–10000	Mandatory to have a proper extraction system and/or dedicated environment when milling composite materials.	Wear proper PPE when machining this kind of material. Some end mills have diamond coating to resist the strong wear given by cutting composites.
Aluminum/ soft metals	Single, double, or triple flutes, up-cut, HSS, or carbide or special coating		Step-down 0.5–1mm, step-over half the diameter of the end mill, feed rate 200–700mm/min, RPM 8000–10000	Coolant may be needed every once in a while. Keep an eye out for material sticking to the end mill, which means your settings are wrong.	Recommended settings are for Fab Lab machines and two- or three-flute end mills. Industrial machines usually have much higher values.
Hard metals	Four or more flutes, up-cut, carbide, and/or special coatings		Step-down 0.5–5mm, step-over half the diameter of the end mill, low RPMs (e.g., 500–4000)	Coolant is often needed, and the machines have dedicated systems for that. Mandatory to have a fully enclosed machine.	Usually not possible with Fab Lab machines, but rather a prerogative of industrial machines.

End mill images in the table are from www.mscdirect.com/browse/Milling/End-Mills?navid=2106227.

Software: Running the Machine

Most branded CNC milling systems will come with their own software packages to control the machine and to generate the toolpaths, called CAM (computer-aided manufacturing). Alternatively, there are options to use different controllers, such as LinuxCNC, a dedicated OS to control CNC machines, or you can use MIT's Mods, for (currently) ShopBots and small Roland mills and (most) MTM machines.

We'll first discuss the details of toolpath generation and then focus on setting up and running the machine.

Toolpath Generation

When working with CNC mills, it is extremely important to choose the right end mill, set the right cutting speeds and depth, and make sure your material is fixed well. Next, choosing your toolpath strategy wisely, and spending some time on the details of how you'll do the cutting, will possibly save you time and tools.

Note that you might hear people refer to individual toolpaths as "jobs" ("You running a job on that machine?", "Yup, roughing now, gonna do a finish after with a 3mm ball nose," "Okay, keep a close eye on it - it's known to lose steps when ramping into your stock").

Let's first look at the options for generating toolpaths for 2D milling (using vectorized files) and then move to 3D toolpaths, which are slightly more complex.

2D toolpaths are used whenever the cutting only involves 2D shapes, for example, cutting out a contour or a pocket. With 2D strategies it is possible to cut at different depths (or Z heights), as long as the height does not change for a single shape. You might also have heard about 2.5D - the difference between 2D toolpaths and 2.5D toolpaths is the Z height. In 2D toolpaths the Z height is constant; in 2.5D toolpaths the Z height varies.

VCarve (a software producing toolpaths we would refer to as 2.5D) allows you to use V-shaped tools, varying the Z axis height to create designs that look like they were carved out with a chisel.

3D toolpaths involve cutting out curves in the direction of the Z axis. All 3 axes move simultaneously to create complex shapes with different finishes. Apart from the limitations of not being able to reach undercuts and inner areas, 3D-milled parts can be comparable to 3D-printed results.

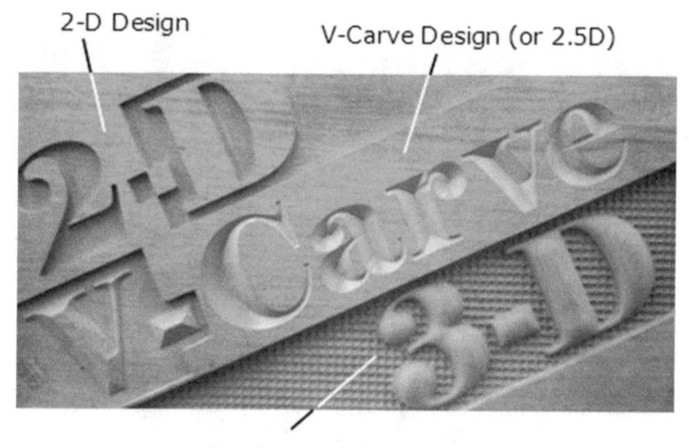

Figure 4-14. *Comparison of 2D, 3D, and 2.5D milling results (`https://static.wixstatic.com/media/0c8839_a367e39eb825486d8ec2312a13c86c9d.gif`)*

Milling Parameters

Before we start with different toolpath strategies, in this section we have a list of the most common milling parameters and their explanation. You will encounter those when setting a milling job with most of the available CAM software, and they are also mentioned in the next part of the chapter.

Feed rate defines the movement speed of the machine head and relative attached end mill. It is usually expressed in millimeter/minute (mm/min), millimeter/second (mm/s), or inch/minute (in/min). Different feed rates (or speeds) are defined depending on the machining operation or machine movements.

RPM, an acronym meaning rotation per minute, defines the rotational speed of the end mill.

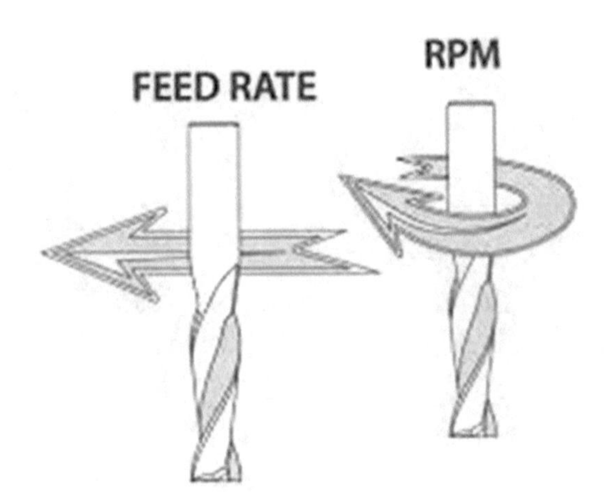

Figure 4-15. *Feed Rate and RPM of an end mill (`https://fabacademy.org/2019/labs/cept/students/karan-tanna/week08.html`)*

Jogging feed rate defines the feed rate during movements not involving any material cutting and at safe distances from any material.

Cutting feed rate defines the feed rate during normal cutting operations. Usually the end mill moves at higher speeds when it is not cutting the materials.

Plunge feed rate defines the feed rate during a "plunge" movement. The end mill plunges when it is penetrating the material vertically, using the bottom of the cutter.

Ramp reed rate defines the feed rate during a "ramp" movement. The end mill is ramping when it is moving at the same time circularly and vertically toward the material.

Step-over is the distance covered horizontally for each single pass of the end mill.

Step-down is the distance covered vertically for each single pass of the end mill.

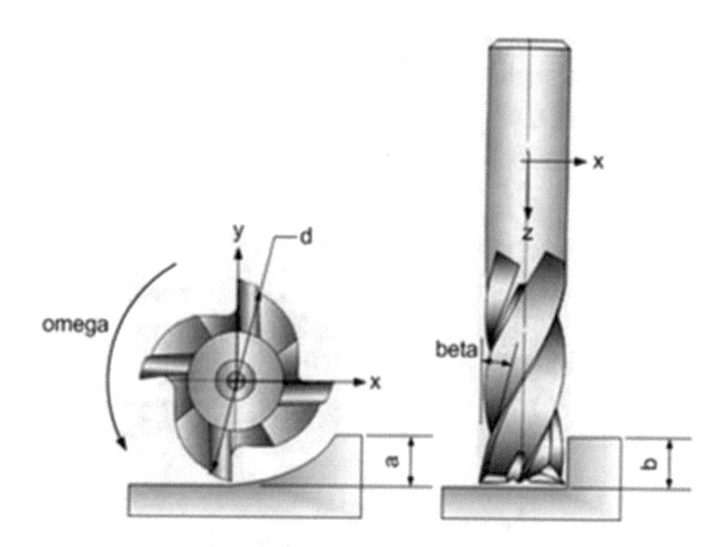

Figure 4-16. *Step-over (left, a value) and step-down (right, b value) (`https://cmailco.wordpress.com/`)*

2D Milling

Once you've created the digital design of what you'd like to build, you need to create the path your tool will follow. In 2D cutting, this means you are plunging (descending) into the material to a certain depth and then moving laterally in two directions to cut out shapes or pockets. As we said earlier, some tools are not made for plunging and need to descend below the level of your material on the side before cutting into it. Check this before using a cutter!

If you are cutting out shapes, you generally have three choices: you either have your tool move along the outside of your line, the inside, or the center on the lines. To understand the difference, imagine you'd like to cut out a piece of wood that is 200mm high and 200mm wide with a 6mm diameter end mill. If you design your square exactly that size, you should cut at the OUTSIDE of those lines, so the piece you take out of the material is the size you wanted. If you cut inside, the hole you'll leave behind will be 200mm by 200mm, and the piece you take out will be smaller in height and width, exactly twice the diameter of your cutting tool. In this example, 200 – (6 × 2) = 188mm. If you cut ON the lines, you remove half the diameter of your tool in both directions, in our case 200 – (3 × 2) = 194mm.

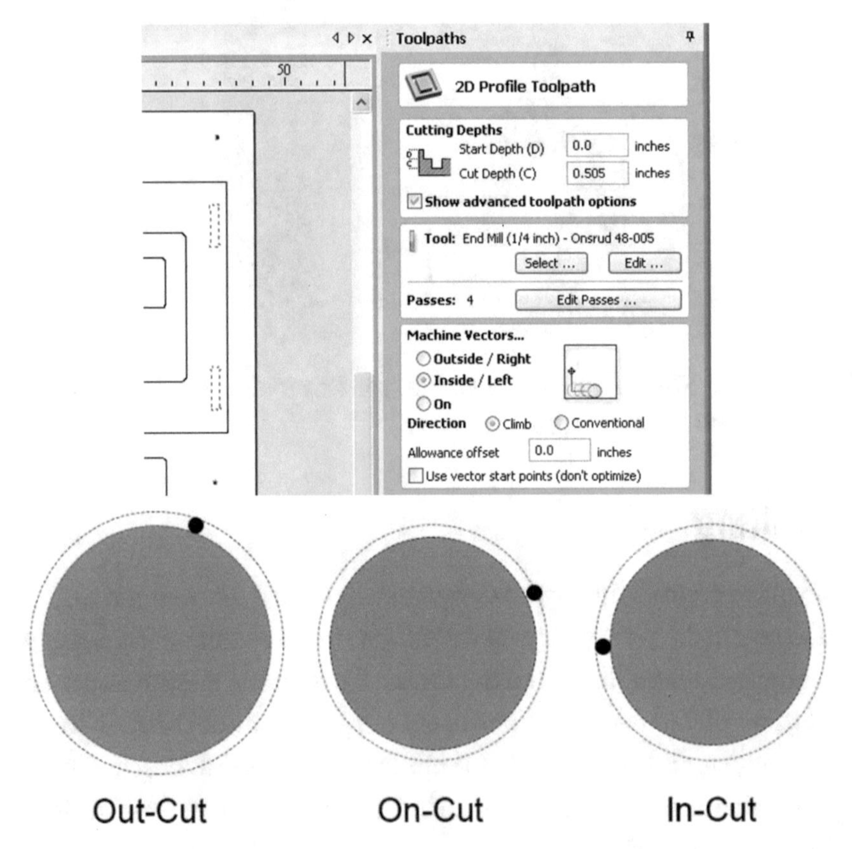

Figure 4-17. *Cutting out shapes (`https://fabacademy.org/2019/labs/cept/students/karan-tanna/week08.html`)*

Next, you can calculate your toolpath to do either climb milling or conventional milling (see Figure 4-18). Note that in Figure 4-18, it's the material that moves, not your end mill, but the physics principle is still the same! If you use a conventional milling strategy, the direction of rotation of your cutter is in the opposite direction of the movement of the material being cut. Climb milling means your cutter rotates in the same direction as the movement of your material. Generally, we could say climb milling is preferred, because it causes less strain on your tool and cutter, giving rise to longer lifetimes of tools and better finishing of the material being cut. On machines that have (or might have) backlash (i.e., they are not rigid), this can be problematic, for your cutter will "pull" the material toward itself, basically pulling the material into the cutter faster than you calculated it should, increasing the chip load. If the chip load becomes too high because of this, you can break tools and even create dangerous situations where parts are flying around the room. Next to that, conventional or climb cutting also has an effect on the finishing when you are machining wood with fibers. Conventional milling, if done in the direction of the fibers in a piece of wood, can pull them loose or even chip them off completely, resulting in parts of the wood being pulled off that should have stayed in place.

If you are making something in a makerspace, make sure the machine is set up right, and use climb milling in general.

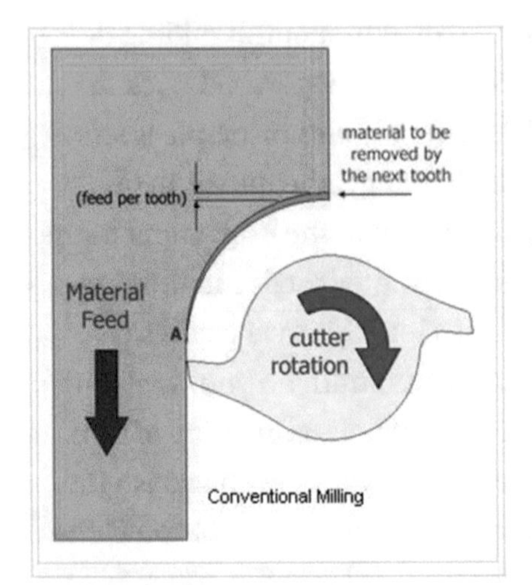

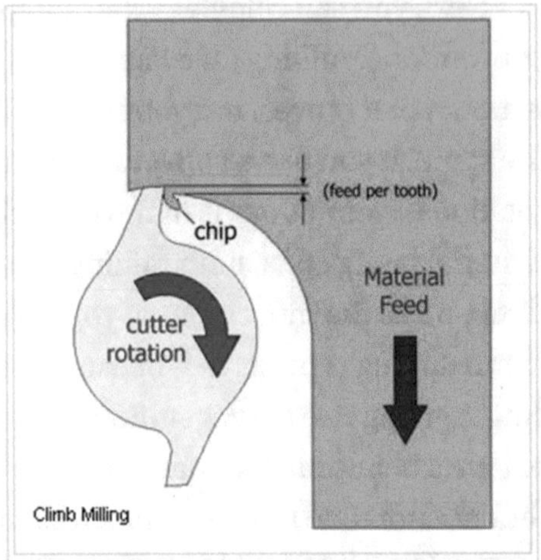

Figure 4-18. *Climb milling and conventional milling*

Before generating toolpaths, add points, known as tabs, that do not get machined away, either in the software or in the design of your pieces. This means there will be parts of the design that will stay attached to the sheet of material you are machining, even at the end. This is to make sure no pieces get detached when machining and fly around the room or get pulled into the tool.

When you are adding tabs, don't just randomly place them around your parts. If you are using solid wood, look at the direction of the grain to make sure you don't place them along the grain (which can then easily split). And depending on the thickness of your material, tabs do not need to be the same thickness. And because you will be optimizing the layout of your pieces, also assure yourself that ALL the tabs have enough solid material around them at the very end.

Figure 4-19. *Cutting tabs manually after milling (`http://archive.fabacademy.org/archives/2017/woma/students/383/week7.html`)*

You'll also want to orient your parts so that you optimize use of your material, but make sure to check your work carefully before starting to machine! I have seen people spend a lot of time optimizing their parts layout and add tabs to attach everything carefully, only to realize that at the end even the tabs are not attached anymore, because pieces are too close together. Bottom line is that you need to make sure ALL of your material is attached well to the machine, even at the end of the machining job. You can use double-sided tape, vacuum (see the following on vacuum tables), screws, clamps, whatever you can think of, as long as your parts are ATTACHED WELL and you make sure your tool does not machine into the things you used to fix your material with. (I have seen beautiful new milling bits plunge into screwheads without a complaint, which means it's impossible to get the screw out again and you'll throw away the cutter. Also, spinning mill bit plus metal screw can equal sparks, adding the risk of fire in the dust extractor. You lose thrice.)

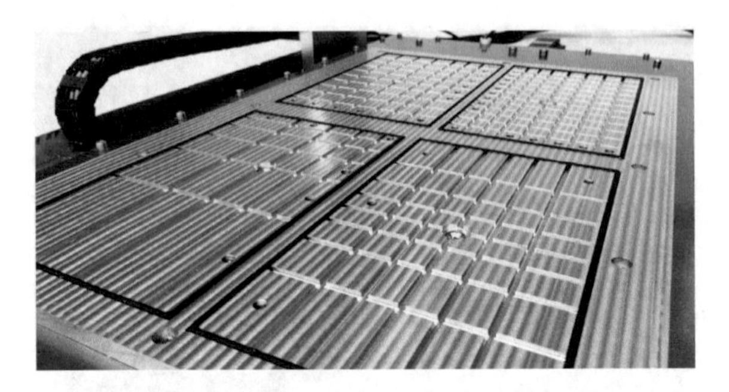

***Figure 4-20.** Vacuum bed (from Daniele)*

Some CNC systems come with vacuum tables, and if yours did not, you could make it yourself. Instead of holding down the material you are cutting with fasteners, you will put it on a table with small holes or a special grid pattern evenly spread over the total surface and a vacuum system that draws air through it. Any flat sheet of material you then put on it covers the holes and gets sucked down to the table, thus eliminating the need for screws, tape, or clamps.

When you are creating toolpaths to machine something in 2D, you might still have different depths to machine to and different machining techniques, like pockets, drills (just plunging, no lateral movement), and contour. In general, we advise you to do all the drilling first, then all the pockets, then interior lines, and then all the exterior lines.

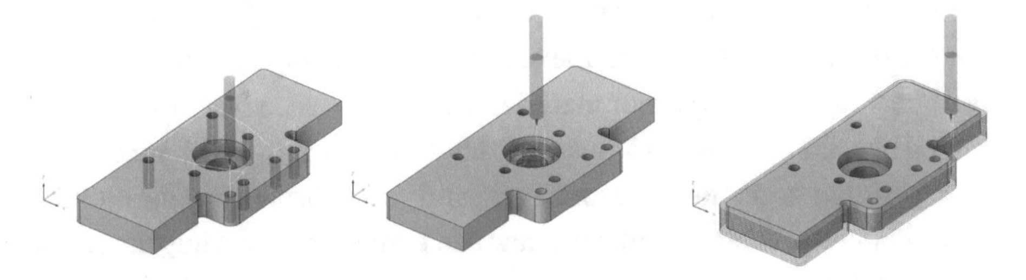

***Figure 4-21.** Examples of common 2D toolpaths, from left to right, shown in the recommended cutting order: drilling, pocket, contour (from Daniele)*

Once you are comfortable with setting up 2D milling toolpaths the right way (see the following on the basic steps to remember), you'll discover that there are still many, many processes to discover. Ramping feed rate, different ways to optimize your cutting time, using different cutters (like V-carve bits for lettering and decoration), changing starting points, plunging differently into materials – again, all this info is available on the Web and in the heads of many people in makerspaces around you. Talk, discuss, and share what you know and what you want to learn. It's a wonderfully rich world that awaits you. :)

Ready to machine? Did you

- Fix your material the right way?
- Choose the right tool, and is it fixed correctly in the machine?
- Calculate and set the RPMs and the feed rates?
- Set the cut depth correctly?
- Simulate your job?
- Make sure your tools cannot touch screws or fixtures?
- Set the starting point (X, Y, and Z) at the right location?
- Turn on your dust collector?
- Put on safety glasses and hearing protection?

3D Milling

Creating toolpaths for 3D milling jobs is slightly trickier and will take a longer time to get right.

The advice is always to start with jobs that require only 2D milling first (and you can do awesome things with just that) before moving on to 3D milling.

If you'd like to machine something in 3D, you can either machine it from only one side (where the difference from 2D milling simply is that you have curves in the Z direction on top of the ones in the two others (X and Y)) or go further and machine two to six sides of a piece of material (machining six sides of a piece is possible even with a three-axis machine, but a real challenge).

Let's look at what you need to do to machine two sides, and we'll let you extrapolate what you are getting into when you want to machine more sides, which will be logical and easy to imagine once you understand it.

Like with 2D milling, you'll have to first create your piece in three dimensions digitally, so you can use that file for the creation of the toolpath. Most machines will accept STL (STereoLithography) files (often used in Fab Labs), whereas the more professional machines will often take STEP (STandard for the Exchange of Product Model Data) or IGES (Initial Graphics Exchange Specification) files. You can easily convert from one to the other, but not without possible losses of information. Recently some CAM software has been integrated directly into CAD solutions and can work directly with the native file format without exporting or importing.

Once you have your object digitally, you can import or add it into the toolpathing software and start by orienting it the right way. You'll want your piece to be oriented so that you can reach the overhangs (parts you tool cannot get to). Once your piece is oriented the right way, you'll be able to set the starting point (origin) of your toolpath in X, Y, and Z. You will then have to specify the size of your material stock (in all directions) and will be able to position your 3D object inside this block.

The virtual stock material should correspond to the real material block you have available for milling. If the physical material is bigger and has not been set in the software, this may cause unwanted collision and potentially break the end mill or damage the machine. If, on the other hand, the material block is smaller than the one set in software, your CNC machine is going to cut in the air, wasting time. If your material does not have a flat top surface, you can choose to put the object you like to create below the surface, so the machine will first flatten the surface before starting on your piece. When machining from two sides, you'll define a line in the Z direction that your tool will machine to, often overlapping a little in both directions, so you'll have a nice smooth finish in the center. As with 2D toolpathing, you'll have to define parts that will stay attached or where the tabs will be.

When milling in 3D, it is common to apply different toolpaths to the same piece to achieve the desired final result. For efficiency, at the beginning "roughing" jobs are executed to quickly remove large amounts of materials from the stock. These are called "roughing" because they are done with large end mills and at high speeds and thus they're not precise. Roughing jobs normally leave a small offset from the milled surface to the final surface. This small offset is then removed by "finishing jobs." "Finishing" jobs are called that because they will arrive at the final wanted surface. Because the finishing jobs remove only a small amount of materials and with small end mills and at slow speed, they're configured to achieve the best surface quality.

Some common 3D milling toolpaths are adaptive clearing, pocket clearing, and parallel milling. Both adaptive and pocket clearing are roughing strategies, while parallel milling is a finishing strategy. There are many more for you to explore in your CAM software!

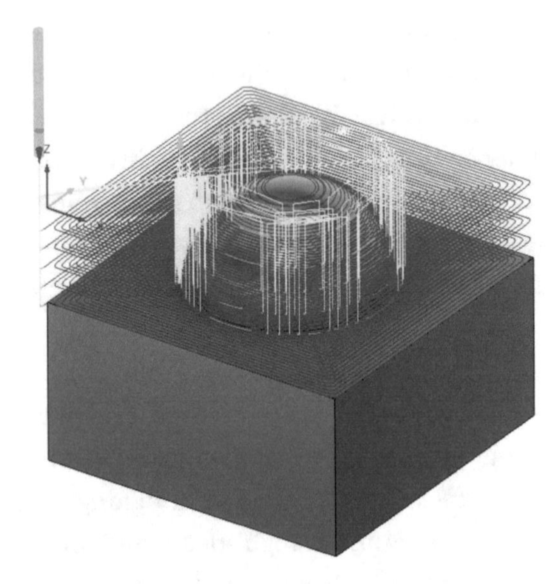

Figure 4-22. *Adaptive clearing toolpath example (from Daniele) - yellow lines are plunges or movements without cutting (also called "air time"), and blue lines are contours*

Toolpath Simulation

After the toolpath has been generated, we highly recommend that you run a simulation to check what is going to happen to your stock. The simulation shows the job movements and the cut applied to the material stock. This is usually shown to the user as a 3D animation where the machine head moves according to the toolpath. Most simulations show you the movement of the tool in real time, allowing you to check the operation at any stage. The simulation will give you quite useful information, such as the job duration (time), initial and ending volumes (quite useful for casting!), distance traveled, and final surface quality. Collisions of the end mill with the machine and the material stock are automatically detected, and you will be warned and advised to change your settings to avoid that.

Figure 4-23. *Simulation of a parallel toolpath (from Daniele)*

Setting Up and Running

Once you have your toolpath generated, you'll need to set up your machine, and you'll be able to run your job. It's important your machine setup and the choices you made in toolpath generation match up: if your Z zero level is on the machining bed mechanically, so should it be in your toolpath. If the Z zero is on top of your material in your toolpathing software, but you mechanically fixed it to correspond to the table top, you'll machine into your bed. This obviously only goes for machines that do not have an automatic homing system, but most small-scale and low-cost machines will not come with this option.

Depending on the software and the machine you use, you'll be able to change the origin position of your tool, according to your needs. If your machine has a system that allows it to automatically find its origin in one or more axes, I'd advise you to always use this when machining something, even if your starting point is different from the machine's mechanical "home." Just let the machine find its origin position, and then move the head to wherever you want to start, and note the position values. This way, if something goes wrong, you'll always be able to find your starting point again.

A lot of mills have a nice trick to find the home position in the Z direction – a little alligator clip is attached to either the mill or another piece of the machine that is connected to the mill so that electricity is conducted via the tool. On most systems this is any metal part on the spindle. You then put a metal plate underneath the tool, and the spindle will descend automatically, until it touches the plate, making an electrical connection. In the software, the thickness of the aluminum plate is subtracted from the position where the tool and the plate touched, and the Z home value is set to match this figure. This will allow you to either mechanically home your machine on your machining bed or on your material. Don't use this technique with V-carving bits or very small mills though; you'll either break the tool or create small holes in the plate. If you are building a CNC mill yourself, a system like this is something you can add to it quite easily.

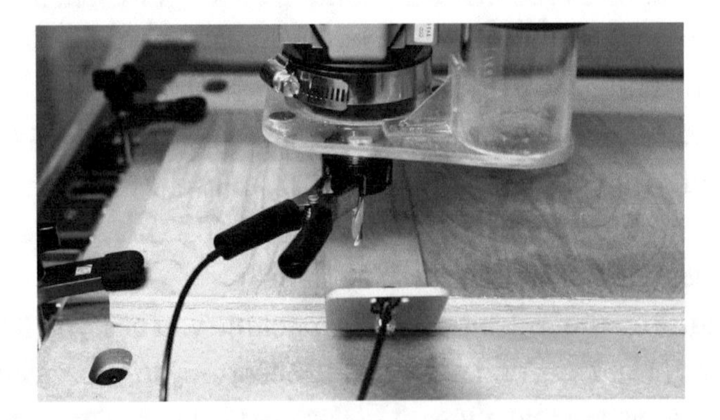

Figure 4-24. *Zeroing using a clip and a plate (`https://i.ytimg.com/vi/O4MAbfXrtHk/maxresdefault.jpg`)*

Whether you set the Z home position on the bed or the material to cut depends on what you are working on and where you want to be precise. If you'd like to cut all the way through your material, it's a good idea to set the Z home on the cutting bed. This way, if your material is slightly thicker than you put into the software, it will still cut all the way through; your first cut will simply be deeper. Don't do this with metals though, because if you cut more (or less) than the amount you used to calculate your feeds and speeds, you might break your tool, your part, or even your machine.

If you want to machine a pocket in the material (to do inlays or fix precise pieces), set the Z home on the top of the material. This way, you'll be sure to cut to the exact depth you set in the software.

For most spindles, it is a good idea to spin it for a couple of minutes before applying force to the tool, that is, cutting stuff. This spindle warm-up time will make sure that the coolant in your spindle is equally distributed, and it will extend your tool life. Check with the good folks who built your spindle or the manual, if this applies.

Safety and Maintenance

Most other machines in your makerspace will have all sorts of safety interlocks. Lasers won't fire unless the door is closed, and knives in vinyl cutters are not very accessible. This is one of the (many) ideas behind a collection of digitally controlled machines, the fact that you never hold the material or tool with your hand while machining, but it's always a computer "doing the job."

Tools Spinning at High Speed Can Shatter or Start a Fire!

The most dangerous machines in your makerspace will be lathes, drill presses, and box cutters, but CNC mills are often open and have less commonly safety interlocks, making this one of the more dangerous CNC machines you'll work with. If you are milling something, with any-size CNC mill, NEVER EVER reach into a spinning tool. People have lost their fingers, or worse, by thinking they could just reach in while the machine was working and remove that little piece of wood or adjust that incorrectly fixed piece of material. Long hair should be tied behind your head or underneath a cap, and don't wear long loose clothing (see Figure 4-25 of a correctly dressed person).

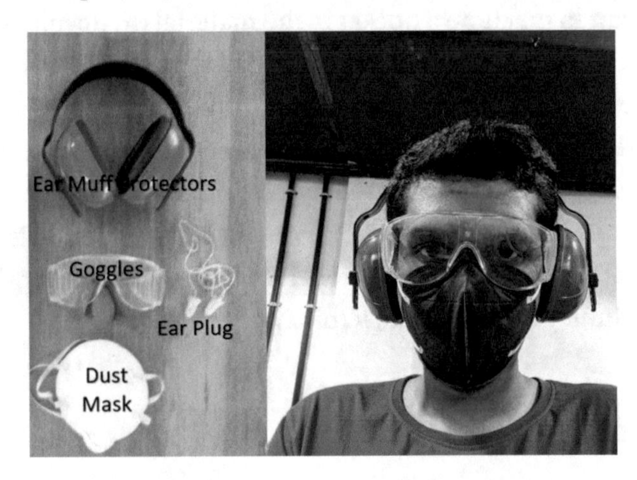

***Figure 4-25.** Correctly dressed person (`https://fabacademy.org/2021/labs/kochi/students/abhinav-ajith/Week%207.html`)*

If you don't fix your material or your tool correctly or you get your settings wrong, you might break a milling bit, pieces of which could go flying around the space you are in. The same goes for materials. If you forget to add tabs or fixings to hold your material in place, the tool, spinning at high speeds, might send (sharp) pieces of material flying around the space. Make sure that you get your settings right, and make sure everyone in the space is properly instructed and clothed when using the machine. Since CNC mills are noisy, you need to use good earplugs. We have four sets of high-quality ear protectors in the lab and a box of single-use plugs if there are more people or visitors. It's also advisable to wear special plastic safety glasses, to protect eyes from small pieces flying around.

Next to these perhaps more obvious dangers, you should invest in a good dust collector. If you are milling wood without one, there will always be small particles in the air of your space that get breathed in by you and others. It's best to place dust collectors outside, if you have the possibility, because most of the standard collectors still release some dust into the space. Dust collectors with HEPA filters can be safely used inside, but they are much more expensive.

If you haven't set up your machine location yet, we recommend you place the CNC mill close to a (safety glass or polycarbonate) window for better light and safer viewing or an aerated area. Also, if the CNC mill is reachable only on one side (e.g., only the front) it makes it easier to monitor people near it.

A fire extinguisher should always be available next to the CNC mill.

So, to sum up, when you are using a CNC mill, wear protective glasses and ear protection, no loose clothing, and no ring or bracelet, and tie (long) hair behind you or use a cap. Then, get all your settings right and, staying close to a stop button, run your job.

Keeping Your Machine in Good Shape

It will extend the lifetime of your spindle if you routinely warm it up before applying force to it. Keep it clean and well greased, and make sure you do not machine abrasive materials without an adequate dust collector. Small dust particles of certain materials, such as composite fiber materials and glass, will possibly damage your tool beyond repair.

The moving parts of your machine should be kept clean and well greased as well. Clean any glide rails, linear guides, and wheels regularly, and use thin oil to grease them. Cogwheels and toothed parts can be greased with lithium.

Applications

Once you are comfortable with this kind of machine, you can make an enormous amount of different things. We'll look at what can be made with small-scale (approximately <50 cm) machines first and then take a look at what possibilities a large-scale CNC mill can give you.

Small but Precise

You can do many things with a small-scale mill that you can also do with a similarly sized laser cutter, such as snap-fit applications and assembling objects. Check out the "Applications of Laser Cutters" section of Chapter 2 for some project ideas and examples.

What you cannot do easily with (most) lasers is make circuit boards. By using very small tools (0.2mm and up), you can machine away the copper on FR1 copper-clad boards and leave only the traces you'd like for your circuit, to create circuit boards for your projects.

If you are creating circuits with an end mill, make sure you are using the right kind of material to optimize the lifespan of your end mill. FR1 or FR2 is the best stock to mill, because either has a layer of copper on top of compressed and hardened paper. It is safer than FR4 stock, which has the layer of copper bonded to fiberglass, which will clog and then break your end mill. Fiberglass dust is also a breathing hazard.

We'll talk more about making PCBs in Chapter 7 on open hardware.

Figure 4-26. *A CNC-milled PCB*

Small milling machines have been used for a very long time by jewelers. They use the machine to create their design in wax, which is then used to form a mold with a material that resists high temperatures. The wax inside the mold is then evaporated, or burned away, and the hole left filled with gold, silver, or any other material you can melt at a not too high temperature. This technique is called "lost wax casting" (or cire perdue).

Another thing to do when you have a small mill at your fingertips is to make molds in wax or other easy-to-machine materials. Blocks of machinable wax that are super-easy to machine are still tough enough to not deform when used. It's not too expensive, and you can melt the waste into a new block. You could start with making a simple one-sided mold, for instance, to make chocolate tablets, where you just machine the positive shape (so you machine, into a block, the tablet shape you'd like) and you pour food-safe silicones into that. If you'd like to go a bit further, you could make molds with multiple parts that fit together, by machining parts of the object you'd like to obtain separately and then creating negatives in silicones with those molds to obtain the final mold, in which you can in turn pour silicones or other materials like concrete and plaster.

In Figure 4-27 you can see the three steps to make climbing hold out of rubber - machining the positive shape, casting a negative mold from that in silicone, and then using that mold to make as many rubber parts as you'd like.

Figure 4-27. *From left to right - CNC-machined positive shape, negative mold in silicone, final pieces in rubber (images by JMM)*

Safety first!

If you are going to make molds for food, like lollipops, ice cream, cookies, or chocolate, make sure you get FOOD-SAFE materials. Mold-making materials are wonderful to work with, but can potentially be dangerous to your health, so check the data sheets and read the safety instructions!

Big and Powerful

Let's now take a look into some of the bigger things you can make with a CNC mill. Most spaces that have a large format mill setup will give you the option to machine materials bigger than 1.5 by 2 meters, giving you enormous possibilities, so much so that we will not be able to talk about everything you can make, but here you'll find some good examples, and you'll just have to be creative after!

The machines you'll be able to use are small though ... Airplane wings and boat hulls are also machined this way, and they need machines that dwarf most mills you'll encounter. Note the man in Figure 4-28 surveying a mill shaping a boat hull.

Figure 4-28. *Mill shaping a boat hull (`www.windpowerengineering.com/over-100-m-reach-lets-cnc-machine-turbine-blades/`)*

Furniture

Furniture is a great example of what can be made with a CNC mill. You can make beautiful and comfortable chairs, sturdy tables, and cupboards to fit all your needs if you take the time to learn to control a CNC mill.

Let's look at two wonderful examples of furniture made in a Fab Lab. Norwegian maker Jens Dyvik (who does even more interesting things than just this; check out his website) has created, and then shared with the world, the layer chair (see Figure 4-29). The design for this chair was done with Rhino 3D and the Grasshopper plugin, making it parametric and allowing you to easily adjust different aspects of the chair, like the width, height, shape of the curve, etc. by manipulating sliders in the software. Once you are happy with the result in the software, you can save the cutting lines, cut them with a CNC mill, and assemble your chair. There are many iterations made on this chair, perhaps most notably the mountain version for a lab in Lyngen, Norway (see Figure 4-29).

Figure 4-29. *Layer chair*

Another maker of furniture that makes very interesting use of CNC mills is Thomas Mouillon, a master of optimization. His work focuses on using as much as possible of the sheets of material, leaving extremely little waste. This means his chairs, tables, bookshelves, and bird seats are "nested" and one cutline often is the outside of not one but two pieces at the same time. See the assembled bird seat in the next image.

Figure 4-30. *Assembled bird seat, designed by Thomas Mouillon*

A nice website to get plans for furniture is Opendesk, where you can go and either download files to machine them yourself or ask a maker close to you to make them for you, a great step toward localized production and giving you access to some great and unique designs.

Houses and Shelters

If you have access to a large format mill, you can not only make furniture yourself, but you could even build a complete house! The Fab House was conceived and built in Barcelona for the Solar Decathlon Europe 2012, winning them the People's Choice Award. As you can see in Figure 4-31, all the pieces are machined with a CNC mill and then fit together to form the final house. You can even download the source files from their website.

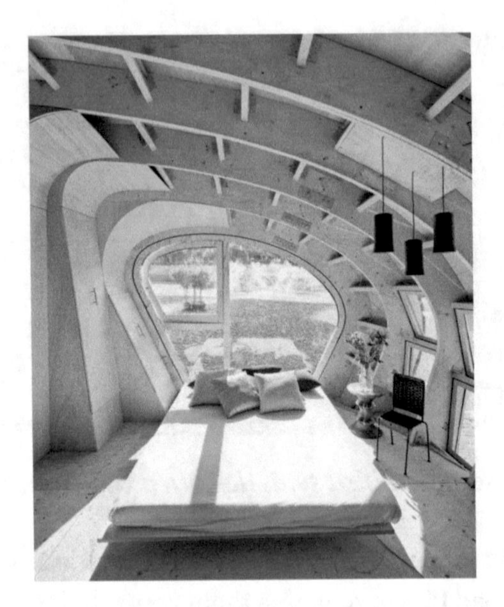

Figure 4-31. *The Fab House (`http://vectroave.com/2010/07/the-fab-lab-house-by-iaac/`)*

Similar to Opendesk, WikiHouse is a website dedicated to sharing plans that can be used on digitally controlled machines to build (parts of) houses and shelters. There are many shelter projects happening, and with the increasing availability of large format milling machines in parts of the world where building shelters fast is a real need, if you work on this, it might be not just for you locally, but you could end up emailing your file halfway across the globe to help out.

Figure 4-32. *WikiHouse plans (`http://spacecraft.co.nz/`)*

Beehives

If you care about our environment, like we do, and you'd like to do something to help bees, you could make a beehive. Keeping bees is a wonderful thing to do and will give you yummy honey as a plus.

The Open Source Beehives project has a nice series of hive plans on the site that you can download and machine, or you can just design a hive yourself and mill out the pieces. Make sure that if you are making beehives or anything else that is destined to be used with live animals, the material does not contain toxic glues or solvents, and it will be able to withstand the weather or moisture you put it in!

Beehives come in different styles, and if you really want to get into this, it's probably a good idea to first find a local group of people who know more than you do. Keeping bees is not trivial, but rewarding in many ways. If you build a beehive in the style of what others around you are using, it will be easier to share tools and resources!

***Figure 4-33.** Beehive (`https://images.indiegogo.com/file_attachments/423049/files/20140310000219-Flyer.jpg?1394434939`)*

Boats

When Ted Hall from ShopBot was still in neurosciences, he was building boats as a hobby. But because he could not find a cheap and robust enough CNC milling system, before building his boat, he decided to build a CNC mill. This took quite some time, but perseverance is an important quality in these matters, and (to make a long story short) he's now no longer in neuroscience, but the CEO of ShopBot, a company building (open source) CNC mills that are used all over the globe.

Figure 4-34. *Ted Hall in circa 1994 with one of the first ShopBot prototypes (boat in the background)*

There are many people building boats using CNC mills, and you'll find all sorts of shapes and sizes. A good starting point is probably building a SOF (skin on frame) canoe or kayak. The frame can be assembled using plywood (which is relatively inexpensive), and the outer hull is then added using fabric or plastic, which is finally treated with resin to make it watertight. This produces beautiful lightweight boats and is a great project to learn different techniques.

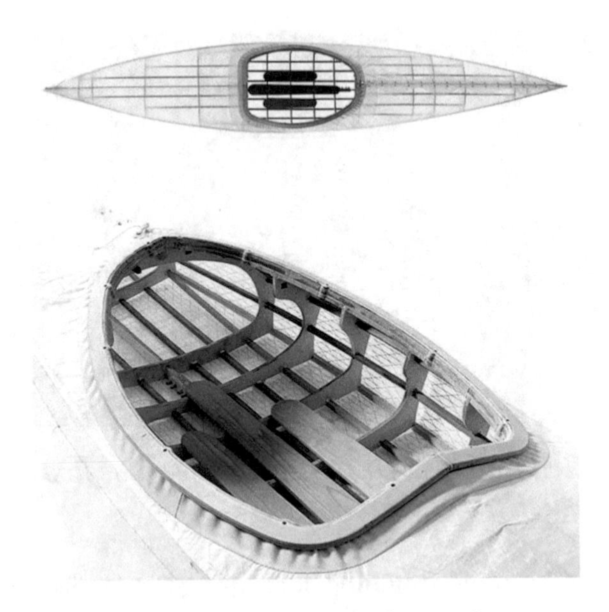

Figure 4-35. *Boat built with CNC mills (`www.pinterest.com/pin/657666351806659325/`)*

Skates and Skis

Many people look to CNC mills when they are building skate decks or even skis, which you can also do completely by hand, but is more precise and repeatable using a mill. If you go the digital way, it also means your deck can be virtually any shape you'd like, as long as the end result is stable and strong enough to withstand the force of you grinding it on a curb.

When making a deck, you can simply cut the desired final shape with a mill, but another reason to use the mill is making molds. Unless you want your deck to be completely flat, you'll need to compress the wood and fibers into a mold, giving it its final shape. Styrofoam works great if you'd like to machine a single precise mold, but another solution is to machine transversal ribs you fit into slots, thus being able to "mix and match" these ribs to create the shape you'd like. To press the wood and fibers into the mold and fix them together, either with simply wood glue or with epoxy, easiest is using clamps, but if you have a vacuum system, you can also create a vacuum bag and compress your deck using the ~1 bar of air we have above our heads (depending on how high in the mountains you are, obviously).

Figure 4-36. *A CNC-milled skateboard (`https://fabacademy.org/archives/2015/eu/students/pugliese.gianluca/exercise12.html`)*

Guitars and Other Stringed Instruments

Creating musical instruments is not easy, not even when you have a powerful CNC mill at your disposition. Positioning the fingerboard correctly on a guitar or making sure the material you use will not deform with the tension of the strings once they are tuned to their final note is a question of calculating well and having the appropriate knowledge of everything that goes into an instrument before starting the build. That being said, if you are up for it, you can indeed make a guitar with a machine close to you.

If you'd like to make a whole guitar, you'll quickly realize the neck is by far the most difficult to build correctly, so make sure you study the impact of different dimensions and different materials before working on it. Machining the body of a guitar is a nice challenge, especially if you'd like to machine both sides (which is often the case, because you'll create pockets for hardware on both sides).

Summary

CNC milling is an enormous field with many possibilities and options. There is much discussion on materials, machines, tools, and milling techniques, and it's a very interesting field to spend some time in, but we don't have enough pages in this book to go deeper into the matter. Sign up to a forum or read more online (ShopBot's forum is great, and the cncrouter-shop website has great tips) and start to discuss with people. You'll learn tons of interesting techniques to improve your work!

CHAPTER 5

3D Printers

Introduction

3D printing, also referred as additive manufacturing, is a fabrication technology used to create three-dimensional objects by adding and solidifying material little by little. In contrast to subtractive manufacturing, where material is removed from a solid block to create the wanted shape, a 3D printer produces an object into an initially empty space, using different methodologies to manipulate and add small amounts of materials.

When 3D printing became mainstream, it was heralded by most media as a new dawn, like something that will replace most production techniques. It is much more likely the future of fabrication will consist of a combination of different technologies and techniques and even biological systems.

Just as microwaves failed to replace kitchens (which some believed would happen when they started to become accessible), 3D printers do not replace other fabrication techniques but are complementary and do offer new possibilities and in some cases speed that is hard or impossible to match with any other technology. It's an exciting field, where changes happen at a very high pace, and the machine that was revolutionary yesterday is normal today.

J-m. Molenaar and D. Ingrassia, *Mastering Digitally Controlled Machines*, Maker Innovations Series, https://doi.org/10.1007/978-1-4842-9849-7_5

Thanks to the rapid evolution it has had in recent times, from a niche and expensive technology, 3D printing has become mainstream for Fab Labs, makers, and hobbyists and has been adopted by some industries requiring the flexibility in shape creation this technology offers. Flexibility in production has also been exploited, especially for on-demand printing of spare parts from raw materials. Experimental 3D printing is exploring many fascinating directions, such as printing houses, footwear, and clothes, healthcare, space, material science, and nanotechnologies. One of the exciting applications that is getting more and more attention is what we refer to as 3D bioprinting, or printing with biologically compatible or active materials to create scaffolds in which we can grow living tissue. We are not yet at the stage of being able to print working organs (although you may have been led to believe we do), and growing or printing meat is also far from mainstream - but these possibilities are getting closer every day, and companies like MeaTech, Novameat and Redefine Meat show very exciting promises for the future.

History

3D printing is older than you probably expect, and it comes in more flavors than you know! It's a vibrant field with an enormous amount of development and innovation going on. Let's take a quick look at where it all started. In this overview of the development of 3D printing, you might encounter some techniques or systems you are not yet familiar with, but not to worry, they are all explained later in this chapter.

The idea of creating three-dimensional objects by stacking layers can be traced back to 1890, when J. E. Blanther proposed the creation of topographical maps (see Figure 5-1). The patent was accepted on May 3, 1892. While this was obviously not 3D printing, it's basically the principle the technique relies on. Only much later in 1972, Mr. Matsubara of Mitsubishi Motors proposed to do the same, but using photopolymers to produce the individual layers. In 1980, Dr. Hideo Kodama of Nagoya Municipal Industrial Research Institute published the first account of a real stereolithography system, but because he did not file the patent in time, he did not get the rights to the technique.

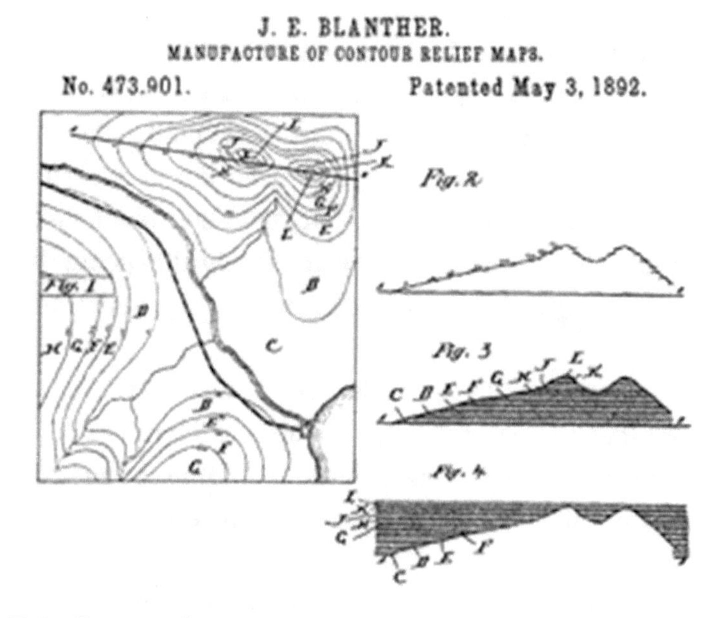

Figure 5-1. *Patent about creation of topographical maps (`www.wtec.org/loyola/rp/03_01.htm`)*

The next step happened in France, where Alain Le Méhauté, Olivier de Witte, and Jean Claude André filed their patent for a stereolithography technique on July 16, 1984. The patent eventually was abandoned by the French General Electric Company (now Alcatel-Alsthom) and CILAS (the laser consortium), because they considered it had not enough business potential.

And then we finally get to the "real" start. In 1984 Charles Hull, who later founded 3D Systems, officially invented stereolithography (SLA), which was patented in 1987. Not long after, the company released the SLA-1, the first commercially available 3D printer.

New techniques continued to be worked on by several groups, and SLS (selective laser sintering) was patented in 1989. The thing that is perhaps surprising is that the technique that you will find in most makerspaces was not patented before 1992, when Stratasys obtained the rights to the FDM (Fused Deposition Modeling).

During those early years of 3D printing, several companies were created, and multiple techniques were being invented and developed.

In 2004, Dr. Adrian Bowyer of the University of Bath in England developed the idea of an open source, self-replicating printer, the RepRap (for Replicating Rapid Prototyper). From that moment on, the world of 3D printing enthusiasts grew rapidly, and with the efforts of people from all over the planet, many different variations on the first printer were designed and built.

Now there are many different variations on the original RepRap, and many printers that are commercially available are based on the first model. Some of them first appeared as a kit and later became commercially available as a fully built system, but many of them are still fully open source and evolving.

While techniques and possibilities continued to evolve both in the home-built and commercially created machines, services around 3D printing also developed fast. Numerous companies offer 3D printing services where you can upload your file and choose the material you want them to use and once your file has been printed it is shipped directly to your home. 3D Hubs is an interesting variety of this, where they don't print the parts on their own machines, but rather function like a platform connecting people with printers to customers who want a part.

Websites allowing you to download files also rapidly grew, promoting the open source movement and sharing of hardware next to the software. Today, it makes sense to have a 3D printer even if you do not (yet) know how to design in 3D because of the thousands of parts you can simply download and print at your home.

3D printing has evolved very fast in the last few years and will probably continue to do so until we possibly move to a new technique. It's an exciting and vibrant field and lots of fun to work with! Let's take a look at what techniques currently are out there and what you can do with them.

How They Work

There are many types of 3D printers, but we'll focus mainly on the ones you are likely to encounter in a Fab Lab, namely, fused filament machines and machines using stereolithography. Let's take a look at all the available types first, because even if you probably won't have access to such machines directly, you can always "use" them by sending files to commercial printers making the part for you. You can have them print your piece in titanium, ceramics, or even gold, if you have the budget.

There are many different techniques in the world of 3D printing, and many more are under development. We can divide the mainly used technologies roughly into seven categories, some with different techniques:

1. Material extrusion
    a. FDM (Fused Deposition Modeling)/FFF (Fused Filament Fabrication)
    b. Paste extrusion
    c. Pellet printing
2. Photopolymerization
    a. SLA (stereolithography) (using a laser)
    b. DLP (Digital Light Processing) (using a projector)
    c. CLIP (Continuous Liquid Interface Production) (using UV light)
    d. DPP (Daylight Polymer Printing) (using an LCD screen)

3. Material jetting
    a. Material jetting (cured with UV light)
    b. Nanoparticle jetting (cured with heat)
    c. Drop on demand (wax binding when cooled)
4. Binder jetting (joined with a bonding agent)
5. Powder bed fusion
    a. Multi Jet Fusion (fused with a bonding agent and energy)
    b. Selective laser sintering (fused with laser)
    c. Direct metal laser sintering/selective laser melting (fused with laser)
    d. Electron beam melting (fused with electron beam)
6. Direct energy deposition
    a. Laser powder forming or laser engineering net shape (fused with laser)
    b. Electron beam additive manufacturing (fused with electron beam)
7. Sheet lamination (fused with a binding agent)

Material Extrusion

Almost all Fab Labs will have an FDM printer, the cheapest and most common technique available. Many printers in this category that are of the DIY variety will be descendants from RepRap (see Figure 5-2), the first open source home-built printer. There is a wonderful arborescence showing all the different machines created over the years, and there is a huge and very active community around the globe working on the evolution of these machines (see Figure 5-3).

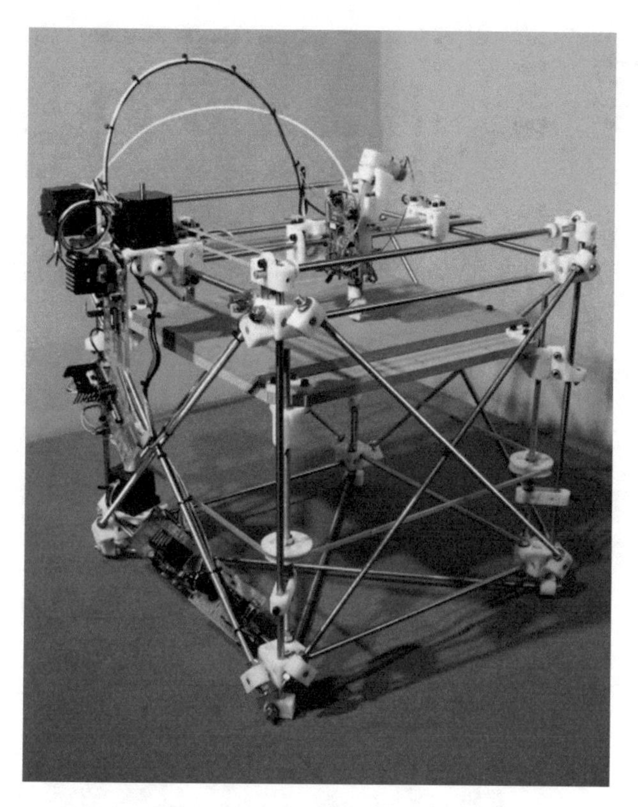

Figure 5-2. *A RepRap 3D printer (https://camo.githubusercontent.com/c6fd884fb08dd829d4f2f6e3dd92eaccf758882b/687474703a2f2f75706c6f61642e77696b696d656469612e6f72672f77696b6970656469612f636f6d6d6f6e732f662f66382f5265707261705f4461727769e2e6a7067)*

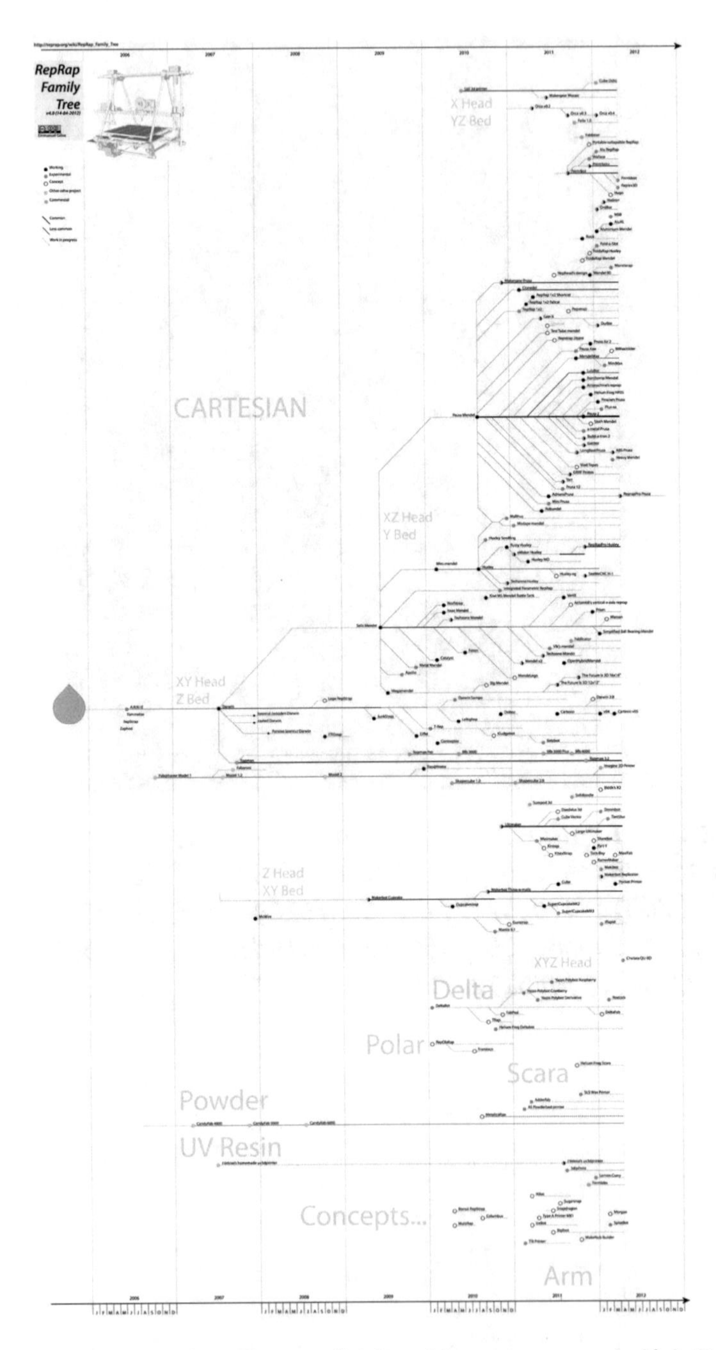

***Figure 5-3.** RepRap family tree (`http://reprap.org/wiki/RepRap_Family_Tree`)*

Fused filament (FDM) printers use plastic filaments as raw material to print. Filaments are rolled in coils that are, when printing, usually attached to the machine itself or placed close by. An FDM printer works by pushing the plastic filament inside a heated extruder nozzle, which is attached to the machine head. While the material is being heated, molten, and extruded by the nozzle, the machine axes move according to the shape to be realized, basically "drawing" with the extruded plastic in thin lines. A 3D-printed object is created by printing 2D shapes for each layer and by stacking up the layers on top of each other. The technique consists of printing a layer, then moving the Z axis, and printing the next layer on top of it. The process is repeated until the height of the wanted object is reached. The molten and extruded plastic resolidifies and bonds to the previous layer. By stacking layers of thin extruded plastic, typically having a thickness between 0.05 and 0.3mm, and by having each layer of a different shape, it is possible to create quite complex objects.

FDM printers are the most common 3D printers found on the market, but also in Fab Labs and makerspaces. Because of the simplicity of the technology used, they are one of the cheapest options for people who want to start with 3D printing. In case you are interested in purchasing an FDM 3D printer, we have compared some of the most important features in the following table.

Features	What Is It?	What Are the Advantages?
Heated bed	The possibility to heat up the bed to a certain temperature. Usually the maximum is 120 degrees.	Mandatory for some materials (e.g., ABS) in order to be printed correctly. Improves the material stickiness on the bed.
Removable flexible bed	A thin flexible sheet, placed on top of the bed. It is usually made with a magnetic material to be easily placed and removed from the bed.	Allows easy and fast removal of 3D-printed parts from the bed. The flexible sheet can be removed with the part attached to it and then bent to let the bottom of the part be easily detached.
Automatic bed leveling	A system using a sensor to probe the bed planarity. A map of points is saved into the machine firmware allowing the machine to dynamically change the Z position while printing the first layer.	Allows precise printing of the first layer, especially with parts having a large base. Avoids unwanted material detachment because of wrong printing height.
Dual extruder	Two extruders are mounted into the machine head. It is possible to extrude two different material colors and/or two different materials.	Allows multicolor or multi-material print. Some printers use the additional extruder to print dissolvable support material.
Direct drive	The motor that pushes the filament into the extruder is mounted as close as possible to the extruder.	Allows the printing of flexible materials. It also offers better control of the extrusion flow and may be needed to extrude tougher filaments.

(*continued*)

Features	What Is It?	What Are the Advantages?
Part cooling fans	Cooling fan(s) are mounted near the extruder and directed onto the 3D-printed part.	Allows the cooling of the last printed layer and/or part area. Cooling is necessary for the correct shaping of some filaments (e.g., PLA or flexible).
Filament sensor	A sensor detects the presence, or not, of the filament into the extruder.	Allows the machine to detect when the filament is finished or it is broken/cut. If a missing filament is detected, the 3D printer stops to allow filament replacement. After the filament has been replaced, it is possible to resume the print job.
Material handling	The printer is able to replace the finished filament and to control the temperature of the filament.	Allows continuous printing without user intervention for replacing the material. Improves print reliability by keeping the material at a certain temperature before printing.
Enclosed printing area	The printing area is partially or completely enclosed. Some printers have a filtering system for the internal emission generated when melting the plastic.	Allows a more stable temperature during printing to avoid unwanted material warping (because of temperature difference). Highly recommended when printing some filaments (e.g., ABS).

(*continued*)

Features	What Is It?	What Are the Advantages?
Temperature-controlled printing area	The printing area has a digitally controlled temperature.	Improves the printing quality of filaments requiring a stable temperature in order to be printed correctly (e.g., ABS).
Wi-Fi	The printer can connect to the local Wi-Fi network.	Allows to launch, monitor, and manage print jobs remotely.
Camera	A camera is placed onto the machine head or in the machine frame.	Often found together with Wi-Fi, it allows the user to remotely visually inspect the status of a print job.

Klipper is an open-source 3D printer firmware that adopts a distinctive approach compared to others by primarily running on a computer rather than a microcontroller. Primarily written in Python, Klipper utilizes a computer, typically a Single Board Computer like a Raspberry Pi, to connect to one or more controllers that manage the motion of the motors. Klipper also implements an API to work with different interfaces, making it easy to manage your printer via WiFi. Additionally, it facilitates wireless file transfer and video streaming from a locally installed camera. We highly recommend Klipper as the firmware for a new printer you plan to purchase or build.

Input shaping, or resonance compensation, is a recent addition to desktop 3D printers that enables the cancellation of vibrations. Before this technique can function correctly, it is necessary to measure the current vibrations, typically achieved by attaching an accelerometer to the printer head. The accelerometer is then connected to the controller, and test jobs are executed. These test jobs gradually increase testing speed and acceleration while the accelerometer records vibration levels, identifying specific frequencies.

Various types of input shaping algorithms exist, contingent on the type of motion system on the printer (e.g., Cartesian or CoreXY). The measured frequencies serve as input to the input shaping algorithm, allowing for the application of vibration cancellation during motion.

A recent market tendency is to have faster and faster Desktop 3D printers, with printers nowadays reaching 300mm/s printing speed and 1000mm/s motion speed. To allow this, many brands are developing or converting their machine design to use corexy, a complex (in comparison to cartesian) motion configuration where motors are stationary and belts are used to move the head at 45 degrees from a single motor. Combining the motion of both motors is then possible to move the head straight.

Bambulab P1P, Prusa XL and Voron are all examples of modern printer designs using CoreXY to achieve very high printing speeds.

Other printers using material extrusion as a working principle are printing soft and pasty materials. In this category printers able to print with clay and food are found. They work similarly to FDM printers, and the main difference is the extrusion system, in this case able to extrude pasty and creamy materials instead of pre-heated plastic. The extrusion works by using a syringe or an Archimedean screw, depending on the viscosity of the material, that pushes the material through a nozzle. The extrusion can also be done using compressed air. Nozzles of these printers are usuallylarger than those of FDM printers, resulting in less detailed prints. Also, food printers are designed to handle food safely, in order to be able to eat the print afterward. Clay printed parts can be fired into an oven to achieve the final part. Parts printed in pasty materials stay soft during the print, not allowing shapes with much overhang.

If you plan to print in multiple colors or use different materials within the same print, we recommend considering a filament material station or, in general, a printer capable of automatically swapping filament. This feature has recently become more affordable and is now available even for budget desktop 3D printers. Additionally, some printers are now incorporating automatic tool changers, which are useful not only for filament swapping but also for utilizing additional tools in place of the printing head.

Recently some pellet 3D printers have appeared on the market. These printers work in a similar way to paste extrusion printers, with the difference of heating up and melting the pellets before extruding them. Pellets are usually stocked into barrels close to the printer, and, while printing, the pellets are pushed (with compressed air) in small batches into the machine head. Depending on the kind of the extruder used, pellet printers can print several kilograms of material per hour. Pellet 3D printers typically use standard industrial plastic pellets (e.g., ABS, PETG, etc.) that are quite cheap and easy to source.

Photopolymerization

All processes in this category have in common that a photopolymer is used. A photopolymer is a liquid material that is cured or hardened with the use of light. By precisely hardening the photopolymer, it is possible to create a 3D object.

A technique that is often available in makerspaces is stereolithography, or SLA. The material used in these printers is resin that hardens when exposed to UV light, and pieces are printed by using a UV laser beam directed up through a transparent container full of resin. Layers are hardened by the laser and stick to the build platform, which rises up every time a layer is finished. Most machines "peel" the layer slowly off the bottom of the build container, so resin flows underneath the build plate, and a next layer can be created.

This technique allows for quite high precision (~25 microns in layer height), but resins are not cheap and have a limited lifespan when in their liquid state. The printers require careful maintenance and handling, especially when it comes to the optics. The machines using this technique are more expensive than FDM printers, but still affordable in many cases, and they allow you to print with different polymers, from very dense to flexible and even materials that can safely be used in the body (for dental work or implants).

CLIP (Continuous Liquid Interface Production) also uses UV light for curing the resin. Using a special membrane, they also print the part upside down but always keep a thin layer of oxygen below the part where the unhardened liquid flows. This allows for much faster printing, because there is no "peel" stage, which is needed in SLA.

DLP (Digital Light Processing) uses a projector like the one you use to watch movies on the wall of your home or project slides at the office. It's very similar to the previous techniques but can be faster, because the layers are exposed fully each time, instead of moving a laser back and forth. These are systems that you could even build yourself (search the Internet for DIY DLP and you'll find examples).

DPP (Daylight Polymer Printing) is a technology using highly sensitive liquid polymer, which is hardened using a standard LCD screen (like small computer screens).

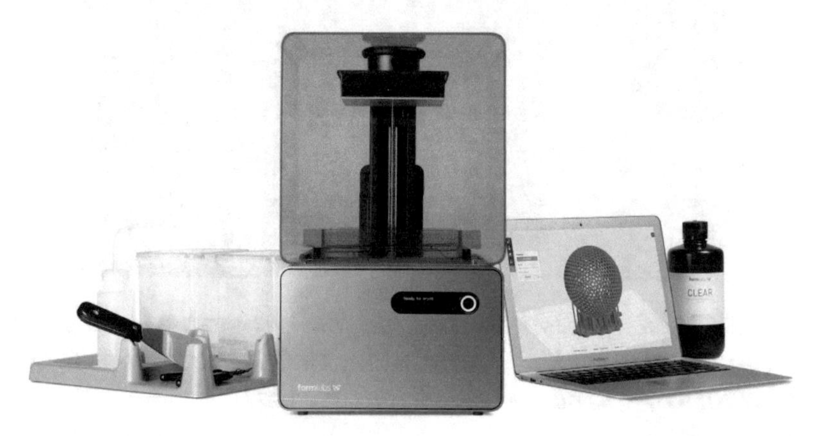

Figure 5-4. *SLA 3D printer from Formlabs (`https://formlabs.com/media/upload/form_1_plus_complete.jpg`)*

Material Jetting

Material jetting technology is very closely related to inkjet printing, using nozzles to deposit droplets of material that are then cured with UV light (producing plastic parts), with heat (producing metal parts), or by cooling of the material (producing wax parts for "lost wax" casting - we'll talk a little more about this later in this chapter).

Binder Jetting

Binder jetting is similar to material jetting, but uses a bonding agent (glue or resin) to fix the particles together. This produces parts in either gypsum, sand, or metal, depending on the machine and bonding agent used.

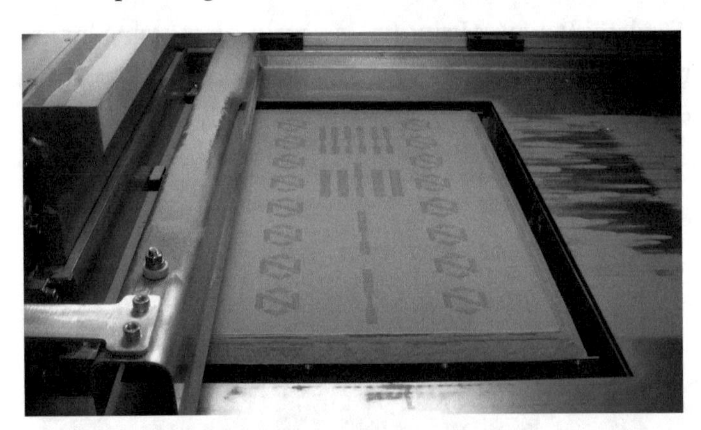

Figure 5-5. *Binder jetting printing platform - note the fused powder with a darker color (`http://3dprintingindustry.com/wp-content/uploads/2015/09/Binder-Imagehighres.jpg`)*

Powder Bed Fusion

Machines of the powder bed fusion variety use powder that is deposited in very thin layers (one grain thick, where possible) on the print bed, which is then fixed with either resin "gluing" the powder together or, when printing with metals, a laser or electron beam. The more expensive machines allow you to use different kinds of metal powder, which is introduced in thin layers into a vacuum chamber, heated to up to 1100 degrees Celsius, and then fusioned where desired using an electron beam. The interesting thing about this technique (and this goes for all powder bed printers) is that the powder that is not fusioned or fixated serves as a support during the printing process, allowing for the creation of very complex pieces. You can print a bolt, with a head at each side, and the nut on the threaded part, being able to turn in both directions, but impossible to take off. You can easily print spheres (with openings to let the excess powder out) inside of other spheres. In a nutshell, creating objects inside of objects is easy.

Direct Energy Deposition

Direct energy deposition also allows you to print with metal, but uses systems that bring the metal in powder form to the position it should be fixed and then fuse it with a laser or electron beam. This allows for more flexibility and is in many ways similar to techniques such as MIG and TIG welding.

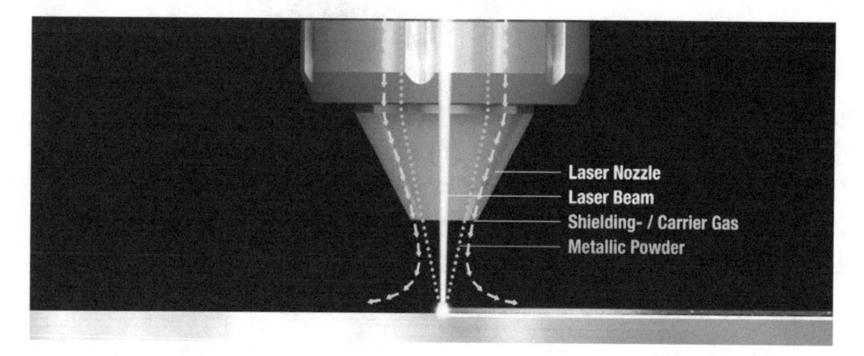

Figure 5-6. *Direct energy deposition process (`www.youtube.com/watch?v=L3CkzQQFZXs`)*

Sheet Lamination

Another quite expensive but equally interesting technique uses standard-sized paper sheets as material to print with. These machines automate a process you can use yourself manually with a laser cutter, namely, stacking cut-out layers to form a 3D object. The thinner the layer, the higher the detail, so using paper gives you nicely detailed products, but would be too tedious to do by hand. This process also allows you to 3D print in color, and the input material is quite cheap. Products can be treated after once printed to become more resistant.

Figure 5-7. *Sheet lamination 3D printer – the Mcor Arke, a 3D printer using simple sheets of paper as material (`https://3dprintingindustry.com/wp-content/uploads/2016/01/mCor-ARKe-consumer-full-color-3D-printer-wood-skin.jpg`)*

Technique	Materials Available	Price (Range) in USD per kg of Material	Often Used In	Pros	Cons
Material extrusion	ABS, PLA, PETG, TPU, PP, PVA, nylon, wood filled, metal filled, carbon fiber filled	$15 for PLA and up to $120 for special filled filaments	Fab Labs, makerspaces, at home, schools	Machines and materials are cheap and easy to use	Generates lots of plastic waste
Photo polymerization	Resins with different properties – durable, flexible, implantable, etc.	$50 for standard resins and up to $500 for special resins	Prototyping facilities, (bio)medical schools and centers	Very interesting and technical materials available, not super expensive	Potentially dangerous materials, needs proper handling
Material jetting	Photopolymers, casting wax	$300–1000 per kg of material	Prototyping, rapid tooling manufacturing		
Binder jetting					
Powder bed fusion		$45–75 for plastics, between $350 and $550 for metals			
Direct energy deposition			High-tech prototyping and fast part replacement	Fast, allows for the creation of tough parts	Very expensive, not easy to find
Sheet lamination			Modeling/design spaces		

Materials

We can generalize by saying you can currently print with anything that can be found in a (semi)liquid state, plastic filament or pellet, or powder form and then hardened using a binding agent, heat, or light.

To say it in simpler words, you can print in plastic, composites (adding fibers to the plastic), gypsum, and metal, and using gel-like materials, you can create biocompatible structures for growth of tissue (more on that in the "Applications" section).

Metals you can use are iron, stainless steel, titanium, chrome, copper, bronze, aluminum, Inconel (an alloy), and precious metals like gold and silver.

Figure 5-8. *3D-printed metallic structure. Metals can be printed into complex objects and shapes (`http://zdnet2.cbsistatic.com/hub/i/2016/04/24/adac9a81-ca89-4643-89ef-9428df718379/168377104c66692cb8ea176e09192065/metal-printed-by-3d-systems.jpg`)*

Using an SLA machine and the right kind of material, you can also create ceramic parts. These are not usable right out of the machine, but need post-processing. To make a cool ceramic espresso cup, for example, you would need to "fire" it after printing, the same way you would do with a hand-thrown cup, bowl, or plate. For that you need a specialized kiln, which slowly increases, holds, and then decreases the temperature to harden the material. You might find a local makerspace with a kiln that you can use.

The resins you can use in SLA machines come in many other types, but all need proper handling and safety rules (see the following). You can find resins that are very tough when cured or stay flexible or even resins that once fully set are even safe to use with food.

The printers you might work with personally will most likely be FDM (fused filament) printers or stereolithography machines. The plastics mainly used in FDM machines are PLA (polylactic acid) or ABS (acrylonitrile butadiene styrene), which is the material Lego blocks are made of. There are many companies developing other plastics, and you can also find plastics that will resemble wood once your print is done or have quite different mechanical properties. Materials that are made up of a mix of plastic and other materials, for example, wood or metals, are called blends.

The following is a table comparing some of the most common materials for FDM printing.

Material/ Properties	Ultimate Strength	Stiffness	Durability	Max. Service Temperature	Price per kg	Printability	Printer Requirements	Additional Features
ABS	40MPa	5/10	8/10	98c	\$10–40	8/10	Heated bed, enclosure recommended	Impact resistant, heat resistant, smoothable with acetone
PLA	65Mpa	7.5/10	4/10	52c	\$10–40	9/10	Part cooling fan	Heated bed may not be required
PETG	53MPa	5/10	8/10	73c	\$20–60	9/10	Heated bed, part cooling fan	Water resistant, chemical resistant, fatigue resistant

TPU/ flexible	26–43Mpa	1/10	9/10	60–74c	$30–70	6/10	Part cooling fan, direct drive extrusion	Flexible, elastic, soft, fatigue resistant
PP	32Mpa	4/10	9/10	100c	$60–120	4/10	Heated bed, enclosure recommended, part cooling fan	Flexible, soft, water resistant, heat resistant, fatigue resistant
PVA	78Mpa	3/10	7/10	75c	$40–110	5/10	Heated bed, part cooling fan	Flexible, soft, dissolvable, fatigue resistant

(continued)

Material/ Properties	Ultimate Strength	Stiffness	Durability	Max. Service Temperature	Price per kg	Printability	Printer Requirements	Additional Features
Nylon	40–85MPa	5/10	10/10	80–95c	$25–65	8/10	Heated bed, enclosure recommended, may require all metal hotend	Flexible, impact resistant, heat resistant, fatigue resistant
Wood filled	78MPa	3/10	7/10	52c	$25–55	8/10	Part cooling fan	Composite
Metal filled	20–30Mpa	10/10	4/10	52c	$50–120	7/10	Wear-resistant or stainless steel nozzle, part cooling fan	Composite
Carbon fiber filled	45–85Mpa	10/10	3/10	52c	$30–80	8/10	Part cooling fan	Composite

Figure 5-9. *Wood-filled filament and part. Filament comes in many materials, colors, and textures, even wood. (`https://go-3dprint.com/wp-content/uploads/2016/04/DSC_0474.jpg`)*

FDM-printed parts can be often post-processed to remove the visibility of the layers and make the part smooth to the touch. Different techniques can be used depending on the printing material. One of the most common procedures uses solvent vapors to smooth surfaces. For example, ABS parts can be finely smoothed with acetone vapors. Sandpaper can be used for most materials, but, because it removes part of the outer shell, it is not recommended for smoothing thin-walled 3D-printed parts. Also, if the parts have been printed with thick layer height, using sandpaper can take quite some time. Coating of 3D-printed parts is also possible using paints or resins.

Software: Running the Machine

Most of the printers on the market today will have their own software package, which only works with their machines. These are similar in many ways though, so we won't look at each one of these packages individually but rather go over the general things you can change when 3D printing a part.

Regardless of the type of printer you might use, you need software to **slice** the object you would like to print into layers to create the toolpath – or, said differently, calculating the moves of the machine for each layer. Some control software uses external slicers, so you can mix and match your interface of choice with a slicer you prefer, but many packages have everything in one interface.

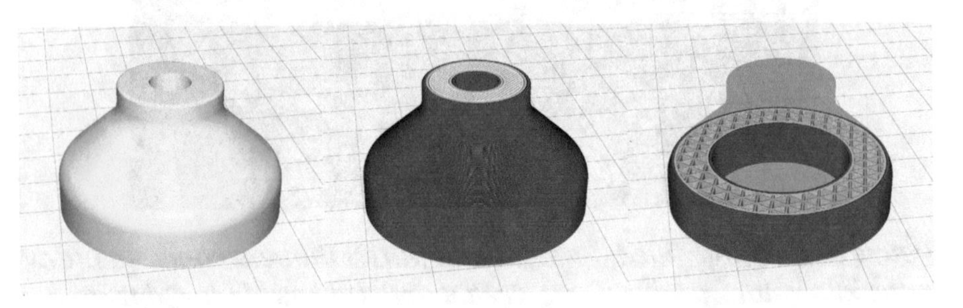

Figure 5-10. *Slicing process, from left to right: 3D model, sliced model, section of the sliced model*

There are software packages available that will function happily with different brands of printers, but not different techniques. So before you start trying out some packages, make sure you know what printing technique you'll go for! If you buy a commercial printer, we would recommend simply using the software provided, unless you want to experiment.

So let's first take a look at what a slicer will do and then how to control your machine and send it the file.

If you have an STL file (some slicers accept different formats), the slicer software of your choice will transform this into a three-dimensional toolpath by cutting it into layers of the thickness you specify. You of course have to take into account the capabilities of your printer, and most software packages will make it easy on you by offering a few "standard" settings, such as low, medium, and high quality. These settings will differ in layer thickness, but also in printing speed, infill, and more.

When working with an FDM machine, the software will not only cut the object in layers in the Z direction but will also create different settings for the outside part of your object and the inside. Oftentimes your object will not have to be filled completely with material to be solid enough for your uses (and this is another one of those advantages of 3D printing - it saves money that way). This means the **infill** can be set to a percentage of the space (so, say, we would like to fill 30% of the space with material), and you can use different strategies to do this.

Look at Figure 5-11 to see some examples. The hexagonal infill is often used, for its nice combination of use of space and strength. Bees are smart!

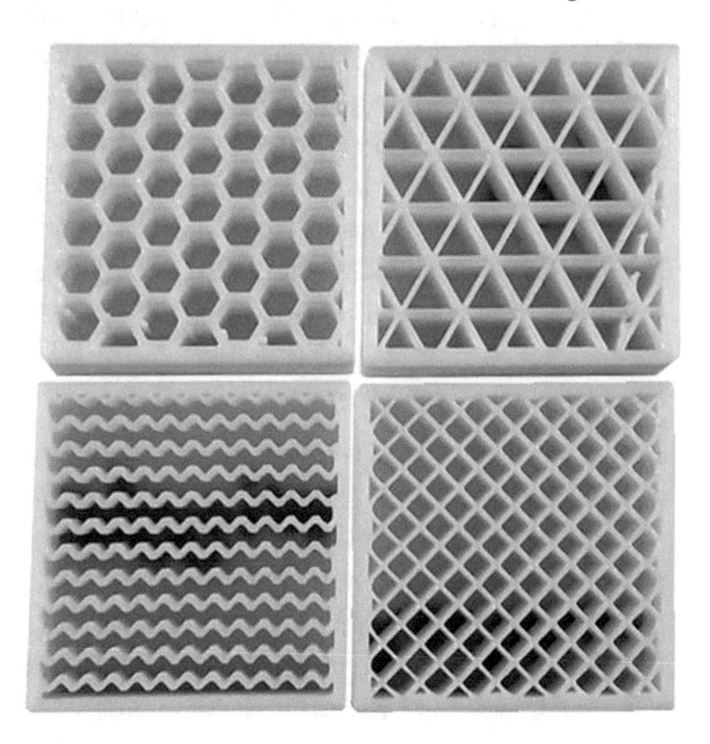

Figure 5-11. *Different infill types (`https://3dprinting.com/wp-content/uploads/2015/09/infill.jpg`)*

There are several settings for FDM, and not all of them are required or used often. For your convenience we have grouped the most important settings for FDM printers in the following table.

Setting	What Does It Do?	What Is the Effect?	Notes
Layer thickness	Changes the thickness of each single layer of the 3D-printed object.	High layer thickness (typically 0.2mm) results in shorter printing times, stronger parts, and lower-quality surface finish. Vice versa, low layer thickness (typically 0.06mm) takes longer to print and makes weaker but higher-quality parts.	Depending on the layer thickness, the same object can be printed using more or less layers. Layer thickness is also a function of the installed nozzle, with the maximum value roughly equal to 80% of the nozzle size.
Shell thickness	Changes the thickness of the object shell. In 3D-printed objects, the shell is the outer wall that separates the object infill from the outside.	High shell thickness increases the object strength, at the price of longer prints and heavier objects. Vice versa, low shell thickness decreases the printing time, making lighter and weaker objects.	This setting can usually be applied separately to the side and the top/bottom shell thicknesses. Very thin shell thickness results in a semi-transparent shell.

(*continued*)

Setting	What Does It Do?	What Is the Effect?	Notes
Infill	Changes the amount of internal object filling and the strategy used to make it.	Usually defined in percentage. Objects with high infill percentage are heavier and stronger. Low infill percentage results in lighter but weaker objects.	The strongest objects are made with 100% infill. Infill strategies can influence speed and stiffness of the objects.
Speed	Changes the movement speed of the printer while printing.	Higher speeds (typically 100mm/s or more) result in shorter printing times at the cost of lower quality. Slow speeds (usually less than 50mm/s) increase the quality, but prolong the printing time.	Different speeds can be set depending on whether the machine is printing the infill or shell or just jumping from one position to another. Maximum speed depends on mechanical, computational, and extruder performances.

(*continued*)

Setting	What Does It Do?	What Is the Effect?	Notes
Support	Enables or disables support for the print job. Supports are needed to hold surfaces with overhangs, if present.	If enabled, surfaces with overhangs will be supported. If not, and your part has surfaces with overhangs, the print may fail or show problems where the overhang is.	A support is an additional structure added to the 3D-printed part by the slicing software, not part of the original design. Depending on the printer, supports are made with the same material as the printed part and snapped off, or they can be made with dissolvable materials (e.g., PVA).

(continued)

Setting	What Does It Do?	What Is the Effect?	Notes
Printing sequence	Defines the strategy used to print jobs involving multiple parts. Usually, it can be set to print one piece at a time or all together layer by layer.	Printing one piece at a time makes the print faster. Printing layer by layer all the parts results in longer printing time and may leave some thin wires between the parts.	Printing one piece at a time may not be possible if parts are placed close together, because the head may crash into them. Therefore, parts may be placed far away from each other, reducing the total amount printable. Make sure the software takes into consideration the size of the machine head to avoid crashes.

When using SLA machines or powder bed printers, you will print the object with a solid infill. If you would print a hexagonal (or another) infill pattern on a printer using resins or powder, you would trap uncured resin or powder inside the pockets of your piece. So on these machines, there is no difference between the outer layer and the inside in terms of printing technique.

Because there are so many different types of printers, we are not going to dive too deep into the settings. We'd need a full book just on that! When starting out we would recommend using the standard settings for the printer, and if you want to experiment, use those as a starting point.

Change one or two settings, print again, and look at the differences. Better? Worse? The same? Once you understand what the settings do, you can move to different parameters, until you have understood them all or are satisfied with your options.

When using powder bed machines (like SLS or material jetting), you don't need to worry about support structures. But if you are using an SLA or FDM machine, you might need to add some.

If you have slanted parts or bridges (parts that will be suspended in the air), you'll need to print a structure underneath those to make sure the printer can actually deposit material in that location. When it comes to angled parts, in general we can say that any angle up to 45 degrees doesn't need support. Beyond that you might get bad results if you do not add support material.

Figure 5-12. *Automatic generation of 3D-printed support, from left to right: the 3D model, the generated support, a section of the support structure. Note the red parts on the bottom on the leftmost image indicate that support is recommended*

Some FDM printers offer the possibility of using different materials for the support and the part you want to print. By using what we call soluble support material such as PVA, or polyvinyl alcohol, which is a water-soluble polymer, you can simply put the printed part with its support structures in a water bath and let the PVA dissolve. Printers not offering this option use what we call "breakaway support," meaning once the print is finished, you need to carefully break, cut, or snip off the support.

Safety

If you have the opportunity to use more advanced machines printing in metal or composites, you will most likely get a training session that explains all the (numerous) safety and health measures you have to take when working with them. But even the home-built printers or ones you buy for your house (that do not come with training) can be dangerous.

3D printing is now so accessible that people tend to forget these dangers. ABS at high temperatures creates toxic particles that are released as a gas (and thus not visible), and PLA will as well (but less so). This does not mean you should immediately stop printing cool things, but make sure you print in well-ventilated spaces, and don't leave your kids hanging over the printer for the duration of the print.

SLA printers possibly pose a greater risk, because the photopolymers used in them are toxic chemicals that should never touch the skin when not fully cured, and many of them are classified as respiratory sensitization category 1 (in the American standardized system NFPA 704), meaning they can cause allergy, asthma symptoms, or breathing difficulties if inhaled.

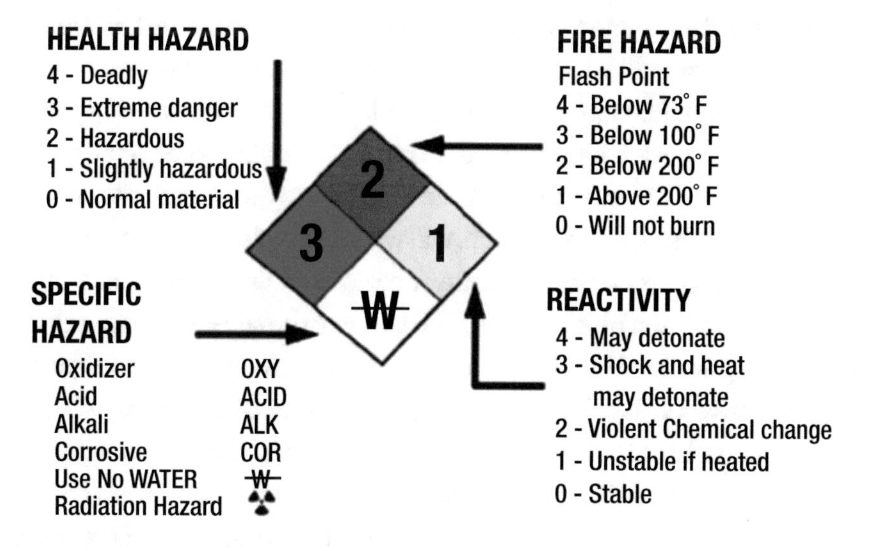

Figure 5-13. *Hazard classification for substances*

Make sure you treat these plastics and chemicals like you would other chemical substances at home or work. Wear gloves when handling resins, make sure you are in well-ventilated spaces, and keep substances out of reach of young ones!

Next to material safety, some machines can also be dangerous. Fingers and hair can get stuck in moving parts, and next to that most FDM printers have parts that become extremely hot but are still easily accessible for fingers and hands and can start fires. We received an email with some images recently showing a burnt-down printer because the hotend (that was not well fixed) dropped onto the printing bed, which was covered with hair spray (which can help with adhesion) and made the machine catch on fire. Always realize you are working with electricity, moving parts, and heat!

Maintenance

The kind of printers that you might get at home or in a makerspace need regular maintenance to make sure they continue to print well. More expensive machines often come with maintenance contracts, and from experience we can tell you it's not a bad idea to take one of those.

If you have an FDM machine, you should make sure the moving parts stay clean and greased. If your machine has belts driving some or all of the movement, also make sure to check the tension on those regularly. Some of the parts of those types of printers will wear out with regular use. You'll most likely need to replace the printing nozzle from time to time, as well as the hotbed (if the machine has one) and some of the sensors. Some printers come with a printhead that is completely enclosed, meaning you might need to replace the whole head if the nozzle has worn out. Others allow you to take off the nozzle only and replace a small part, which is a lot cheaper.

When it comes to SLA printers, it's of vital importance to keep them clean of uncured resin. Most of the resins used in these types of machines are cured with UV light and will (slowly) cure when they are in daylight.

This means that if you drop some of it on parts of your machine (or workbench, tools, whatever you have lying around), it will harden on that surface and be very difficult to remove. All the resins have an expiration date and become unusable sometime after it. Because of the resin price, we recommend always making sure it does not go to waste. Resins must be properly disposed of because of their toxicity.

Some SLA printers have a glass window that the laser shines through, which should not only be kept spotless but also scratch-free. If there is even a small scratch or some dust, the laser beam can be diverted to the wrong spot, resulting in unexpected printing results.

SLA printers use transparent containers to hold the uncured resin. These can be reused a few times, but are ultimately consumables and not cheap. When thinking about getting a printer, make sure you take that into account!

Applications

3D printing is a welcome addition to the toolset we discuss in this book, because of its possibility to create pieces that are extremely difficult, or even impossible, to build any other way. Next to that, fused filament 3D printers are currently one of the most abundantly accessible and affordable machines around you, so wherever you are, you'll probably find one close to you.

Usage in Industry and Commercial Applications

The market for 3D printing has been growing rapidly in the past years. In 2021, the global market was estimated at US $16.54 billion and is expected to grow to $62.79 billion in 2028. In industrial and commercial settings, you'll most likely hear "additive manufacturing" instead of 3D printing – for all means and purposes, it's the same thing.

Stereolithography is most popular and accounts for around 11% of the total market. Next is FDM followed by the other techniques. Companies in aerospace, car manufacturing, and healthcare sectors often need specific materials, which leads to further development of the less generalized technologies.

The obvious use of 3D printing in industry is for parts that are one-offs like medical devices. Ninety-eight percent of hearing aids made by Starkey (`www.forbes.com/sites/rakeshsharma/2013/07/08/the-3d-printing-revolution-you-have-not-heard-about/#84f0f81a6b5a`) are made with 3D printers, and other companies use the technique similarly. See Figure 5-14 of a few parts just printed by Widex, a Danish company offering prosthetics and hearing aids.

Figure 5-14. *3D-printed hearing aids (`http://disruptiveinnovation.se/wp-content/uploads/Picture22.jpg`)*

Next to that, a lot of prototyping and testing is now done with 3D printing in the automotive industry, aerospace, architecture, education, and entertainment and for consumer products.

Industry is very interested in the development of this technology because of the cost advantages.

It generally creates less waste, you can have a lower inventory you need to stock, labor costs go down because less production steps are needed, quality control is easier since the product remains "digital" until the last step, and finally the setup is often cheaper.

Most of 3D printing is done in product development and prototyping. With 3D printing technologies changing with the speed of light, we might see an increase in what's possible locally and switch to more decentralized manufacturing using these techniques. The potential change in time to market for different products means it is a very exciting and quickly changing field. But the science fiction examples of machines at home that make almost anything are still quite far off, and it's probably not just 3D printing that will develop those!

Bioprinting

There is a lot of active research toward the use of these technologies in the biomedical world. 3D bioprinting is a technique where scaffolds, often in the shape of the desired object, are created out of biologically compatible material.

The idea is to create a shape in which we can put active cells, which will then grow into the shape that was printed, forming an organ or piece of the body. This is still ongoing research, but has potentially great applications in the medical world and also in the food industry! Imagine you could use a 3D printer in your home to print a shape that you then sprinkle some cells on to grow meat, without the need to end the life of an animal. Who's up for some hamburgers, freshly grown in your own kitchen? Sounds like science fiction? There are multiple companies working on exactly that or even using different substances to directly print a steak.

What You Can Make

Master Yoda, or "Test Print Realize This, You Must"

One of the things you'll almost have to print when you build a 3D printer is a small Master Yoda. It's like the "Hello world"[1] of 3D printing. This stems from the moment where a "test object" was needed once the construction of a printer was completed and the open source (geeky) community adopted Master Yoda as their figurehead. If you'd like to really test your printer and at the same time display something that you'll find is impossible to build with another machine, you should print the Voronoi Yoda you can see in Figure 5-15.

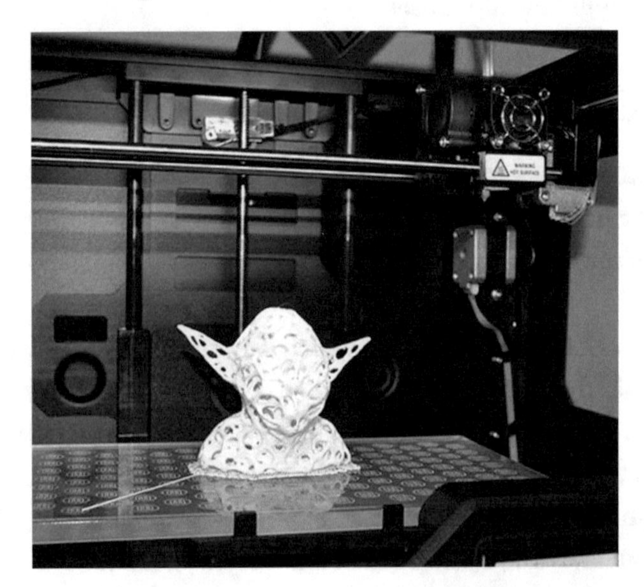

Figure 5-15. *3D-printed Voronoi Yoda (`www.3dizingof.com/3D-Printing/wp-content/uploads/2014/03/3D-printed-3D-Voronoi-Yoda-by-Dizingof-510x453.jpg`)*

[1] A Hello world program in computer programming is often the first program made by people learning to code. It's simply a program created to output the words "Hello world" onto screen.

Another Machine, or Machines Making Machines

Certainly at the beginning of the RepRap/home-built 3D printer movement, a lot of printers were built using other printers to create some of their pieces. The wonderful FoldaRap (see Figure 5-16) is built using pieces that can be printed with the machine itself. "What came first?" you ask. "The print or the printer?" As Neil deGrasse Tyson (@neiltyson) tweeted, the egg came first, but it was laid by a bird that was not a chicken. The first machine was made using a machine that was not a FoldaRap, but once you have one functional 3D printer, you can print most of the next one or any other machine you'd like to build. Milling machines, vinyl cutters, machines to plant seeds - imagine it and print it.

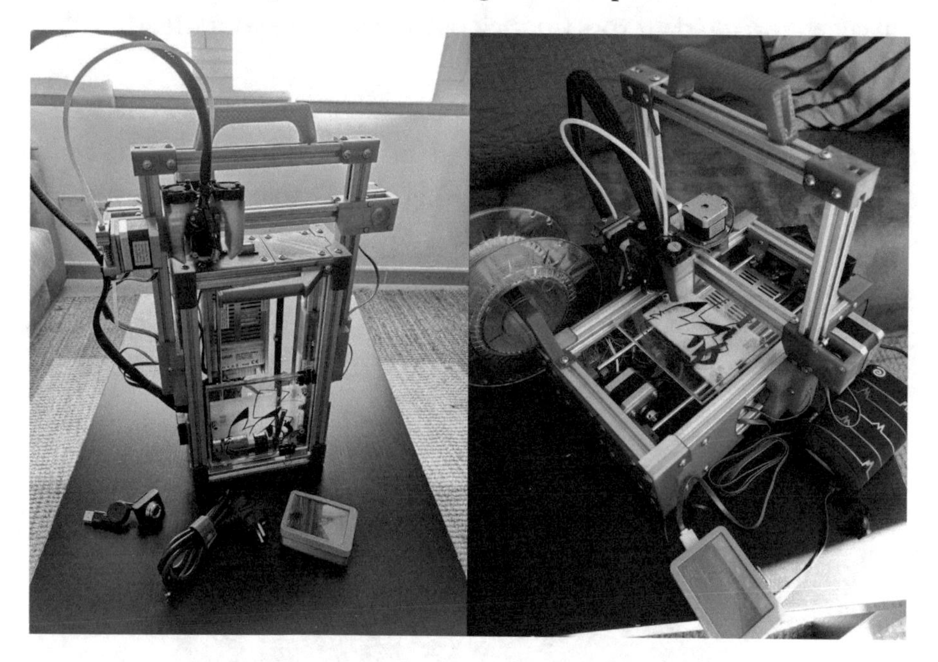

Figure 5-16. *FoldaRap*

Molds

A nice thing to do when you have a 3D printer is to use it to not make the final piece but a mold (or, often, the mold for the final mold). For instance, you can print some skulls (we developed an exhibit on skeletons in our science center, no morbid fascination here) and then create a mold with those using food-safe silicones to pour chocolate into. Anna from the Fab Academy made some awesome skull molds, and one of my colleagues duplicated the idea and added gold spray paint on top. Golden chocolate skulls look (and taste) quite exquisite.

There is a nicely done mold generator on Thingiverse, where you can put in your 3D object (doesn't have to be a skull, you know) and it will generate a mold for you. Check it out and surprise your friends with personalized cookies and lollipops.

Next to food, you can also use plaster or other curable materials to create the final object. What's nice about this is the expansion of the types of materials you can use - from very strong and durable to flexible to soluble!

Figure 5-17. *3D-printed skull molds*

Printing with Food

The printers used in research around bioprinting most often use a syringe to extrude materials. This means you cannot print very large objects (or you would need an enormous syringe), but it does allow you to use semi-liquid materials, such as dough or chocolate paste. By filling a syringe with pancake dough and printing on a hotplate, you can create customized pancakes, on which you can then print some chocolate spread before topping it off with strawberries. Those you'll need to add by hand though or with a robotic arm.

Figure 5-18. *3D food printing. Left is mashed meat, and right is creamy cheese*

Metal Casting

Either using an SLA machine and some specialized resin or using a simple FDM printer and PLA material, you can create pieces to use in lost wax casting.

You would use the printed piece to create a mold out of plaster, which you then put in an oven or kiln to "burn" the wax or PLA away. Now you can pour molten metal into the mold, cure it (which also needs a kiln), and then break the mold to reveal the final piece. A "cheap" way to "print" metal pieces at home! If you want to do this, you need a proper setup to harden the plaster mold while burning out the print. Simply heating it up in an oven would make the mold brittle and unusable. On top of that, the wax or PLA evaporates and creates some toxic fumes you definitely do not want in your oven!

***Figure 5-19.** Example of metal casting done with 3D-printed parts and silicone*

Hold: Hooks and Holders

3D printers can be wonderful if you'd like your laptop to sit just a bit higher to optimize viewing pleasure for that latest *Star Wars* flick or if you accidentally broke the handle on your drawer, fridge, or car. Having your soap rest on a personalized soap dish in your bathroom or your cup collection hanging from hooks stylized by yours truly – it's easily done with a 3D printer.

We also still live in a time where if a small part of an appliance you use in your home breaks, it's not that easy to replace and often also not cheap! But once you have (access to) a 3D printer, you can print a new knob for that washing machine or a new door handle for that fridge quite easily!

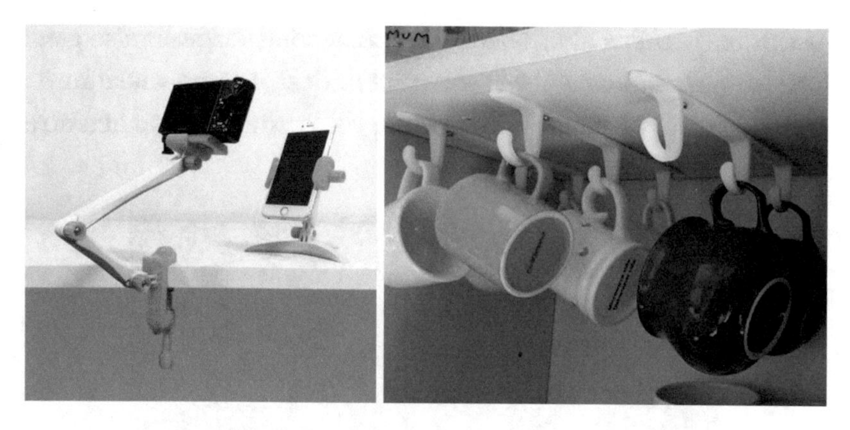

Figure 5-20. *Example of 3D-printed holders and hooks*

Timekeeping with Shadows and Lights

Because of the possibility to print complex hollow objects, you can 3D print parts that create very specific shadows or projections when light falls through them. A designer called Mojoptix designed the sundial in Figure 5-21 that actually shows the time in numbers by creating shadows with the sunlight falling through it.

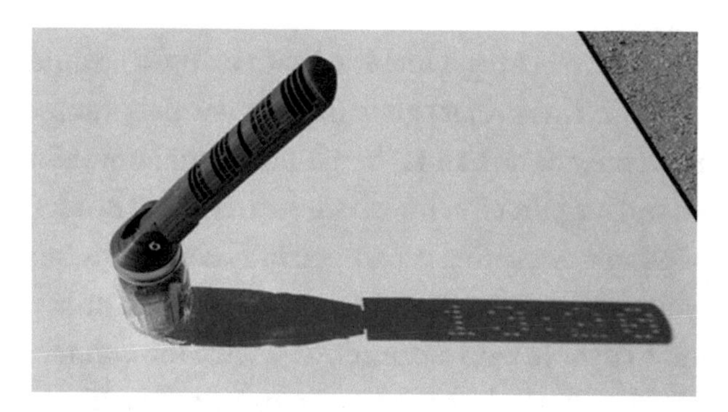

Figure 5-21. *A 3D-printed sun clock (`http://42mzqz26jebqf6rd034t5pef-wpengine.netdna-ssl.com/wp-content/uploads/2016/02/3d-printed-digital-sundial-sun-clock-mojoptix-12-550x292.jpg`)*

The principle of creating shadows or projecting shapes is also great to apply to lamps or lampshades. If you print or design some, make sure to use bulbs that don't heat up, or make sure your print cannot catch on fire or melt!

Figure 5-22. *Shadow projected through a 3D printed model (`https://3dprintingindustry.com/wp-content/uploads/2014/12/lamps3.png`)*

Helping Hands

A wonderful project you can get involved with using 3D printers is Enabling the Future. This project grew out of a few people creating assistive devices (prosthetic hands) for children (and now adults) who are missing a hand, or part of it, for whatever reason. It is now a vibrant community of people designing prosthetic hands that you can download and print on your own printer. They have a website that links people needing a hand to people with a printer, and once the connection is made, it often doesn't take long before the person has a newly 3D printed hand to try out. If you have a printer at home, sign up, so that if someone needs a hand, you can give one!

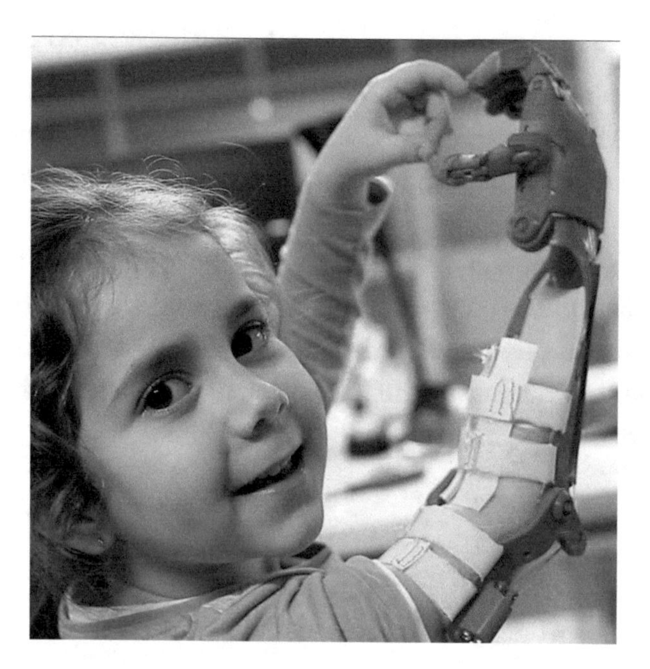

Figure 5-23. *3D-printed prosthetic (`http://enablingthefuture.org/category/featured-stories/`)*

To sum up, 3D printing is a fast-changing and broad field of techniques, possibilities, and applications. The very low cost of many printers and ease of use really make them wonderful machines to start making things with. So whether you are interested in making lamp shades, scale models, prosthetic devices, or even bigger things like guitars, start designing and printing!

Summary

3D printers are more and more affordable for you to create 3D objects. 3D printing, also referred to as additive manufacturing, allows rapid prototyping of complex shapes not possible to manufacture with other digital fabrication techniques.

From printing simple plastic parts to solve a small problem at home to flexible production of spare parts, 3D printing is a well-established technology in makerspaces and Fab Labs, starting to become used also in other fields such as metal processing, food shaping, and medical applications.

Now that you know about the different kinds of available 3D printers, ranging from printers you can build yourself at home to industrial printers, and their features, possible materials, and applications, you can start looking online for interesting things to print, or even better, start designing some custom objects yourself!

CHAPTER 6

Other Machines

This chapter provides a succinct overview of a variety of machines, beyond those discussed in detail in other chapters of the book. While some of these machines may be found in makerspaces, others are predominantly used in industrial settings due to their cost, size, or specialized purpose. This overview is not exhaustive, but it aims to provide a comprehensive understanding of the various techniques available, should the need arise for scaling production or working with materials that cannot be handled by more readily accessible machines.

In addition to the specialized machines explored in this book, there are an increasing number of multi-functional machines that incorporate multiple techniques and tools. An example of this is DMG Mori's Lasertec 65, which serves as both a 3D metal printer and a CNC mill, switching between tool heads as needed for each operation. The concept of having machines that are a set of axes with interchangeable tool heads is being actively researched and developed. It's possible that in the future, a single machine could be reconfigured and equipped with various tools and processes to meet a wide range of needs by adjusting its axes and changing tool heads.

Nadya Peek from MIT is working on a platform that allows you to quickly prototype machines this way; See the next images for older and more recent machine.

J-m. Molenaar and D. Ingrassia, *Mastering Digitally Controlled Machines*, Maker Innovations Series, https://doi.org/10.1007/978-1-4842-9849-7_6

Figure 6-1. *Prototyping machines - the MTM Snap by Nadya Peek (https://2e0a24317f4a9294563f-26c3b154822345d9dde0204930c49e9c.ssl.cf1.rackcdn.com/3661066_1425202476174_be72b180_m.png)*

Figure 6-2. *Recent prototype with multiple toolheads*

Let's start by taking a look at cutting techniques (some of which will also allow engraving) other than CNC milling and laser cutting.

Plasma Cutting

Plasma cutting is a technique using fast streams of hot plasma (superheated, ionized gas - examples you know are the sun, neon signs, and lightning bolts) to cut through electrically conductive materials.

Handheld plasma cutters are available at a reasonable cost; however, they are more dangerous compared with handheld routers due to the nature of the technique used. Mounting a plasma torch onto a CNC-controlled system results in a CNC plasma cutter, which offers greater precision and ease of repetition, but at a higher cost.

The limited availability of plasma cutters compared with lasers is due to the need for a more secure and complex setup, which many Fab Labs cannot afford. If interested in obtaining a plasma cutter, you should be prepared to invest a minimum of $1,000 for a handheld cutter or at least $5,000 for a CNC cutter. Additionally, you must secure the workspace, acquire necessary safety equipment, and purchase consumables and gas.

Waterjet Cutting

Waterjet cutting is a precision cutting technique that employs a highly pressurized water stream or a water-abrasive mixture to cut through various materials including glass, stone, ceramics, plastics, and wood. The water stream that comes out of the nozzle has an extremely high pressure, up to 100,000 PSI or 6894 Bar, and uses consumable parts to maintain its proper operation. The cut's width or kerf is determined by the nozzle's diameter, typically ranging from 1 to 1.3mm (0.04–0.05 inches) for abrasive cutting and 0.18 to 0.33mm (0.007–0.013 inches) for water-only cutting. Waterjets are ideal for cutting materials that lasers or plasma cutters cannot handle. Acquiring this versatile tool requires a significant investment, with machine costs around US $80,000 and additional expenses for safety equipment, cutting consumables, and materials.

If you're considering investing in a waterjet cutting machine, it's important to budget for the associated expenses beyond the machine purchase, such as safety equipment and a suitable workspace. Additionally, you will need to take into account the operational cost of the machine, which can amount to approximately US $50 per hour, excluding the cost of materials. Despite the considerable financial investment, the versatility of waterjet cutting makes it a worthwhile option for certain applications.

A company named Wazer has successfully introduced waterjet cutters for a lower price point, approximately US $6,000, after receiving the notable amount of US $1.3 million in funding through a kick-starter campaign, surpassing their original 100,000 goal. While there are concerns regarding the reliability and quality of products launched through crowdfunding campaigns, it is promising to see initiatives like this working toward democratizing digital fabrication by offering more affordable access to complex and typically expensive machines.

Figure 6-3. *Mike Holden Glass – tessellation series*

Electric Discharge Machining

Electric Discharge Machining (EDM) is a metal removal technique that utilizes rapid electric discharges to vaporize metal between electrodes and then flush it away with deionized fluid.

Two primary types of EDM include Sinker EDM and Wire EDM. Sinker EDM is used for creating complex molds and three-dimensional parts by lowering a shaped electrode onto the material being machined and creating discharges. Wire EDM uses a thin conductor wire, often brass, that moves through the material in one direction to cut through extremely hard metals, which can be 16 inches or more in thickness depending on the wire and machine used.

The absence of pressure from the cutting tool allows for the production of small and precise pieces without deformation. Additionally, the process yields a high-quality surface finish, and with advanced machines, complex 3D geometries can be created in materials that are otherwise difficult to machine.

Wires as small as 0.02mm in diameter can be utilized, resulting in kerfs of that size. However, the wire is a consumable, as is the water used to flush out the minute metal particles from the machine. This results in a costly process that requires significant setup and operational time. Second-hand EDM machines can be bought for approximately US $5,000, but it should be noted that yearly wire costs can easily add a few thousand dollars to the expense. You will have other considerations, such as space and safety, that must also be taken into account.

Figure 6-4. *EDM machine*

CNC Lathes

Digitally controlled lathes are similar to CNC mills, with the difference being that the workpiece being machined is held in a rotating chuck instead of being affixed to a flat surface. In this process, cutters and blades are brought to the surface of the workpiece to remove the material. These machines are primarily used for cylindrical objects. Though you might have seen lathes before in various sizes, which are manually operated, the difference here is the digitization of the process, making it easier and safer to repeat.

Hot-Wire Cutter

A cost-effective alternative to other cutting machines is the hot-wire cutter, which can even be fabricated with relative ease. It is not as versatile in terms of material options, being mainly restricted to foam cutting. Nevertheless, it is a good option for producing intricate mold shapes, form studies, and demonstration pieces. The cutting is carried out by a wire, often nichrome or stainless steel, that is electrically heated and then driven through the foam by motors, producing precise shapes from a solid block. Complex objects can be produced using a hot-wire cutter with multiple axes.

***Figure 6-5.** Pieces made with an hot-wire cutter (`www.foamlinx.com/image-files/sample_cuts2_small.JPG`)*

Robotic Arms

Increasingly, teams and individuals are utilizing robotic arms, such as KUKA or Universal Robots, for object fabrication. By equipping the robotic arm with various end effectors, you can create a CNC machine with added degrees of freedom, enabling more intricate operations. This increased complexity necessitates additional programming and safety precautions, and consequently, these machines are more commonly found in university labs and research centers.

However, they are becoming more affordable and offer exciting possibilities for creating large-scale objects. While smaller robotic arms are relatively easy to transport and have a significant working area, these arms may not be readily available in small makerspaces. In this field, books and scientific papers are emerging, showcasing the trend of attaching extruders (for 3D printing), spindles (for CNC milling), and even chainsaws (for cutting).

Sewing Machines

Sewing machines are designed to stitch together different types of fabric using thread, enabling the creation of clothing, bags, wearables, and other items. Unlike the other machines discussed in this book, sewing machines are not digitally controlled tools, which means that the design process is not computer based. However, they remain highly accessible and offer an interesting complement to other machines.

You can incorporate laser cutters for engraving or cutting personalized gear, and wearables can be produced. Sewing machines are available in various shapes and sizes, and it is important to consider the frequency of use before purchasing. Industrial sewing machines are faster and more powerful, allowing for the use of thicker and harder materials like leather. Simple, compact machines can be found for around $100, while more professional machines can range in price up to the thousands of dollars.

Embroidery Machines

Embroidery machines are designed to create colorful and intricate designs on fabrics using different colored threads. These machines are more advanced compared with sewing machines and are relatively more expensive, even at the entry level. Embroidery machines are equipped with multiple needles that allow the use of multiple colors in a design, but the number of needles available determines the maximum number of colors that can be used. Although embroidery machines are quite expensive, they are impressive and fascinating to use and observe in action.

Figure 6-6. *Embroidery machines (`www.neptunerenewableenergy.com/wp-content/uploads/2016/08/GG758_915_FLAT_COMPUTERIZED_EMBROIDERY_MACHINE_634567717143105675_1.jpg`)*

Summary

Not all machines in this chapter are commonly encountered, and some are only used for very specific purposes. For those in need of specialized parts, there are options to have them fabricated using these tools by paying for the service. Many cities have fabrication shops equipped with waterjet cutters or EDM machines.

However, there exist many other highly specialized machines that perform a series of complex tasks to achieve a specific outcome. These machines are often part of larger toolchains that fabricate and assemble parts into the final product. Many factories use robotic arms in conjunction with huge presses and automated systems to produce millions of identical products. Conversely, the idea behind many makerspaces is to have a space and machines that facilitate the creation of countless unique objects based on a myriad of different ideas.

CHAPTER 7

Design Approaches

A design approach defines the strategy for where to start and what to design first, based on how different parts of the design influence and interact with each other. Whether you are building a digital fabrication machine or are just thinking about adapting a machine, it is useful to have a design approach as a guideline. A machine may consist of many parts, and it's often hard to tell where to start. In our experience simple design approaches consist of setting priorities and requirements, used to design specific parts. Once these parts are designed, the rest of the design can be derived from and adapted to them.

Where to Start?

If you keep reading the following, you'll find that each of the design approaches gives you an indication where to start.

Where to start? We recommend taking one of these two approaches, either inside-out or outside-in. Here are some factors that might influence your decision:

1. Space limitations might lead to you choosing outside-in.

2. Conversely, if this is your first build, you might choose inside-out and adapting an existing OS machine.

J-m. Molenaar and D. Ingrassia, *Mastering Digitally Controlled Machines*, Maker Innovations Series, https://doi.org/10.1007/978-1-4842-9849-7_7

Read on for a more in-depth exploration of each approach, benefits and drawbacks, and examples of the process.

If you don't follow any of the ones described in this book, you may decide yourself what the best starting point of your design might be.

A good start is thinking about the machine requirements, for example, the machine type, the working area, or the available space in your shop or Fab Lab. Given the machine working area, you might start with the machine linear guiding system, because it is easy to design the rest of the machine parts around the needed travel distances. If you start by designing the housing, it may lead to less machine space because of unexpected space for unforeseen devices or parts. This approach can be useful when limiting the machine footprint to the available shop space. If you wish to build a machine using old or recycled parts, then those can constrain the next steps of the design because of compatible other parts and mounts.

Figure 7-1. *A laser cutter made with recycled parts from other laser cutters (Lucio Pentagna Guimarães Neto)*

Depending on the complexity of the machine you would like to make, you can make it directly by hand or by designing it in CAD. When integrating components or checking spacings, fittings, etc., a CAD design can help you quite a lot before having any physical part in your hands. When you use digital fabrication machines to create parts, you need to start from a digital model, and thus a CAD design is needed. A CAD model is also important for documentation, as it can be used by others for reproduction or improvements.

Standing on the Shoulders of Giants

Standing on the shoulders of giants, or starting with and reusing the experience and the developments of others for your machine design, often gives you a great head start. Whether the existing machine is open source or a proprietary design, it is always useful to have a look at it and investigate how it is made. This is easy if the machine is open source, because CAD files, assembly instructions, and helpful pictures are often available. For commercial machines, pictures of the inside may be available for maintenance procedures or uploaded by users, for example, in specialized forums. Even if pictures may not contain specific information or the text around them is not explanatory, you can still find a lot of details. An expert eye can estimate the type, size, or brand of the parts, while others can at least get the basics (e.g., belts and pulleys instead of gears). If you have the chance to physically observe the machine and even remove some of the external panels, it can help you understand how parts are physically made and connected to each other mechanically, electrically, hydraulically, etc.

By observing the machine, either physically or virtually, you will find that machines of similar type and range may use similar parts, systems, and configurations. Checking the machine similarities can help identify the basic concepts per machine type and think about how to integrate them into your design. Starting from an open source machine design is, in general, our recommended approach. As you will read near the end of this book, proficient makers have spent years trying to make their own open source machine, often improving their designs with several versions and variations over the years. In addition to that, with an open source design, you embrace the concept of distributing the design of your machine to anyone interested. And if you're open to starting from someone else's existing design, you will be happy if someone in the future tries to improve your design. In open source designs, modifications can be made with the mutual goal of improving the design. At the time of writing, popular platforms for open source machines are websites such as Wikifactory, GitHub, Fab Academy archive, OpenBuilds, Thingiverse, and Hackaday.

Figure 7-2. *A range of different open source 3D printers from Reprap (RepRap)*

Inside-Out

An inside-out approach consists of designing a small machine part inside the machine body and then designing the parts around it, iterating the process until the overall design is complete. The parts already designed influence the design of the nearby parts, for example, for fitting and motion purposes. An example comes from the development of LaserDuo. The main requirements of the machine were the working size of 1500 × 1000mm (X = 1500mm and Y = 1000mm). The X axis of the machine was designed first as the part to be used to design all the others. The closest part to the X axis was the Y axis, and this led to the design of the Y axis before any other part. The Y axis design took into consideration the provided attachments from the X axis, its size, and the laser optics. The Z axis followed the Y axis, then the inner frame, electronics, and the housing. The shape and the appearance of the frame and the housing were not clear at the beginning but resulted from the chaining of all the machine parts requirements.

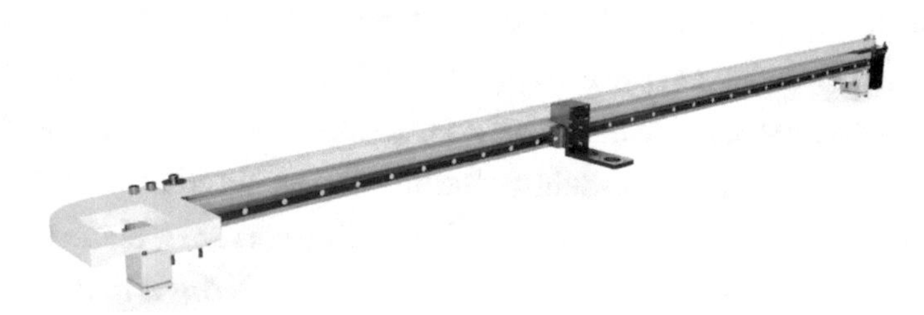

Figure 7-3. *CAD drawing of the LaserDuo X axis design*

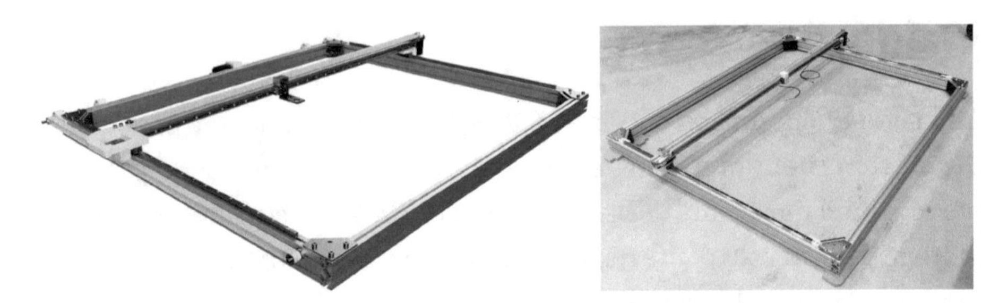

***Figure 7-4.** LaserDuo Y axis, with integrated X axis - CAD on the left, actual on the right*

Outside-In

The outside-in approach consists of first designing the machine part that will contain or attach all the others together and then designing contained or attached parts. Machine parts where everything attaches to or that contain everything are typically the frame and the housing. Similarly to the inside-out approach, in the outside-in approach, the process iterates, designing first the closest parts to the container part until the overall machine is designed. An example of an outside-in approach is the design of BigFDM. In BigFDM the machine frame was designed first, with a specific size to fit the specifications of a shipping service (related to the overall costs sustained by the client). The Y axis, contained in the top of the machine frame, was subsequently designed. The Y axis, in turn, contained and attached to the X axis, which was designed as the next part. The process continued until all the parts were designed.

Figure 7-5. *The frame of BigFDM, containing all the rest of the machine parts*

Figure 7-6. *The X and Y axes of BigFDM, designed to fit inside the top part of the frame*

Focused

A focused approach sets specific features as the most important for the machine design. There can be several features that stand out and that make different machines appealing or desirable, for instance, for different materials or scenarios. Some examples are a vacuum bed or a tool changer for the CNC milling machine, a glass laser tube or a movable Z axis for the laser cutter, and a clay extruder or automatic bed leveling for the 3D printer. Because of their differences and required parts and systems, it is often worthwhile to design these features from the start and to then design the rest of the machine around them, especially if you think that those will be essential for the use of the machine. Implementing some specific features, usually expensive commercially, is one of the benefits of building your own personalized machine. These features may require you to shape the machine to its surroundings or to integrate other systems for it. Some generic examples of the requirements and additional systems for some features are given in the following:

- A vacuum bed for the CNC milling machine requires an air-tight sealing, holes for the air pipe, a vacuum pump, etc.
- A clay extruder may require a compressor, storage for the clay, a syringe/lead screw extruder, etc.
- An automatic bed leveling system for a 3D printer may require a metallic bed (for inductive probes), a precision switch to be mounted on the head, etc.

Figure 7-7. *A 3D printer with automatic bed leveling with inductive probe and aluminum bed (Daniele Ingrassia)*

Reproducibility

An important aspect that can deeply influence your design, especially in the case of the open source machines, is its reproducibility. Following a design approach for reproducibility does not necessarily exclude other approaches, but can be considered widespread in machine construction.

You need to produce documentation so others can reproduce it. To start with the reproducibility approach, first think of a target group of people that could reproduce your machine. For example, Fab Labs share an inventory, with every Fab Lab having laser cutters, CNC milling machines, 3D printers, etc. In this case if you manufacture your machine with the tools and the machines available in a Fab Lab, then you can be reasonably sure that other Fab Labs can replicate it. Another consideration can be the availability of the parts used to build the machine. You can specify ready-made parts that can be sourced as commonly as possible, rather than using raw materials to create your parts. Enabling as many people as possible to replicate your design can boomerang back to you a lot of improvements and feedback about your machine. However, remember to factor in the effort and time you need to invest into the documentation, to publish the machine files online, and to manage a possible community.

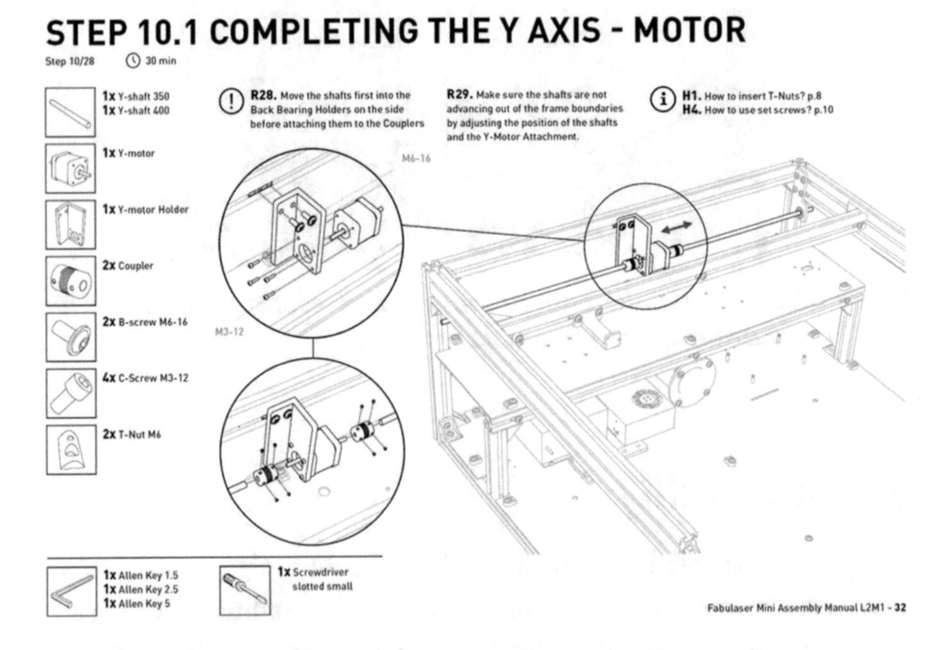

Figure 7-8. *Assembly instructions of an open source laser cutter machine (Fabulaser, Daniele Ingrassia)*

Technical Details and Parts Guidelines

Now that we have looked at different design methods, we will dive into more technical aspects of building a machine. We will take a look at the different base materials you can work with and explore the benefits and drawbacks. After that we will look at mechanical parts you will need to create your machine – anything from nuts and bolts to bearings and guides. After materials and mechanical parts, we get into electronics and control systems.

These parts of the book are designed to help you understand your options and thus are not necessarily created to be read from A to Z – look at this more as a reference guide when you are looking at elements you may already have or things you can purchase locally. It's a good idea to read through it quickly before you start to imagine your machine and come back to get the exact details once you need them for the part you have found.

For each of the subsequent paragraphs, there will be a section helping you select the right materials or parts according to the machine you would like to build or the desired results. Going through these suggestions will help you understand what we normally use in different scenarios, creating a basic understanding that you can use to cover most of the machine building that can be done in makerspaces or Fab Labs. All the described materials and parts have been selected because they are available almost everywhere, easy to work with, and great for small and/or low-cost machines.

Base Materials

It is common to incorporate custom components into a machine build, as this provides the opportunity to tailor the design to specific requirements, implement unique features, and gain hands-on experience with fabrication technologies. To fabricate custom parts, raw materials must be obtained. A variety of materials are readily available for purchase that may be suitable for building machines, and the selection of a specific material should be based on factors such as stiffness, workability and/or machinability, cost, and other relevant characteristics. This section outlines some commonly used base materials for fabricating machine parts in Fab Labs and makerspaces.

Plastics

Plastics are a commonly used and easily manageable material for creating custom machine parts. For the production of strong and accurate components, milling is the preferred method, followed by laser cutting and 3D printing. However, if complexity is the primary consideration, we recommend the following order of fabrication techniques: 3D printing, CNC milling, and laser cutting.

One of the most suitable plastics for machine building and CNC milling is acetal (also known as POM). This material is easy to mill and offers high mechanical strength with a degree of elasticity. Additionally, it has a low friction coefficient, partially due to its self-lubricating properties. Acetal can also be laser cut, typically up to a thickness of 8mm using an average laser cutter.

Figure 7-9. *A block of acetal (Daniele Ingrassia)*

As an alternative to Acetal, HDPE can be considered as a cost-efficient option for CNC milling. Although it lacks the rigidity of acetal, it can still be milled with precision, and it is usually much cheaper than acetal. However, it is not suitable for laser cutting due to its tendency to melt. Acrylic, also known as plexiglass, is another material that can be CNC milled, but there is a risk of melting if the cutting conditions are not carefully controlled. Thin sheets of acrylic are brittle and not suitable for applications that require bending, while thicker plates offer improved strength and rigidity. Although acrylic is more expensive than acetal and HDPE, it performs well with laser cutting and results in a smooth edge finish. Acrylic plates up to 10mm in thickness can typically be laser cut.

Figure 7-10. *An acrylic sheet (Daniele Ingrassia)*

Teflon (PTFE) is a softer plastic than acetal, acrylic, or HDPE, having above all the advantage of offering the lowest friction among those and other common plastics. Teflon can be CNC milled, being careful to properly use feeds and RPMs to avoid melting. Teflon can also be laser cut, with best results with thin sheets. Teflon cannot be glued with anything else, unless specific primers are used, and it is best suited to try out sliding parts or for parts requiring low friction (e.g., bushings).

If the part to be fabricated requires overhangs, and especially in case of hard-to-reach cavities, 3D printing is the most suitable technology. Many different kinds of polymers can be printed today, with different results and properties. For detailed information about the 3D printing materials, please refer to Chapter 5. If traditional FDM printing is used, the machine builders must take into account the direction of the layers, where tension force could cause delamination both immediately and over time. In terms of precision, FDM 3D-printed parts always have a certain amount of shrinkage, and also achievable precision is much less than CNC milling. We recommend using FDM 3D printing only for parts when high complexity and low precision are required.

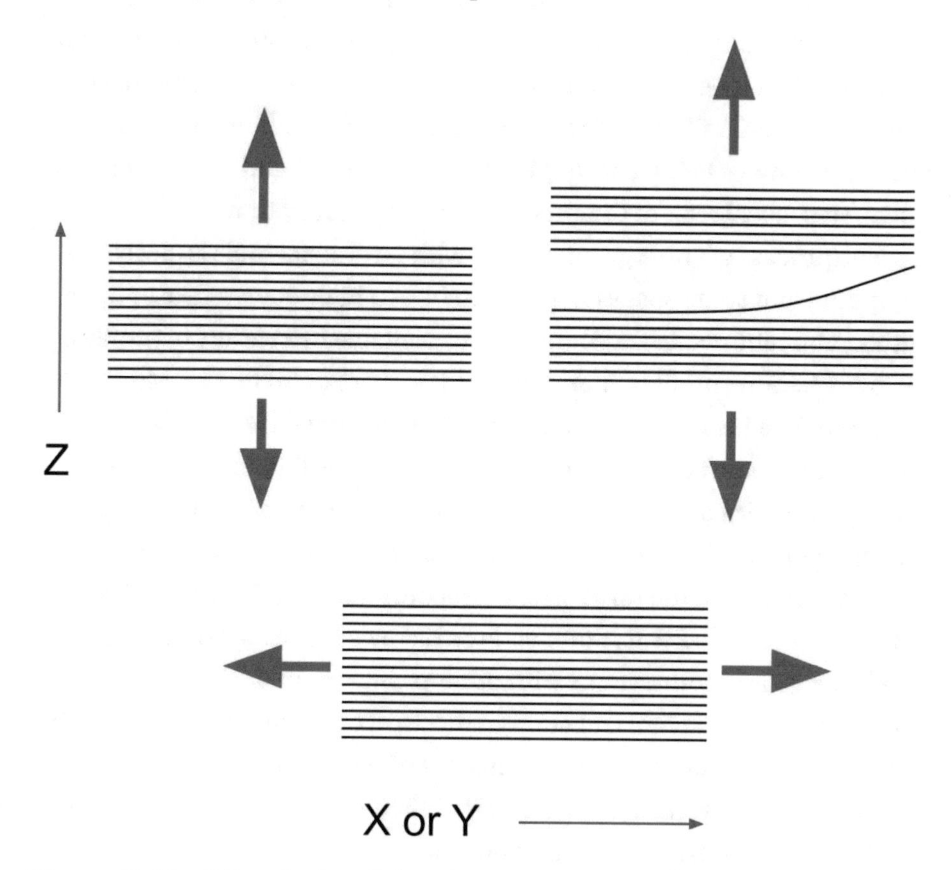

Figure 7-11. *3D printing delamination example (Daniele Ingrassia)*

It is best to avoid using plastics in high temperature or fire-prone environments as they may not withstand such conditions.

Metals

Aluminum

In makerspaces or Fab Labs, access to machinery capable of working with metals is often limited, but there are options to work with aluminum and other soft metals, such as brass. Aluminum, being a strong material, is suitable for CNC milling with mid- to low-end CNC milling machines, with weaker machines being able to mill it at a slow speed and with small step-down/step-over (refer to Chapter 4 for further information).

The process of cutting and drilling with traditional tools is always an option, and some spaces might even have a high-powered laser fiber cutting machine available. Aluminum is available in a variety of profiles, including simple profiles, modular profiles, sheets, and blocks. Modular profiles offer a flexible approach to constructing machine frames and come in two main standards: Bosch and Item. The difference between these profiles lies in the slot shape and dimensions, with the Item profile having a smaller slot size of 2mm (1mm for 20 × 20 profiles) compared to the Bosch profile of the same size. We recommend Bosch profiles if larger fasteners are needed (e.g., 6mm vs. 8mm screws for 40 × 40 profiles), creating stronger connections with other profiles or materials. The availability of a wide range of combinations, accessories, and connection possibilities with these aluminum profiles provides ample design freedom for attaching and securing parts. For DIY CNC milling machines and laser cutters, we recommend using aluminum.

Steel

Although steel presents challenges during machining processes with typical equipment found in Fab Labs, it remains a popular and cost-effective option for building machines. Steel boasts much higher strength compared with aluminum, making it ideal for construction of structural components, machine housings, and mechanics. Steel is frequently utilized painted or coated (to avoid rust) and comes in the form of simple profiles and plates that can then be cut, drilled, and adapted by hand or even be bent to create housing structures. When building larger machines and structures, steel is highly recommended even in the absence of digital machining equipment such as a waterjet cutter, as it can still be drilled and cut using conventional tools. The process of galvanization adds a thin layer of zinc to steel to protect it from rusting, as an alternative to paint, making it also usable in the open. Galvanized steel is usually more expensive than plain steel. Welding galvanized steel releases toxic gases and can be done with protective gears and in a protective environment. Steel (and aluminum) can be powder coated, a coating usually stronger and tougher than paint.

Figure 7-12. *A base frame that uses galvanized steel square pipes (Daniele Ingrassia)*

Brass and Copper

Slightly harder than aluminum, brass is a metal that can be CNC milled with typical Fab Lab milling machines and that can also be used with traditional hand tools. Used commonly to manufacture hydraulic and air fittings, brass can be used to make parts that are stronger, but heavier, than aluminum ones. Copper is more malleable than aluminum and brass and can be milled, as can a soft aluminum alloy. Brass and copper can both be used to manufacture parts for FDM 3D printer extruders, such as the heating block and the nozzle or nozzle adapters.

Figure 7-13. *Custom heating block from CNC-milled aluminum (Daniele Ingrassia)*

Aluminum Composite

Aluminum composite is a plate material made of two thin layers of aluminum, glued to a thicker middle layer of plastic. A highly suitable material for CNC milling and fabrication with traditional hand and bending tools, aluminum composite is an ideal choice for constructing machine housing and light structural elements. Aluminum composite is available in sheets, usually ranging from 2 to 8mm in thickness, and offers a range of color options and surface finishes, making it an ideal material for exposed surfaces on a machine. Although CO_2 and fiber lasers cannot cut it, CO_2 lasers can be utilized to engrave on the material, making it suitable for labeling and signage purposes. Additionally, vinyl stickers can easily be applied to its surface. Aluminum composite is also used for signage, and it is usually much cheaper than aluminum.

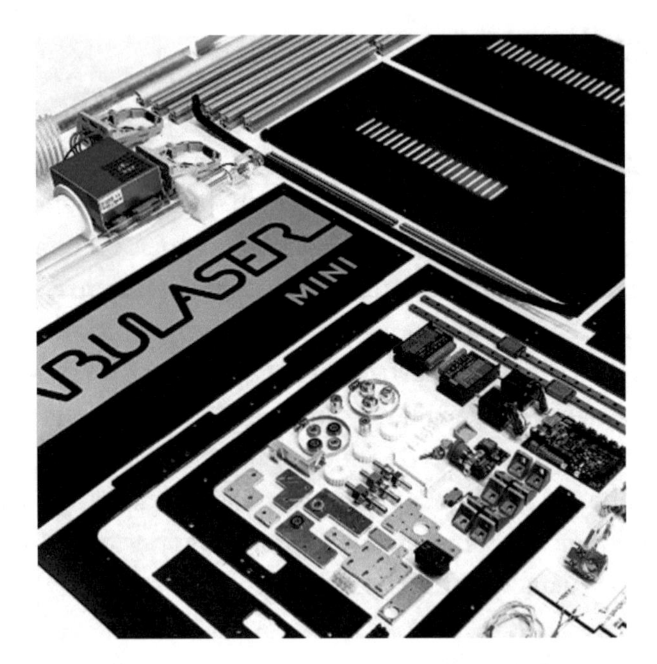

Figure 7-14. *An open source laser cutter kit with black housing (black panels) made out of CNC-milled aluminum composite (Daniele Ingrassia)*

How to Select Base Materials for Your Machine

With plastics one has to consider that they mostly have a relatively low melting temperature, and because of that it is best not to use them close to an area where the temperature can rise (e.g., the bed of a 3D printer) or laser can easily melt it (e.g., in the housing of a laser cutter). However, plastics are usually one of the easiest materials to work with makerspace machines. Acrylic is easily cut with a laser and can be adopted for transparent housings and windows. PLA and other filaments can be used to make complex parts, for example, frame connecting parts, supports, and even some mechanical parts that will not be subjected to stress. Acetal, HDPE, and other engineered polymers are great to use with a CNC mill, to make very strong and precise parts. Acetal is great to machine custom gears or as housings for bearings. In general if your machine does not require high rigidity or does not have to work with lasers, plastic is a great choice for several parts.

Metals on the other hand can be quite handy for higher temperatures (e.g., a copper block for the 3D printer nozzle) or to stop CO_2 laser beams or when higher rigidity is required. Among the metals presented, aluminum is the most useful because of the good compromise between being machinable with small machines and having relatively low weight and high strength. Other metals such as steel and stainless steel may not be so easy to work with, limiting their usage of what can be done with ready available shapes (e.g., steel beams) and simple modifications such as drilling, tapping, and cutting. Aluminum is therefore a highly recommended material for housing, frame, and mechanical parts for machines such as laser cutters and CNC milling machines. We recommend CNC milling the aluminum, either 2D milling sheets or 3D milling blocks, to manufacture rigid and long-lasting parts of your machine. Aluminum and copper are also best for parts that can dissipate heat (e.g., the heatsink for a 3D printer extruder).

Mechanical Parts

Static

Fasteners

Fasteners commonly represent one of the most simple and effective ways to join parts, with the drawback of increasing the amount of parts needed for an assembly. Lots of different types of fasteners exist, and this book would not be enough to show off all of them, so we have selected some of the most common and useful ones for machine building. Fasteners are manufactured according to standards, and often they also have, together with the standard, a representative name. When looking to buy fasteners, we'd recommend to first search them by the standard, to make sure they fit the standard dimensions. Different standards exist with the most common being ISO (International Organization for Standardization) Metric Thread, DIN (Deutsches Institut für Normung), and BS (British Standards). These can have common standards, where a fastener can be identified with two codes, and tables can be used to look up code conversion. DIN, ISO, and BS are also used for many other standard parts, where fasteners are only a subcategory.

Fasteners can be made of lots of different materials, including brass, aluminum, plastics, and titanium, just to name a few. Each different material will give different properties, for example, plastic bolts can be electrical insulating or titanium bolts extremely robust. The most common materials are steel, galvanized steel, and stainless steel.

Within a standard fasteners are identified by diameter and/or length. For bolts both are used, but for washers and nuts, only the internal diameter is usually sufficient.

Bolts

Each size of screw can be supplied with different thread pitches (distance between thread rings). If the pitch is not specified, then those are the normal pitches for the standard. For special applications (e.g., the bolts to regulate the mirror of a laser cutter), finer pitch can be used.

DIN 912, also called cap bolts or socket head bolts, are bolts fitting an Allen key and having a cylindrical head, typically used when it is necessary to fasten from the top and where the head can fit into a pocket in the material. These can't be fastened directly from the side.

DIN 933, also called hex bolts, have a hexagonal head and can be fastened by using a spanner key or a socket key. These can be fastened directly from the side and also from the top. The head of these can be embedded into a pocket, given enough space for a socket key to fit.

ISO 7380, called button head bolts, are similar to the DIN 912, with the difference of having a rounded head instead of a cylindrical one. These can also be fastened with an Allen key and only from the top. A variant with an even larger head exists, called ISO 7380-2. In both ISO 7380 and ISO 7380-2, the large head can be used as a substitute of a washer, or you can think of them as bolts with an integrated washer.

ISO 7991, also called countersunk bolts with a socket head, have a conical head and require holes with a conical shaped beginning to fit. This type always fits completely inside the material resulting in a flat surface. Similarly to the DIN 912, these can be fastened only from the top and using Allen keys.

DIN 7505, or wood screws, are the typical screws used to join wood parts. These can either be directly screwed in wood without holes or be helped by a drive hole. Being similar in shape to a countersunk screw, this type used a cross screwdriver to be fastened.

Figure 7-15. *From left to right: ISO 7380-2, DIN 7991, DIN 912, ISO 7380, DIN 933, DIN 7505 (Daniele Ingrassia)*

Nuts and Spacers

Nuts are normally used to tighten a piece of material to the bolts. The material is typically in between the screw head and the nut.

DIN 934, also called hex nut, is one of the most common nuts. Its shape is basically a hexagon and can be fastened by using either a spanner key (from the side) or a socket key (from the top).

DIN 985, also called locknut, is almost the same as the DIN 934, with the difference that it has a plastic ring on one side. When tightening, the plastic ring locks the screw by means of friction and prevents the screw from coming out easily. If a locknut is a bit loose, it will still hold the screw in place, till the screw comes out of the plastic ring.

Nuts for aluminum profiles are special nuts designed to slide and to be inserted inside the slots of aluminum profiles. Usually called T-slot nuts, those are kept from rotating from the slot of the aluminum profile itself, not requiring to be held when fastening. Some of those are spring loaded to stay in place in case of vertical slots.

Spacers, also called standoffs, are special types of nuts used to make room between the screw head (or a nut) and the contact surface, typically used to attach PCBs to a plate or when distancing is needed between plates. Spacers have different shapes, with some that can tighten (e.g., DIN 934) and some that are just cylinders with an inner thread.

Figure 7-16. *From left to right: hex plastic spacer, T-slot nut, T-slot nut with a spring ball (×2), DIN 985, DIN 934 (Daniele Ingrassia)*

Washers

Washers are used to increase the contact surface of the screw head (or nut) for stronger tightening (e.g., for softer materials). They can also be used as spacers.

DIN 125 is one of the most common types of washer, consisting of a ring slightly larger than the diameter of the fitting screw. They are normally equivalent to the diameter of an ISO 7380-2 head.

DIN 9021 are larger washers, which further extend the contact surface.

Figure 7-17. *From left to right: DIN 9021, DIN 125 (Daniele Ingrassia)*

How to Select the Fasteners for Your Machine

Fasteners are mainly selected using basic parameters such as size and type. For all the ready-made parts you're going to have in your machine, you are forced to at least match the screw thread diameter. Examples are bolts to mount the electronics (power supplies, drivers, etc.) or mechanical parts (bearing housing, motors, spindle, aluminum profiles, etc.). Deciding on the shape of the screw head is usually less restrictive and sometimes just depends on aesthetic preference or space constraints in situations where things can collide or need to be integrated (e.g., choosing a shorter head as the button head). If the parts of your machine are entirely designed and made by you, such as a CNC-milled piece of aluminum for the frame of a CNC milling machine, then the entire choice can be driven by the strength required and the space available. The strength of a screw is directly proportional to its diameter and thread pitch, but can also depend on the material. A general rule of thumb is that bolts should be coupled to tapped holes of at least 1.5/2 times their diameter, especially if done in soft metals. So if a screw is 3mm diameter, the depth of the tapped hole should be at least 4.5 to 6mm. Washers are required to increase the screw footprint on a surface (if the space is available), and locknuts are needed when vibration and motion parts are involved. Plastic bolts can be used for fragile electronics such as PCBs and controllers, while normally steel bolts are used. Stainless steel bolts may be used for additional strength and resistance to corrosion.

Profiles

Different kinds of profiles can be used to build structures, machine frames, and axes. With profiles are usually defined metal extrusions of different shapes and lengths.

Simple profiles have basic geometric open or closed shapes, such as L-shaped, U-shaped, square, rectangular, etc. The most common materials are steel and aluminum profiles, with the aluminum ones easy to be cut or reworked either with machines or by hand. Profiles are mostly hollow and represent a good compromise between weight, stiffness, and cost. Profiles with basic shapes are normally the cheapest, but you must consider the amount of work you may need to adapt them to your needs and attachments.

T-slot aluminum profiles are aluminum profiles having T-shaped slots in one or more sides. As mentioned previously, there are two main types of T-slot profiles, Bosch and Item (from the respective companies). Differences are mainly the slot size being larger (given the same cross-section size) in the Bosch type. These types of aluminum profiles offer higher strength than the simple profiles, and they can fit T-slot nuts and accessories, allowing usage and mounting flexibility in a lot of different ways. T-slot profiles can also be tapped on the side and can even be integrated with electrical parts (e.g., cable ducts). Standard shapes have square cross section and one slot per side, with 20 × 20mm, 30 × 30mm, and 40 × 40mm being the most common. Of each square size, it is possible to order multiples, for example, 40 × 80mm or 30 × 120mm. For each multiple of the size, there is an additional slot, for example, in the 40 × 80mm, there are two slots in the 80mm side and one in the 40mm side. A drawback of the T-slot profiles is that they likely increase the number of parts of your machine, due to the connecting elements required (T-nuts, bolts, brackets, etc.).

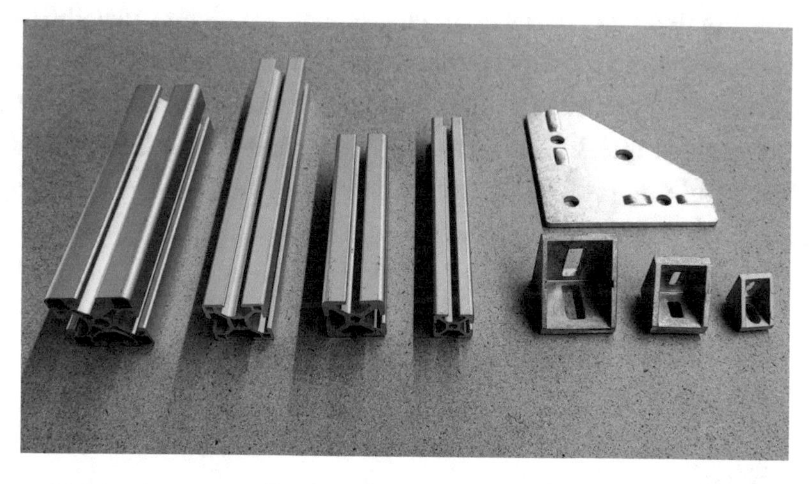

Figure 7-18. *A range of T-slot aluminum profiles and accessories. From left to right: different brackets (20 × 20, 30 × 30, 40 × 40), an L connector plate, profile 20 × 20 (Item type), 30 × 30 (Item type), 30 × 30 (Bosch type), 40 × 40 (Item type) (Daniele Ingrassia)*

How to Select the Aluminum Profiles for Your Machine

The first question should be if you really need an aluminum profile or if you can use custom parts. Using aluminum profiles can speed up the building of large frame structures that can be mounted, integrated, and expanded easily. Although that sounds promising, the drawback is the high amount of parts required for the connections, plus the high price of all the parts summed up together. You can quickly calculate how many parts you need to attach standard profiles together and how much would it cost for you to produce the same part or if the standard size of a profile is the right fit for you in order to decide whether to use an aluminum profile or not. For large parts, exceeding one or two meters, usually there is no way for a hobbyist to make them (you will need larger machines, not easily accessible), so using an aluminum profile may be the only choice. This can, for example, be the case of a large format CNC milling machine or laser. Aluminum profiles are not recommended if there are not many connected parts needed (e.g., a lid) or specific size and fittings are required (e.g., to position two linear guides at a custom distance).

Dynamic Parts

Bearings

Bearings are mechanical elements that constrain motion and reduce friction between moving parts. All machines require bearings to move their axis and any other moving part. Bearings are everywhere where motion is, in every motor, in every linear guide, and in every rotating shaft. In this book we describe the most common type of bearing that you can use to build your machine, considering two basic types of motion: linear and rotatory motion. In order to select the proper bearings for your machine, you need to understand the main parameters involved. Amount and direction of the loads, rotation speed (rotation per minute or RPM), usage environment, and dimensions can be some of the most used selection criteria. For cylindrical bearing we consider two basic types of applied loads: axial and radial. Axial loads are forces applied along the bearing axis, while radial loads are forces applied to a right angle of the bearing axis. Loads are measured in Newtons (N).

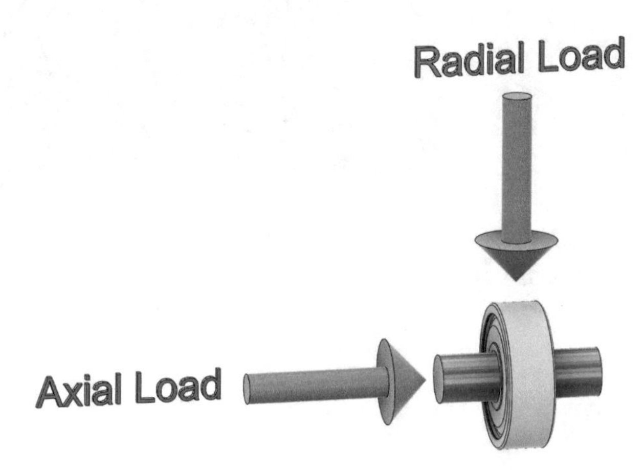

Figure 7-19. *Axial and radial loads (Daniele Ingrassia)*

Bushings

Bushings are one of the simplest types of bearing, basically consisting of low-friction material mechanically constrained between moving parts. Typically the materials used are durable, can resist high temperatures (eventually generated by the friction), and often resist corrosion. PTFE, or Teflon, and derived materials are typical examples of materials used in bushings. Note that bushings can also be made by mechanically joining two or more materials (e.g., one serving as housing). Bushings typically have a cylindrical shape and can be used either for linear or rotatory motion. Depending on the type of material used, bushing may require lubrication (check the manufacturer datasheet). When you are building machines, bushings can be used for linear motion moving very light loads. Nowadays it is possible to find linear guides with plastic bushings.

***Figure 7-20.** A solid bushing and bushing with metallic housing (CC from* `https://en.wikipedia.org/wiki/Plain_bearing#Bushing`*)*

Ball Bearings

Ball bearings are a type of bearing that employs multiple spheres to reduce friction between rotating components. The dimensions and number of spheres vary depending on the type and size of the ball bearing. The spheres and body of the ball bearing are typically constructed from steel; however, alternative materials such as plastic, ceramics, or other materials capable of withstanding the necessary loads and friction may also be utilized. Ball bearings can be procured in a variety of configurations to suit the specific environment in which they are employed, including without protection, with double-sided rubber sealing (2RS), or with metal shielding (ZZ).

Figure 7-21. *Various types of ball bearings with metal and plastic protection (Daniele Ingrassia)*

Deep Groove Ball Bearings

Deep groove ball bearings are utilized in applications where heavy radial loads and a limited amount of axial load are present. As one of the most widely used types of ball bearings, they are generally readily available and cost-effective. The axial load capacity is typically approximately half of the maximum radial load capacity. The spheres are contained between an inner and an outer ring and rotate within the races of the rings. Deep groove ball bearings are commonly employed in stepper motors, electric motors, skateboards, and rotating shafts where axial loads are not a significant factor.

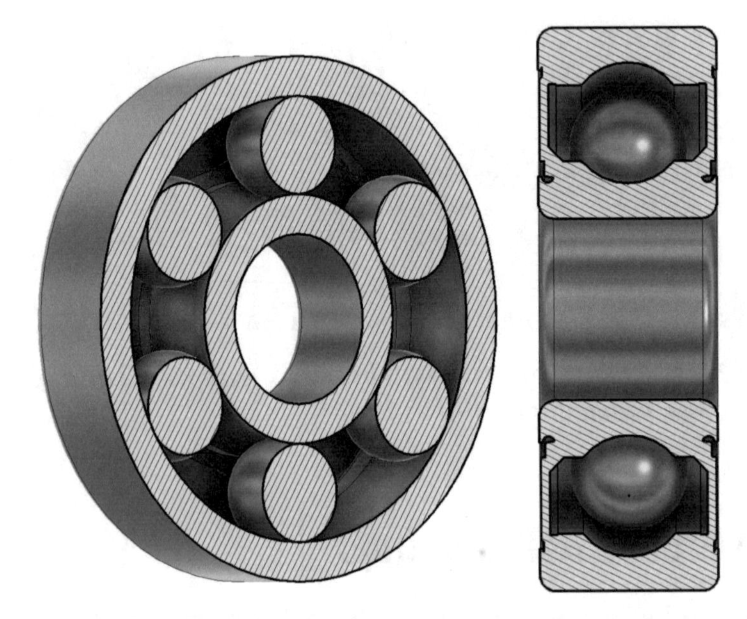

Figure 7-22. *Cross section of a deep groove ball bearing (Daniele Ingrassia)*

Angular Contact Bearings

Angular contact bearings are similar in design to deep groove ball bearings, but with the added capability of accommodating higher axial loads due to the angled shape of their races. These bearings are capable of handling radial loads from any direction, although unidirectional variants also exist, with the load-bearing side specified by the manufacturer. To further enhance their axial load capacity or as an alternative to the angled race design, angular contact bearings can also be manufactured with a double row of spheres. These bearings are ideal for applications where both high radial and axial loads are anticipated. They are frequently utilized in CNC milling machines to support ball screws and to attach lead screws.

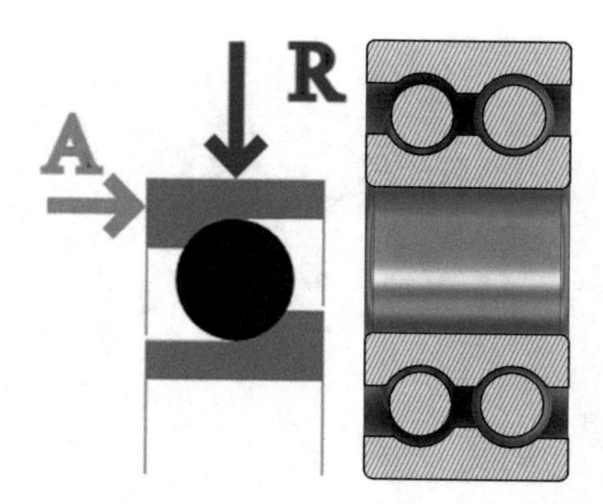

Figure 7-23. *Races inside an angular contact bearing and a double-row angular contact bearing (Daniele Ingrassia + CC `https://commons.wikimedia.org/wiki/File:Schema_Ball_bearing,_angular_contact_single.svg`)*

Thrust Bearings

Thrust bearings are meant only for axial loads. Standard thrust bearings cannot withstand any radial force. They usually consist of two parallel discs that rotate remaining coaxial to each other. If one ring of balls is present, then one disc stays fixed, while the other rotates. If two ball rings are present, then we are talking about a double-rotation thrust bearing, and in this case the two outside discs can rotate independently.

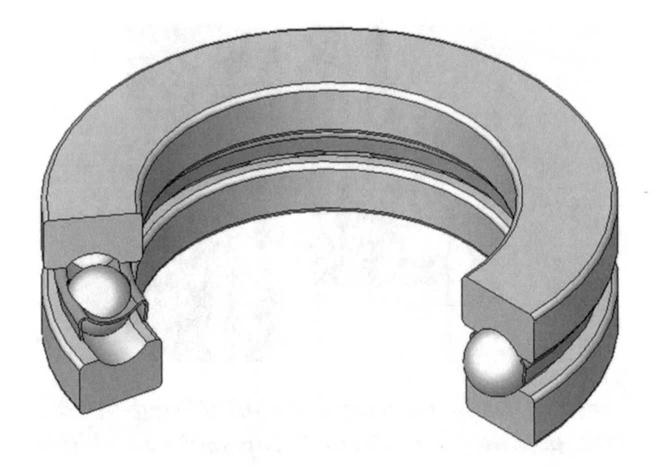

Figure 7-24. *Thrust ball bearing (https://commons.wikimedia.org/wiki/File:Thrust-ball-bearing_din711_120.png)*

Roller Bearings

Roller bearings are bearings using small cylinders instead of balls as rolling elements. In general, this kind of bearings rotate more slowly than ball bearings, but perform better for impacts and shocks. Different variants exist, such as the cylindrical, needle, and tapered roller bearings. The tapered type can stand both axial and radial loads. The cylindrical type is only suitable for high radial loads. The needle type is similar to the cylindrical, but is much more compact in size.

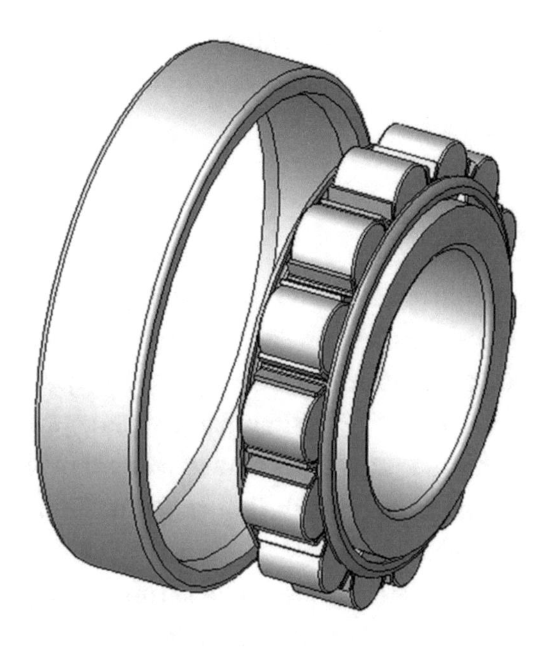

Figure 7-25. *Cylindrical roller bearing (`https://commons.wikimedia.org/wiki/File:Cylindrical-roller-bearing_din5412-t1_type-n_ex.png`)*

How to Select Bearings for Your Machine

Nowadays ball and roller bearings are commonly available and accessible to makers, making the choice of bushings avoidable in most cases. To support rotating shafts with side (radial) forces, we recommend deep groove ball bearings. An example of this is when a single motor is used to actuate the two belts of the Y axis of a 3D printer, with the bearing supporting the rotating shafts. We recommend axial angular contact bearings to support ball screws or lead screws, where there is load applied along the screw itself. This is, for example, the case with ball screws in a CNC milling machine or large format 3D printers' Z axis lead screws. Unless your machine has to deal with very heavy load (which is not often the case with a DIY CNC milling machine) or unless the bearings are very small, you can freely select the bearings according to the size of your shaft and of your bearing housing.

Bearing Housings

Bearings are commonly inserted into niches and pockets by the means of press fit. In turn, these niches or pockets belong to larger parts. There are a number of standard parts where the bearings are ready press-fitted, called bearing housings. The bearing housings usually use screws to be attached, basically allowing the bearing to be mounted without press-fitting it. As we will also see in the next paragraph, the housings are also used to enclose bearings for linear guides.

Pillow blocks (also called plummer blocks) are bearing housings that can be bolted to a surface and typically used to support a rotating shaft. These housings are bolted to surfaces parallel to the axis of rotation and are usually made of cast iron. Pillow blocks are available in different standard shapes and vary in height, width, diameter of the bearing, etc. Some pillow blocks can account for shaft misalignment, allowing the bearing to tilt its body inside the block. Flange types of bearing housing, sometimes also called flanged bearing, are bearing housings also bolted to a surface, in this case perpendicular to the axis of rotation. These housings also support a rotating shaft and can support shafts from their start/end.

Figure 7-26. *A range of bearing housings. K08 (bottom left), UCPA 201 (bottom right), BF10 (top right), UCP 201 (top left) (Daniele Ingrassia)*

How to Select Bearing Housings for Your Machine

Bearing housings are mainly selected according to how they are mounted and their specific features. Most of them allow you to mount a shaft onto a surface, for example, to support your 3D printer or laser cutter's Y axis shaft. The mounting can be done either perpendicularly or alongside a plate. Special bearing housings are needed for ball screws for CNC milling machines, containing axial bearings.

Linear Guides

Linear guides are mechanical devices that restrict motion to a single direction. They consist of a linear bearing and a surface for the linear bearing to move on. A linear bearing is a bearing specifically designed for linear motion.

When paired with an actuator system, linear guides are a critical component in the motion of machine axes. They are widely used in digital fabrication machines and traditional hand-operated machines, such as lathes, drill presses, and milling machines, to ensure precise positioning during motion.

Different types of linear guides exist, ranging from commercially available options to self-made designs, depending on factors such as load, speed, size, reliability, and mounting requirements. Generally, machines requiring higher loads, such as CNC milling machines, necessitate stronger linear guides, while machines that demand high speed and low loads, such as laser cutters, require lighter, more agile linear guides.

Similar to bushings and ball bearings, linear guides can use components such as sliders, spheres, or other rolling elements. Unlike ball bearings, which can be challenging to produce in a makerspace or Fab Lab, some examples of self-made linear guides exist. Linear guides are typically available with different levels of preload or with adjustable preload. Higher preload results in more precise movement but with higher friction, while lighter preload offers lower precision but with reduced friction.

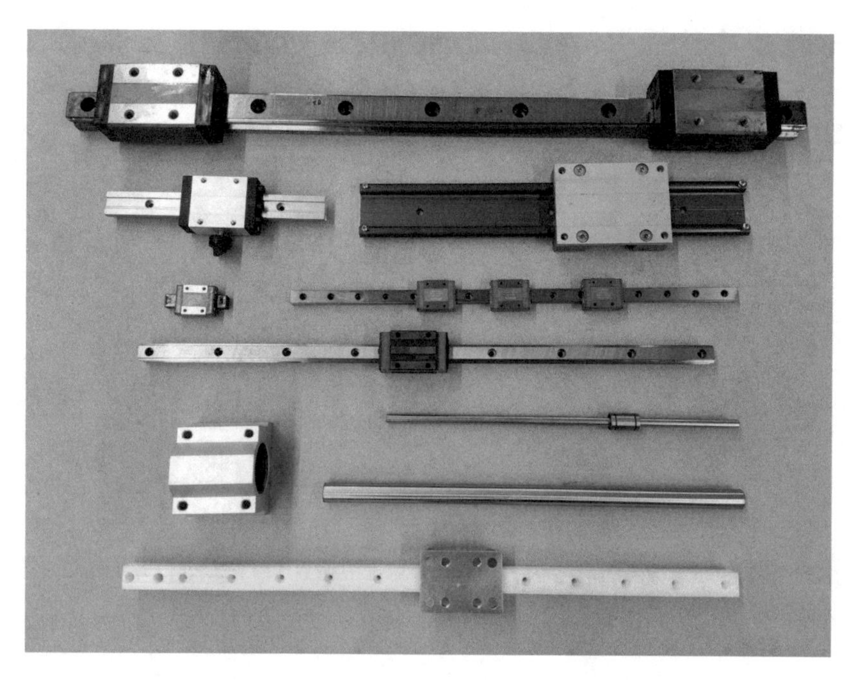

Figure 7-27. *Various linear guides (Daniele Ingrassia)*

Dovetail

Dovetail guideways are a type of mechanical device that restricts motion to one axis and are typically used in heavy-duty metalworking machines, both CNC and non-CNC. These guideways are made of two interlocked blocks that slide against each other, offering increased stiffness compared with linear guides with rolling elements. However, the increased stiffness comes at the cost of higher friction and a requirement for more frequent lubrication.

The large machined surfaces in contact, along with the stiffness, make dovetail guides ideal for dampening shocks and vibrations that can cause damage to other types of guides with rolling elements. Due to their substantial size and weight, as well as the high friction, we recommend dovetail for slow machines that require very high loads. Dovetail guides require a solid surface to be mounted on and typically support a single sliding element.

***Figure 7-28.** Dovetail guide of a cross-slide on a lathe (Daniele Ingrassia)*

Shafts

Linear shaft guides are composed of high-precision metal cylindrical components that are coupled with cylindrical linear bearings. They are highly sought after for their high-speed capabilities and competitive cost. They are commonly used in machinery such as 3D printers and laser cutters. The cylindrical shaft and cylindrical linear bearings are offered in various shapes and sizes, offering versatility in machine design.

The simplest form consists of a shaft and cylindrical linear bearing with a cylindrical outer shape, which can be press-fitted into a custom-designed part. The shaft is usually supported at its ends by shaft holders or custom designs. Additionally, the shaft can be purchased with an underlying support, known as a supported shaft. In this configuration, the linear bearing is open on one side to allow it to slide while accommodating the support. This arrangement is optimal when loads are applied from any direction except the bottom, as the linear bearing is also open on the bottom.

Figure 7-29. *Supported linear shaft (Daniele Ingrassia)*

Linear bearings are available in a range of housings with varying shapes and lengths to meet specific requirements. The load-bearing capacity of a linear bearing increases with its length, but it also requires a longer shaft for the same travel distance. The common types of linear bearings include flange-mounted (round or square), surface-mounted, and adjustable. To reduce friction, most linear bearings for these guides utilize recirculating spheres; however, bearings made of sliding materials are also available for purchase.

***Figure 7-30.** A cylindrical linear bearing, long version with square flange mount (Daniele Ingrassia)*

***Figure 7-31.** A cylindrical linear bearing with housing for attaching to a flat surface (Daniele Ingrassia)*

In order to enhance load capacity and support heavy components, it is a common approach to incorporate multiple bearings and shafts. Linear shafts can operate without the need for a bottom support in certain configurations, and they can also facilitate rotational movement of the bearing on the shaft. The load-carrying capacity of these linear guides can vary, depending on the diameter and length of the shaft(s) and the type of linear bearing utilized.

Roller Guides

The Roller Guide is a linear guide system that employs rolling elements to achieve linear motion. It consists of a cart or carriage that rolls on a guiding rod. The Roller Guide is a cost-effective option and has gained popularity, particularly in cheap 3D printers. The rolling elements typically used are common ball bearings, while the guiding rod is often made of aluminum, allowing the machine frame to be used as the linear guide. While this configuration is possible, the rolling cart has limitations in terms of attachment points. To avoid play during motion, the ball bearings are shaped with a V-ring (concave or convex), and the guiding rod is designed with a corresponding negative shape. This design can be easily modified or customized with V-slotted aluminum profiles or added components to an existing rod. The Roller Guide is not capable of handling high loads, but is suitable for medium to high speeds, making it ideal for 3D printers and some laser cutters. Increasing the number of rods, carts, or rolling elements can improve the load capacity.

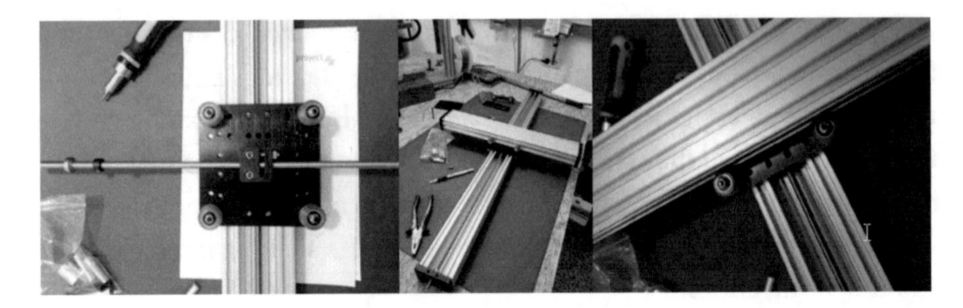

Figure 7-32. *Roller carriage, loose and installed in a V-shape slotted profile (Gerhard Matthisen, Fab Academy)*

Figure 7-33. *A machine made with laser cut roller guide carriages (FabLab UAE)*

Rails

Linear rails are a popular type of linear guide, along with linear shafts. They consist of a custom-shaped rail and a carriage that slides on it. Different configurations and shapes of both the rail and carriage are available. The most common type uses a hardened steel rail and a ball-recirculating carriage, offering a combination of high speed and high load ratings. This compact guide is suitable for a variety of digital fabrication machines, including fast laser cutters, vinyl cutters, and heavy-duty CNC milling machines. Linear rails are highly reliable, and the durability of the guide depends on the type of rail used. Carriages made with sliding material blocks and aluminum or plastic rails are also available. Depending on the width of the rail, carriages can have one or two recirculating ball tracks. Multiple carriages can be used on a single rail, and multiple rails can be used for a single machine axis. Linear rails require an underlying surface for support, making them one of the most expensive types of linear guides. A special variant of the linear rail is available in a curved shape, useful in case your design involves motion in curves or, for example, as a way to move around tool holders (for a tool changer) or the stock on the bed.

Figure 7-34. *Linear rails of a custom-made CNC milling machine (Daniele Ingrassia)*

Self-Made

If commercial linear guides do not meet your specific needs or if cost or accessibility is a concern, you may consider fabricating your own linear guide. One approach is to explore open source linear guides and modify or replicate them. Another option is to replicate commercial guides, which can be challenging. It is important to note that creating linear guides with similar precision and rigidity as commercial counterparts can be difficult without access to professional manufacturing equipment, such as an industrial CNC milling machine. Nevertheless, if precision and load requirements are not extremely high, fabricating your own linear guide can be a rewarding experience and offer the flexibility to customize the design. One popular method involves using deep groove ball bearings that roll on a surface, such as attaching multiple bearings to a plate or connector and using the side of an aluminum profile. Another approach involves creating positive and negative V-shaped materials that slide on each other.

Figure 7-35. *Chamfer rail with an integrated motor made out of acetal (Jens Dyvik)*

Figure 7-36. *Self-made examples of roller guides (Daniele Ingrassia)*

How to Choose Linear Guides for Your Machine

Linear guides are mainly chosen using the following parameters: strength, cost, and mounting possibilities. If you have enough budget, linear rails are the preferred choice for most purposes. They can be very strong for a CNC milling machine, but also quite light and fast for 3D printers and laser cutters. As a drawback, rails always need a flat reference surface to be mounted onto and also many screws. Wider linear rails are stronger, with CNC milling machines usually having 15–25mm rails and 3D printers and laser cutters using a mix of 15mm and 9/12mm. We recommend linear shafts, being attached at the two edges, for fast motion where less strength is required, with the advantage of having a lower price than rails and flexibility to be attached without an underlying surface. While rails can mount the load only at their top, linear shafts can have bearings with different housings, allowing you to attach the load in different ways. Linear shafts are usually employed in 3D printer Z axes and laser cutter Y or X axes. We recommend roller guides for light loads and if there is a fitting aluminum profile already available in the machine design.

Actuators

To give motions to your machine and projects, you'll of course need a motor, but also a mechanical actuator. With an actuator you can translate the shaft rotation of the motor into linear motion and other types of movements. Here we'll talk only about the common actuators used in machine building. These are characterized by different ways of being attached and coupled and can be suited for speed, strength, backlash, etc. Backlash is defined as the amount of lost motion in a mechanism, because of gaps between parts.

Toothed Belts and Pulleys

A machine that uses toothed belts and pulleys usually requires either high speed or it moves a light load. Pulleys and belts can be used to achieve linear motion or to translate rotation to another location. By changing the size of the pulley, the transmission ratio can be changed, to, for example, achieve higher speeds or higher precision. To work together, belts and pulleys must match in terms of pitch (distance between teeth), width, and profile type. Different belt and pulley profiles exist depending on torque, power, and speed requirements.

A common profile used, especially for larger machines and industrially, is HTD (acronym meaning High Torque Drive). HTD belts and pulleys come in 3, 5, and 8, and 14mm pitches, with a range of widths from 9 to over 100mm. GT2 is a profile widely used in small machines, especially 3D printers and small laser cutters. GT2 belts offer very low backlash movements and low load on the shafts. Usually found in 5 and 10mm width and with 2mm pitch, GT2 belts and pulleys are one of the cheapest ways to implement a belt-driven system. Belt-driven systems can also be combined with other systems, to decouple and change the ratio of the motion from the motor shaft.

Figure 7-37. *A range of belts and pulleys, HTD-3M (closed belt), HTD-5M (top belt), GT2 6mm and 10mm (belts inside the closed belt), GT2 pulleys (first and third from the right), HTD pulleys (Daniele Ingrassia)*

Rack and Pinion

Racks and pinions are used when a high amount of torque must be transferred. Racks and pinions are typically used on large machines, where a long range of motion is required (e.g., meters) and where other actuators are not suitable. Racks and pinions can either be found with straight or helical teeth. Helical-shaped racks and pinions usually run smoother than straight ones and require lower initial torque to start rotation, but generate additional axial loads and are generally more expensive than straight racks. As for gears, racks and pinions are dimensioned by module. Module is calculated by dividing the gear diameter with the number of teeth, and it defines the size of a gear. Racks and pinions have a noticeable backlash, higher than belt-driven systems. Most large format CNC milling machines in Fab Labs use rack and pinion systems.

Lead Screws and Ball Screws

Screw-driven systems use screws and nuts to transform rotation to linear motion. Typically, the screw is rotating while the nut can't, with the result of the nut moving in a direction, depending on the rotation and threading direction. In machine building, commonly used screws are lead screws and ball screws. Lead screws have a trapezoidal threading profile and normally use brass or plastic nuts. Lead screws have large backlash when changing direction, which is sometimes reduced by using a spring loaded anti-backlash nut. Because of the backlash, lead screws are mostly used vertically supporting a weight. In this way the nut is always pushed down by gravity and always in contact with the threading, eliminating backlash. Differently from lead screws, ball screws use nuts having channels with recirculating balls (similarly to rail linear guides; see the "Rails" section). Ball screws, regardless of the working position, have negligible backlash and ensure smooth motion even with high loads on them. Ball screws are also more precise than lead screws. Lead screws are normally cheaper than ball screws and are commonly found on Z axes of 3D printers (including large format ones). Ball screws are mostly used when higher loads are required, typically for CNC milling machines.

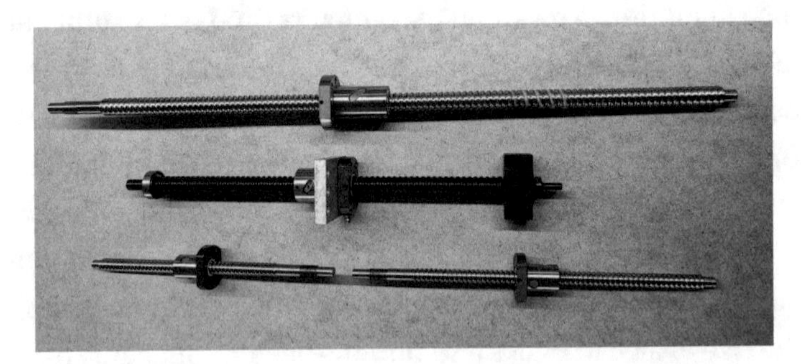

Figure 7-38. *A range of ball screws, 1204 in the bottom line (12mm diameter 4mm pitch), 1610 middle and top line. (Daniele Ingrassia)*

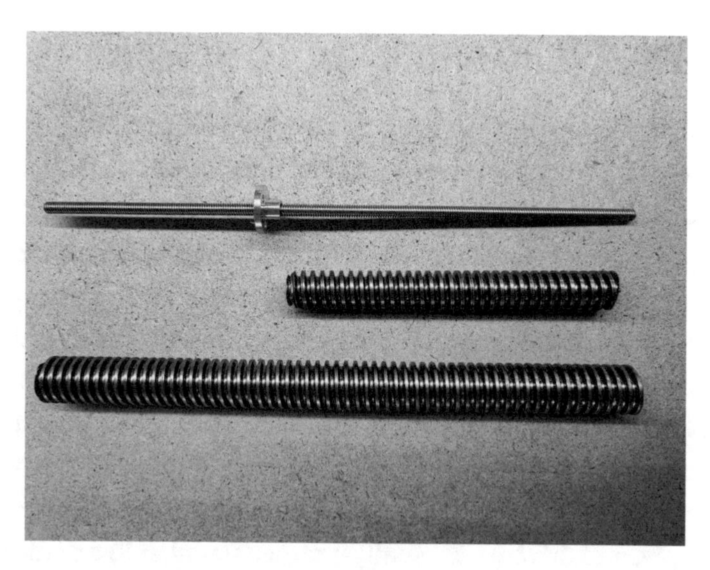

Figure 7-39. *A range of lead screws, 20 × 4 bottom line (20mm diameter, 4mm pitch), 16 × 4 middle line, 5 × 1 top line (Daniele Ingrassia)*

How to Choose the Actuator for Your Machine

Belts are the fastest and lightest option if you need fast motion, such as in X and Y axes of a 3D printer or laser cutter. Type and size of belt can be driven by RPMs and load required. For small machines usually GT2 belts, in the width of either 5 or 10mm, are recommended. Belts will fail when higher loads are required, such as in CNC milling machines. For CNC milling machines, ball screws are desirable, because of the very low backlash and high transmissible torque. For longer travels ball screws can easily wobble (more than 1–1.5 meters) requiring expensive bigger diameters, and thus rack and pinion is preferred, especially in the case of making large format CNC milling machines and laser cutters (X and Y axes). Lead screws can be a cheaper alternative to ball screws, especially if used only vertically, and are useful as Z axis actuators for 3D printers and laser cutters.

Electrics, Electronics, and Software

In addition to the mechanical structure, a controller, motors, and motor drivers are typically employed to automate the motion of a digitally controlled machine. The drivers and the controller use electrical power to work, which is usually provided as DC (direct current) from a power supply connected to a wall outlet in AC (alternate current). The electrical power is distributed in the machine using electrical cables. Machine end effectors (e.g., a spindle, a laser, a knife, etc.), limit switches, sensors, connection interfaces, a screen, and many other accessories or options are attached to the controller, depending on the type of machine. While limit switches and sensors are placed in specific locations around the machine, the controller, power supply, and drivers are usually grouped together in a dedicated space, either integrated in the machine or in a separate electrical box. Recommendations are at the end of this section.

Cables

Cables are used to carry electricity around the machine and can be selected according to the type of signal or amount of power they need to transport.

Generally, we can identify the following cable properties:

- Number of cores – The number of individually isolated cables packed in a single one, with each core able to carry a separate signal or power line.
- Cross-section area – How thick the cable is, defining how much current the cable can carry. The larger the area, the more current it can carry.
- Isolation – Type of isolation used, defining the maximum usable voltage.

- Shielding – Either present or not and of different types, helps shield the cable against electrical noise, either coming from the cable itself or the surroundings.

There are two main cable categories, power cables and signal cables. Power cables are used to transport high current at high voltage, requiring a large cross section, while signal cables usually work with low voltages and low current and have small cross sections. Shielding is more commonly found in signal cables than power cables. To be effective, shielding should be connected to the negative of the line they are carrying. The number of cores varies depending on the amount of signals or power lines required. Length is an important factor in any cable, because the longer the cable, the higher the resistance. A high resistance on a cable (e.g., a very long or very thin cable for the application) may cause the cable to overheat in case of power cables or to weaken/lose data on the signal cable. One can find information about the amount of power or the type of signal on the device specifications sheet or directly written on it.

Figure 7-40. *Different cables, from left to right: AC cable 1 × 1.5mm^2, shielded signal/data cable 8 × 0.34mm^2, motor power cable 4 × 0.5mm^2, AC cable 3 × 1.5mm^2 (Daniele Ingrassia)*

Power Supplies

A power supply is normally used to convert AC to DC, in order to power the machine electronics, such as the controller, the motor drivers, sensors, etc. You can select a power supply according to the power needs of your electronics, which, in many cases, are mainly driven by the power required for the motor drivers.

The typical specifications of the power supply are the following:

- Input ratings – These are normally the same as your wall power outlet and vary depending on which region of the world you are in:
    - Input voltage – Usually 110V or 220V or both
    - Input frequency – Usually 50Hz or 60Hz or both
    - Input current – Not always specified
- Output ratings – Typically DC values that match the power requirements of your electronics:
    - Output voltage – For example, 12V, 24V, 48V, etc. Must match the voltage required by your electronics.
    - Output current – For example, 5A, 10A, etc. Must exceed the current needs of your electronics. The more it exceeds, the less stress on the internal elements of the power supply, ensuring longer life.

Figure 7-41. *Power supplies of different form factors (Daniele Ingrassia)*

In case you need to power different devices with different voltages, for example, the controller at 5V and the motor drivers at 24V, you can either use two different power supplies, one with an output of 5V and another one for 24V. Or you select a 24V power supply and use a voltage step-down converter, which converts 24V to 5V. Similar to power supplies, DC-DC step-down converters have output voltage and current ratings, with the difference that they take DC input instead of AC. Dimensions of power-supplying devices are proportional to electrical power, with the most powerful devices usually being the largest.

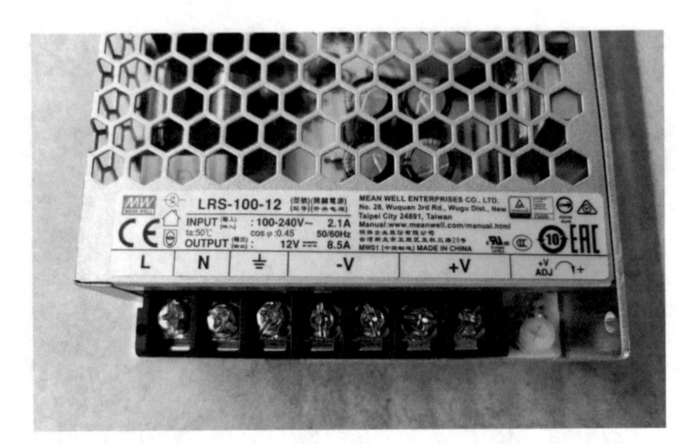

***Figure 7-42.** Details of the power supply specification label (Daniele Ingrassia)*

Controllers

A machine controller is an electronic device that implements the machine control. It is normally used to convert G-code commands into automatic movements and to manage the machine functions (e.g., control a laser or a spindle, perform the homing, etc.). Different types of controllers exist specifically designed for different types of machines, such as laser controllers, 3D printer controllers, etc. In simpler machines, the controller usually consists of a PCB hosting a microcontroller, input and output connections, and integrated components to drive other machine devices (e.g., a screen). In this form the microcontroller, an embedded computer in a small chip form factor, performs all the operations to implement the machine functions. This type of controllers typically read the G-code from the user computer connected to the machine or from an SD card interface. More complex machines can also employ the use of a compact or industrial computer. The computer is used to give the user a more complex interface and to calculate advanced machine motion, and it is paired with a microcontroller that generates all the low-level signals required to apply the motion. In both the preceding cases, the microcontroller also generates the required signal for the machine-specific end effector. Controllers also manage the interface with the user using the machine. The interface can either be physical or offered via network (e.g., Wi-Fi or LAN). Many controllers nowadays support touchscreen and Wi-Fi. Some controllers have integrated motor drivers in the same PCB reducing the space required for the electronics, but mostly only able to drive small-size motors. Standard controller boards or single-board computers can be sometimes used as controllers, either as they are or with an additional shield or adapter board.

Figure 7-43. *Controllers, from left to right: a single-board computer (Raspberry Pi), a 3D printer controller, a laser controller (Daniele Ingrassia)*

Motors and Motor Drivers

Motor drivers are used to control the machine motors. Different types of motors exist, also with different specifications for the same motor type. The drivers are chosen according to the type of motor used and also to the motor specifications. In digitally controlled machines, motors that can precisely control their motion are used, and thus drivers for those are selected.

***Figure 7-44.** Stepper motor drivers, from left to right: A4988 (top) and DRV8825 (bottom, both best suited for Nema 17 motors), TB6600, and DM556 (Daniele Ingrassia)*

The most common type of driver is a stepper motor driver. This type of drivers require DC voltage to the powered and can be set up for a range of stepper motor types. Stepper motors are DC electrical motors that move the shaft in a number of steps. These motors normally have 200 (1.8 degrees) or 400 steps (0.9 degrees). A stepper driver can drive a stepper motor in microstepping by subdividing the control signal in smaller voltage step variations. As the name suggests, microstepping is small steps and allows the stepper motor to increase the number of steps for revolution in multiples of the steps possible. Without microstepping, a stepper motor works in full step mode. Given the same transmission ratio and increasing the microstepping, the motion resolution increases accordingly. Common microstepping modes are 1/8, 1/16, and 1/32, giving, respectively, 1600, 3200, and 6400 steps for revolution in case of a 200 steps per revolution stepper motor. While increasing the microstepping increases the resolution, the motor maximum speed and torque decrease, reducing overall motor performance. Too high microstepping can also cause the motor to lose accuracy. A stepper motor driver can adjust the maximum current according to required motor current. Stepper motor driver settings are usually applied using dip switches or can even be set up by software. Controllers interface with stepper drivers usually using STEP, DIR, and ENABLE signals. The STEP signal sends the number of steps to move and at what speed. The ENABLE signal is used to enable or disable the motors (if a motor is enabled, it holds the shaft in position). The DIR signal defines the direction of rotation, clockwise or counterclockwise. More advanced drivers offer to communicate to controllers via network protocols, allowing the change on the fly of the parameters. Stepper motors are sold in standard NEMA sizes, defining the cross-section dimensions and mounting hole positions. Each stepper motor has a torque rating and can be configured with different shaft sizes or types. Normally, the larger the motor, the more torque available. Some types of stepper motors and drivers offer closed-loop control, meaning that an encoder is constantly checking that position corresponds to the wanted one from the G-code.

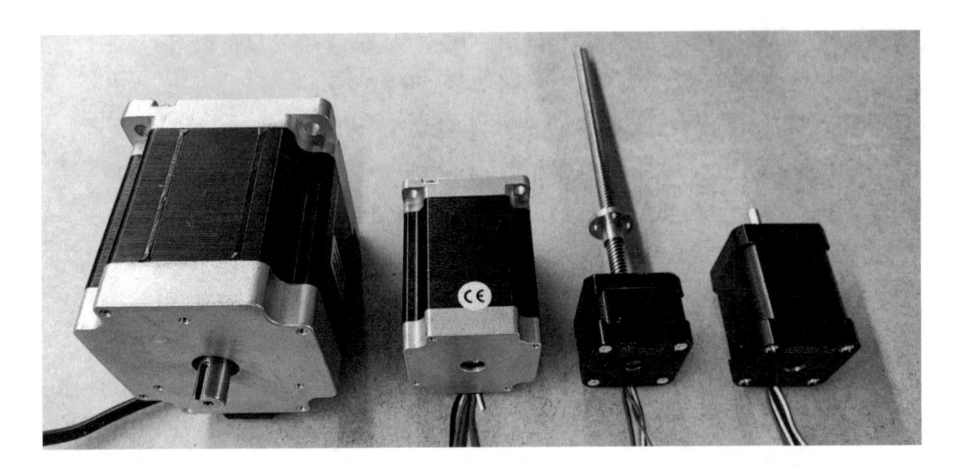

Figure 7-45. *Stepper motors, from left to right: Nema 17, Nema 17 with integrated lead screw, Nema 23, Nema 34 dual shaft (Daniele Ingrassia)*

Sensors

Depending on the type of machine, sensors can be selected for different reasons and usage. Limit switches, used to safely stop the machine motion when going out of the motion range, are a typical example of sensor usage. Limit switches, sometimes also called endstops, are most commonly a mechanical switch or inductive probes (only for metal parts). Other types of endstop exist, for example, using optical sensors, capacitive sensors, hall effect sensors, infrared sensors, etc. 3D printers use different types of sensor for the automatic bed levelling, with sensor types similar to ones used in the endstops, but with the difference of being very precise in detecting the bed distance. Different sensors have different connection, power, and output signal requirements. Make sure that your controller, firmware, and power are compatible with the used sensors. Each sensor has pros and cons, for example, mechanical switches are cheap and easy, while they do not give a high accuracy and require physical touch of the part. Inductive probes can sense a piece of metal without touching it, but can't work with non-metal materials and require higher voltage than usually controllers work with to operate. Be sure to evaluate sensor accuracy and requirements beforehand to match your machine needs.

Figure 7-46. *Sensors, from left to right: a tool length sensor for a CNC milling machine, an inductive probe, a microswitch (Daniele Ingrassia)*

How to Choose the Electronics for Your Machine

When working with cables, one should always check the ratings given by the manufacturer to check if the voltage and the current required match your use. Normally signal cables are thin, while power cables are thick because of the higher current. We recommend cables with shielding for signal cables close to motor cables, inside a CO_2 laser cutter using a glass pipe with very high (and noisy) voltage, and motor cables, which are usually very noisy.

The choice of motors and motor drivers depends on different factors, mainly, the torque and the speed required, the weight, and the space available. For desktop-size 3D printers and laser cutters, we recommend Nema 17 stepper motors. For CNC milling machines and larger 3D printers and laser cutters, we would opt for large Nema 23 or 24 stepper motors. In every case it is important to check the motor and the shaft dimensions for proper mounting and coupling into your machine.

When supported by your controller, we recommend non-contact endstops for durability and reliability. The controller choice depends on the type of machine, with ready-made 3D printer controllers, laser controllers, and CNC milling controllers. If you go with open source firmware, we recommend controllers supporting Marlin or Klipper for 3D printers and grbl or grbl-hal for CNC milling machines and laser cutters.

Good luck and may the force be with you.

CHAPTER 8

Safety and Space Setup

It's very important to keep your machines in good shape, which can be a challenge if your space has many different users. Both security and good maintenance start with informing all your users and everyone working with the machines to follow some basic rules and to talk to people about their responsibility when using the tools. People who consider your makerspace to be a collection of machines to rent and that you'll clean up after them are not going to make sure the machines stay in good shape.

If you want to create a collaborative space, make sure to explain to all users they are responsible for the space and its tools!

This chapter lists some of the important elements to consider when creating a new Fab Lab or makerspace and offers some tips on how to deal with those topics. We cannot offer detailed information on all of these subjects, because rules and regulations are different depending on the country, region, and context in which you create the space (i.e., in your personal garage vs. in a college or school).

Check with your local officials (government, police, firefighters, etc.) to understand and implement the correct rules for the space you will be operating in!

J-m. Molenaar and D. Ingrassia, *Mastering Digitally Controlled Machines*, Maker Innovations Series, https://doi.org/10.1007/978-1-4842-9849-7_8

Layout

When creating the layout for your future space, there are a few important elements to consider.

First of all, you need to make sure there is enough space around the machines to safely operate them, but also to evacuate the space quickly if the need arises. Small spaces can house quite a lot of machines if you place them in a smart way – 3D printers can be stacked, and vinyl cutters can be on top of the storage for the materials and consumables.

Another element to think about is flow – or how people move around in your space. Make sure the consumables for the laser cutter are not in the path of someone standing in front of the CNC mill or that you need to wait for people to finish using some power tools if you need a handful of screws. More complex is thinking about larger groups – will you be welcoming school classes in your space? Make sure there is ample space around machines to safely tour the room(s) and have enough room for curious young learners to cluster around the laser cutter, without accidentally pushing the off button for the fume extractor.

Also, think about the materials that are used with certain machines. Large CNC mills used for milling wood and plastics should not be close to tools used for metalworking (even power tools like angle grinders), and spaces for working with chemicals (e.g., composites for making skateboards) are best not situated next to a machine or somewhere with a lot of people working without masks and protection.

Lastly, many of the machines in a lab make quite a lot of noise ... Even five 3D printers running at full speed can be annoying if you are trying to have a meeting or if you want to focus on that small electronic circuit you are soldering.

Electrical

When it comes to the electrical installation, it's always best to hire a local technician, go over all the machines and tools you will install, and have them make sure your installation is correctly set up to handle the different loads.

It's good practice to be able to switch off power to machines individually, in case you need to work on them and want the rest of the lab to stay operational. Additionally, some labs cut off power to more dangerous tools while leaving others on, during moments users are "alone" in the lab.

Laser cutters are sensitive to power fluctuations, and the lifespan of a laser tube will be shortened significantly if you cut off power to it in the middle of a job – think about installing a UPS (uninterrupted power supply) if your location has regular power cuts. Think of these systems as very large batteries that charge themselves when power is on and take over if there is a power cut. If you have the budget for it, it's also useful to add these to any 3D printers you might have, so they can continue to function in case of a power loss.

Larger tools might need a different voltage than what you have available. In the United States (where 110V is the standard in homes), many workshops will have 208 volts available as well. Some machines, though, require 240 or even 460 volts. Make sure to check this before purchasing a machine.

Similarly, most smaller machines will run off single-phase power (110 or 220), meaning you have two wires and a ground. Some larger tools need three-phase power, which is three wires, plus a neutral. Again, check what the machine you want needs and whether or not your space can provide it.

Waste Disposal

How to separate trash may depend on the city or country where you're in, but at least some distinctions are basically the same for all shop floors having machines. When it comes to metals, it is common to separate aluminum chips (from CNC milling) and scrap parts from other metals. Aluminum can most likely be directly sold to metal collection centers giving you some money back. Other metals can be mixed and also brought to centers or sold as scrap metal.

Machine oils and other oils are not to be disposed of in traditional trash but should be brought to the closest official waste disposal site, or sometimes you can convince your local car shop to take it. Avoid mixing metal chips with wood chips, as metal chips can still be hot and generate fire.

Usually plastic trash is just for packaging materials (e.g., food containers, cellophane) but not the large amounts of acrylic, acetal, or other plastics your lab might generate. For those one should ask the local waste disposal site or local government.

If you receive boxed shipments, you may reuse the cardboard to try out designs with the laser cutter before cutting more expensive materials.

Resin from SLA or DLP 3D printers must be disposed of as special trash and whenever possible should be disposed of only when fully cured (you can let it cure with the sun a little bit before trashing it).

Air Handling

Many vendors will tell you their filters are so amazingly awesome that they really filter out all the bad particles in the air from your laser or other machines, so you can expel the air right back into your space.

Our advice would be to take this with a grain of salt and expel the air outside. It is very important to use a proper filter, after which the air should still go outside of your space.

For laser cutters, we advise adding a pre-filter to your extraction unit, which can contain simple insulation material, to catch larger elements and particles. After that, a HEPA filter is recommended, even though they are quite expensive and need to be changed regularly.

People often underestimate the amount of particles released in the air by 3D printers. When printing with thermoplastics, quite a lot of small particles are released into the air, and if breathed in on a regular basis, these can cause harm.

The best solution to this is to place all 3D printers you have in a separate air-controlled space or to add (transparent) boxes around all of them, which have air handling connected to them (so filter and then outside).

Floor Types/Load

Some machines, especially metal milling machines, can be quite heavy and require floors able to support their weight. It is therefore a good idea to inform yourself about the load capabilities (measured in weight per area) before placing a specific machine. If the floor cannot support the weight, it is sometimes possible to purchase loading plates that extend the load to a larger area, thus allowing lower floor load ratings. A wooden floor is also not recommended with heavy machinery.

Additionally, Fab Labs tend to be messy spaces, and users will drop stuff on the floor from time to time. Having a floor that withstands heavy objects falling on it (think hammers, corners of large sheets of material) without creating a hole or a dent is a must. You will most likely end up with chemicals (resins) and paint on the floor in some of the areas. Either set up those spaces with separate protection, or simply make sure all your flooring is okay with that.

Makerspaces should be somewhat messy, but it's better if it is easy to clean up!

Fire? What to Do?

Fire! We have had it happen, and it won't be the last time a machine burns down and perhaps even takes a building with it.

First rule of make club: DO NOT LEAVE THE LASER CUTTER ALONE.

But there may be other elements in a space that cause a fire – sparks from metal cutting, overheating 3D printer nozzles that get in touch with chemicals used for better bed adhesion, or embers from too hot CNC tooling getting sucked into the dust collector (yes, we also had that one happen, and no, it was not pretty).

Before you start to use any machine, you should do a few things:

- Make sure you have fire extinguishers, which are checked and easy to find, for ALL possible kinds of fire: electrical, liquid, etc.
- Have emergency exit routes clearly marked and free of obstacles.
- Train those responsible for the space what to do in case of a fire.
- Make sure people who use a machine know how to do so correctly.
- Separate machines and tools from flammable materials (no welding in the wood shop).
- Have proper insurance.

As mentioned, many different elements can cause a fire, but as long as you don't use metal grinders in your wood cutting space, risk is limited. The best way to deal with fire is to not have it happen, so include a moment to talk about risk and mitigation in ALL training sessions you organize.

There are different fire extinguishers for different types of fire, as you can see in Figure 8-1. You should make sure to have at least one CO_2 extinguisher next to your laser cutter, but also a powder-based extinguisher somewhere else in the space, which is not close to the laser and clearly labeled to not be used on the machine.

Fire Extinguisher Type

Fire Type		Powder	Foam	CO²	Water	Wet Chemical
CLASS A	Solids (e.g. wood, plastic, paper)	✓	✓	✗	✓	✗
CLASS B	Flammable Liquids (e.g. solvents, paint, fuels)	✓	✓	✓	✗	✗
CLASS C	Gases (e.g. butane, propane, LPG)	✓	✗	✗	✗	✗
CLASS D	Metals (e.g. lithium, magnesium)	✓	✗	✗	✗	✗
ELECTRICAL	Equipment (e.g. computers, servers, TVs)	✓	✗	✓	✗	✗
CLASS F	Cooking Oils (e.g. cooking fat, olive oil)	✗	✗	✗	✗	✓

Figure 8-1. *Fire extinguisher types*

You should also have one or several fire blankets in the space, which can be used to cover a machine when there is a fire or materials or even a person, might that need arise.

We hope you will never encounter a situation where you need these items or this knowledge, but with many users and busy makerspaces, these risks are always present. It's better to be properly prepared and ready than to find out too late what you would have needed.

Lastly, most fire departments are more than happy to swing by your space and review your situation. Yes, they will be harsh if you are not set up right, but better a slap on the wrist than a burned-down makerspace.

Insurance

We obviously cannot tell you exactly what insurance to get, as this changes per country and situation. Some countries do offer shared insurance for makerspaces (like Germany and France), while others simply share knowledge about the best options – do check with other makerspaces in the area or in your country how they set it up.

First of all, make sure you and your users are insured. Many spaces offer the option to become part of the organization of the lab in an official way, allowing you to include them in a general insurance. If you cannot do that, another option is to explain to people their options and have them sign a waiver – making sure you are covered if somehow they did not get proper insurance.

Second, you want to make sure you and your tools are insured against any kind of fire or damage caused not by human intervention.

When looking around for insurance options, make sure to ask what the regulations are – you might very well not be paid out in case of a problem if your space was not correctly set up or if, for instance, you did not have the right fire extinguisher next to the machines.

Labeling/Signs

Labs can become messy and full of enthusiastic people making all sorts of wonderful things. Labeling and proper signs can help with multiple elements of running a successful and fun makerspace.

Mark where tools are supposed to be – so no one can tell you they "didn't know where to clean it up" – and even mark some of the tools, so people know they belong to the space ("Oh, that's not my box cutter?").

Mark storage for hazardous materials and potentially dangerous tools – you don't want to mix your resins for 3D printing with those used in composites.

Add floor marks indicating safe and proper distance from certain tools – it's much easier to enforce people to keep proper distance from a running CNC mill if there are clear markings around it.

Add reminders above and around machines – don't leave the laser alone when it's running! Wear proper ear protection when using the CNC mill! Never use the lathe when you are alone in the lab! And son. Be creative, and make it look nice, but serious enough to remind people of the important rules of the space.

Label your machines. Many Fab Labs are visited by new people who want to learn about the machines and their possibilities. Next to advising them to read this book, it's a great help to add signs showing what machines are and do. Yes, YOU know what a 3D printer is, but most people still don't!

PPE

We recommend having a range of personal protection equipment (or PPE) available in your space, depending on the machines you have.

This should be available for any user of the space and explained during training sessions. Check the equipment regularly, because masks to use with chemicals that are beyond their lifespan and gloves with holes are not going to help you maintain your space and its users.

Here's PPE per machine/process (elements not listed do not require PPE):

Laser cutter – If it's "home built," make sure you have proper eye protection, which means glasses specifically made for blocking the wavelengths from the type of laser you are using.

CNC mill – Ear protection, gloves, and eye protection. Also make sure that those with long hair either put it away in a cap or tie it up securely behind their head.

3D printing – For FDM there is no need for PPE, but resin (SLA) printers and power bed printers need gloves, respiratory protectors, and eye protection.

Molding and casting – Respiratory protection, gloves, eye protection.

Composites/layup – Respiratory protection, gloves, eye protection.

Electronics – Make sure your working tables are properly grounded.

Others – We recommend having ear protection for those sensitive to noise (even a laser cutter with air extraction can be noisy) and several sizes of gloves, for general use.

CHAPTER 9

Where to Go from Here

When computers became available in the home, it still took a while for people to see the use in their daily lives. Imagine your life without a computer today – hard to do, isn't it?

Even though advertising companies have used phrases like "everyone is a maker," in reality there are not that many makers around, but perhaps that will change. The tools to make almost anything you like are widely available and ever easier to use, but all of them still need dedication and take time to master.

The possibility to create prototypes and experiment with fabrication ourselves is clearly changing the way we work and live. Platforms like Kickstarter allow for almost anyone to start a business, however weird their ideas. But thinking that a successful crowdfunding campaign or a product that goes "viral" is a great opportunity for the ones involved, don't forget it might go too fast. A friend of mine explained how in the beginning of a well-known 3D printer company, they mostly had to focus on "damage control" – meaning the company grew so fast and so sudden that it wasn't easy to find good solutions while holding on to one of the main initial ideas, being open source. There is a huge difference between running a company with six people and running one with 60, and if you planned for fabrication (and packaging, shipping, after-sales) for 2000 products, but you need to make 200,000, your life is going to be messy.

The original version of the chapter was revised. A correction to this chapter can be found at https://doi.org/10.1007/978-1-4842-9849-7_10

J-m. Molenaar and D. Ingrassia, *Mastering Digitally Controlled Machines*, Maker Innovations Series, https://doi.org/10.1007/978-1-4842-9849-7_9

And it's not only fabrication that is changing rapidly. Ever more powerful computing is available in our homes and our pockets; synthetic biology is changing the way we create medication, fuel, food, and perhaps one day even products; and strong AI is just around the corner, or already here, depending on whom you speak to. The world is bright and exciting in many ways, but also often filled with pain and suffering. Learning new skills, which were not long ago only available if you went to a university, can be rewarding not only for you but also for people who do not have the luxury of being able to buy what they need, if you apply them to better the world around you.

Developing Ideas, Projects, and Business

If you have been making things for a while and you reach the stage where your objects (be it speakers, skateboards, smart home devices, or whatever) no longer look like prototypes, you might start to wonder if you could start a business. Or perhaps you have a great idea and realize you could prototype the electronics yourself and feasibly create a super-cool product you can market.

There are resources online that can help you navigate the complex environment of fabrication, find funds for a startup, or accelerate your company. The best way to start is to try and find communities of people who do (or have done) things like you want to do and quiz them. How did it start? What went wrong? Do they regret learning some things only at the end? Are you the kind of person for this project?

If you really think you are ready to get your product on the market, check out what companies offer solutions for your type of idea. You can find companies called **accelerators**, which offer programs with planned end dates and basically will try to grow your company as fast as possible to get ready for the first round of seed money or VC (venture capitalist) money (see Figure 9-1), or **incubators**, which often do not have an end date and try and help you become successful at a speed that's right for you and your project.

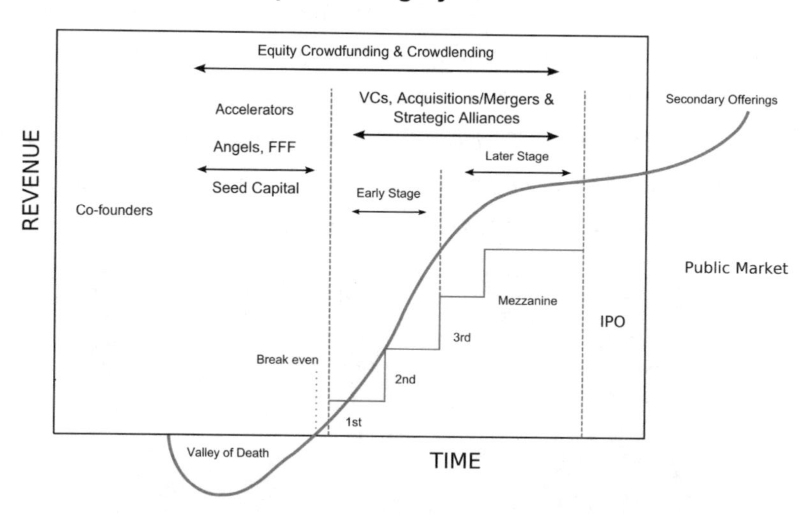

Figure 9-1. *Startup financing cycle (`https://upload.wikimedia.org/wikipedia/commons/thumb/8/8e/Startup_financing_cycle.svg/2000px-Startup_financing_cycle.svg.png`)*

These services are not free (duh), and there are different models that are offered. Read up on VCs; first-, second-, and third-round funding; equity; angel investors; and crowdfunding solutions before diving into the world of being an entrepreneur.

So got all the entrepreneurial mumbo jumbo and you are ready for the ride? The perhaps best-known accelerator for hardware is HAX, based in Shenzhen, China (where you most likely will end up anyway if you go the current way of fabricating large volumes). But they are by no means the only one. You can reach out to NextFab, Make in LA, AlphaLab Gear, Techstars, Y Combinator, ReadWrite Labs, PNP IOT, Usine.io, Ecomachines, Lemnos Labs, Hardware.co, R/GA Accelerator, PCH Highway 1, Alchemist Accelerator, Industrio, Buildit, and many more.

If you are the "self-made" type of person, you can of course also fly to Shenzhen (or a closer-by place with a factory) and try to make a deal for fabrication of your product in large volumes.

Shenzhen is a truly amazing place if you like building stuff and has literally everything you might need. Fifty thousand resistors? One hundred thousand LEDs? You can just pull them off the shelf and walk back to the hotel. Andrew Huang, better known as Bunny, has compiled a great handbook for going there. *The Essential Guide to Electronics in Shenzhen* has translations for anything you might need, as well as maps and guides; it will help you navigate the immense markets and options.

Figure 9-2. *Shenzen's Hua Qiang market – LEDs by the millions (photo by JMM)*

Resources and Discussion

If you are already making things or you are just starting out to use the tools and techniques discussed in this book, you are not alone. There are myriads of forums and online platforms where people share ideas and how-to's, and almost every major city has at least one Fab Lab, makerspace, hackerspace, or open workshop of some kind.

Some of these are part of global networks, like the Fab Lab Network. All of them will be filled with people who will be happy to share their knowledge with you.

If you really want to become a master of all that is digital fabrication, check out the Fab Academy. Spun out from an MIT course (that is still running each fall semester), it's a globally distributed series of classes taught by Professor Neil Gershenfeld via video conference, which you can follow in hundreds of Fab Labs across the globe. Classes range from laser cutting, 3D printing, CNC milling, and vinyl cutting to making electronics and programming, molding and casting, composite materials, and much more.

Next to open makerspaces, you will be able to find educational resources such as the Fab Academy. You should also check when the next and closest Maker Faire or similar event is organized. These events group makers of all ages and skills and are filled with amazing projects that will inspire and often thrill you!

What's Next

We are at the end of the book, so what's next? If you enjoyed the book, this is only the beginning - there is much to learn (even if you already know a lot) and much to build.

Don't hesitate to spend a decent amount of time getting proficient with one or more CAD and CAM programs (see a list in the annex for choices) and hanging around Fab Labs and hackerspaces in your surroundings. There are many websites with cool example projects, and trying some of those will greatly improve your skills.

Correction to: Where to Go from Here

Correction to:

Chapter 9 in: J-m. Molenaar and D. Ingrassia, *Mastering Digitally Controlled Machines*, Maker Innovations Series
https://doi.org/10.1007/978-1-4842-9849-7_9

The original version of Chapter 9 was inadvertently published with the Google Sheet link at the end of the chapter. It has been removed from all renditions.

The updated version of this chapter can be found at
https://doi.org/10.1007/978-1-4842-9849-7_9

J-m. Molenaar and D. Ingrassia, *Mastering Digitally Controlled Machines*,
Maker Innovations Series, https://doi.org/10.1007/978-1-4842-9849-7_10

Annexes

1 - Machine capabilities

machine	capabilities	materials	Additional needs
CO2 or Diode Laser Cutter	2D	**Cutting:** wood and derivatives, (some) plastics, cardboard, paper **Engraving:** glass, ceramics, stone, some metals (depending on the laser)	Compressed air, filter and/or turbine for extraction of fumes
CNC mill	2D and 3D	**Cutting:** wood and derivatives, plastics, some metals, composites **Engraving:** glass, ceramics, stone	dust collection
Vinyl Cutter	2D	plastics, paper, copper tape	none
3D printers	3D	Nylon, PLA, ABS, Resin, Gypsum, Gold, Silver, stainless steel, Titanium, paper	proper ventilation

J-m. Molenaar and D. Ingrassia, *Mastering Digitally Controlled Machines*, Maker Innovations Series, https://doi.org/10.1007/978-1-4842-9849-7

2 - Software

3D Modeling Software	Type	Recommended for	Level	License	Operating System
3D Slash	3D Modeling, CAD	Quick creation of simple 3D model online.	Beginner	Free (basic) / Monthly fee	All, Web Browser
AgiliCity Modelur	SketchUp plugin	Urban agglomeration design	Intermediate	Commercial	Windows, Mac
Autodesk AutoCAD	Drafting, CAD	2D sketching, 2D/3D CAD	Professional	Commercial	Windows, Mac, Android, Browser
Autodesk Inventor	CAD	Mechanical 3D modeling, Parametric Design, Product Design, Simulation, CAM	Professional	Commercial	Windows
Blender	3D Modeling	3D Design, Animations and Visual Effects, Rendering	Professional	Open Source	All
Bricsys BricsCAD	CAD	2D/3D Parametric CAD, Building Information Modeling	Professional	Commercial	All

(*continued*)

3D Modeling Software	Type	Recommended for	Level	License	Operating System
BRL-CAD	3D Modeling, CAD	Ballistic and Electromagnetic analysis	Professional	Open Source	All
C3D	Modeling toolkit	3D CAD, CAM, Computer Aided Engineering	Professional	Commercial	All
Cobalt	3D Modeling, CAD	Product Design	Professional	Commercial	Windows, Mac
CATIA	CAD	3D CAD, CAM, Computer Aided Engineering	Professional	Commercial	Windows
SolidWorks	CAD	Mechanical 3D modeling, Parametric Design, Product Design, Simulation	Professional	Commercial	Windows
FreeCAD	CAD	Mechanical 3D modeling, Parametric Design, Product Design, Simulation, CAM	Intermediate	Open Source	All

(continued)

3D Modeling Software	Type	Recommended for	Level	License	Operating System
Fusion 360	3D Modeling, CAD, CAM	Mechanical 3D modeling, Parametric Design, Product Design, Simulation, PCB design, CAM	Beginner	Free for educators and hobbists / Commercial yearly fee	Windows, Mac
IronCAD	CAD	2D/3D Mechanical Design	Professional	Commercial	Windows
KeyCreator	3D Modeling, CAD	2D/3D CAD	Professional	Commercial	Windows
LibreCAD	CAD	2D CAD and Sketching	Intermediate	Open Source	All
NanoCAD	Drafting, CAD	2D/3D Mechanical Design	Intermediate	Commercial Yearly Fees	Windows
Onshape	3D Modeling, CAD	Mechanical 3D modeling, Parametric Design, Product Design	Professional	Free (basic) / Commercial Yearly Fees	Web Browser

(continued)

3D Modeling Software	Type	Recommended for	Level	License	Operating System
OpenSCAD	CAD	Scripted 3D CAD	Intermediate	Free	All
ProgeCAD	CAD		Professional	Commercial	Windows
PTC Creo (formerly Pro/ ENGINEER)	CAD, CAM		Professional	Commercial	Windows
PunchCAD	CAD		Intermediate	Commercial	Windows, Mac
QCad	Drafting, 2D		Intermediate	Free	All
Rhinoceros 3D	3D Modeling, CAD	2D/3D CAD, Parametric Design, Architectural Drawings, Industrial Design	Professional	Commercial	Windows, Mac
RoutCad	CAD, CAM		Professional	Commercial	Windows
Sculptris	3D Modeling, CAD		Beginner	Free	Windows, Mac
ShapeManager by Autodesk	3D Modeling kernel		Professional	Commercial	n/a

(continued)

3D Modeling Software	Type	Recommended for	Level	License	Operating System
Siemens NX	CAD, CAM, CEA, PLM		Professional	Commercial	Windows, Mac, UNIX-like
Siemens Solid Edge	CAD		Professional	Commercial	Windows
SketchUp	3D Modeling, CAD		Intermediate	Free	All
SpaceClaim	CAD		Professional	Commercial	Windows
TinkerCAD	3D Modeling, CAD		Beginner	Free	Web Browser
TurboCAD	CAD		Professional	Commercial	Windows, Mac
VariCAD	CAD	2D/3D Mechanical CAD	Professional	Commercial	Windows, Linux
VectorWorks	CAD	Depending on package, for Architecs, Landmarks, Spolight	Professional	Commercial	Windows, Mac

File viewers / conversion	Function	Level	Price	System
Netfabb	Slicer, STL Checker, STL Repair	Intermediate	Free / $225 per year	All
3D-Tool Free Viewer	STL Viewer, STL Checker	Intermediate	Free	Windows
MakePrintable	STL Checker, STL Repair	Intermediate	Free	Web Browser
MeshLab	STL Editor, STL Repair	Professional	Free	All
Meshmixer	STL Checker, STL Repair, STL Editor	Professional	Free	Windows, Mac

3D printer software / Slicers	Function	Level	Price	System	Link
Cura	Slicer, 3D Printer Host	Beginner	Free	All	**https://ultimaker.com/en/products/ultimaker-cura-software**
CraftWare	Slicer, 3D Printer Host	Beginner	Free	Windows, Mac	https://craftunique.com/craftware/
KISSlicer	Slicer	Beginner	Free /$25 /$35	All, Raspberry Pie	http://www.kisslicer.com/index.html
MatterControl	Slicer, 3D Printer Host	Beginner	Free	All	https://www.matterhackers.com/store/l/mattercontrol/sk/MKZGTDW6
Repetier	Slicer, 3D Printer Host	Intermediate	Free	All	https://www.repetier.com/
Slic3r	Slicer	Professional	Free	All	http://slic3r.org/

OctoPrint	3D Printer Host	Professional	Free	All	http://octoprint.org/
		^ High = have to build/compile/program - intermediate = have to install (plugin etc.)			

CAM	Function	Difficulty	Price	System / Language	Link
This list is not complete - but shows some free CAM software available. There are many commercially availabe programs, ranging from hundreds to thousands of euro's in cost.					
cncOnline	2D CAM	High	Free	Python	**https://github.com/hugomatic/hugomatic**
ACE Converter	2D DXF to g-code	High	Free	Windows	http://www.dakeng.com/ace.html
Aptos	3D CAM	High	Free	Linux	https://sourceforge.net/projects/aptos/
Blender CAM	CAM plugin for Blender	Intermediate	Free	All	http://blendercam.blogspot.com/
CamBam	2.5D CAM	High	Free	Linux	http://www.cambam.info/ref/ref.linux/

CAMVOX	3D CAM	High	Free	All	http://camvox.sourceforge.net/
dxf2gcode	2D CAM	High	Free	All	https://sourceforge.net/projects/dxf2gcode/?source=navbar
HeeksCNC	3D CAM	Intermediate	Free	Windows	https://code.google.com/archive/p/heekscnc/

Machine control	Function	Difficulty	Price	System	Link
This is list not complete - but shows some free or low cost Machine controll software. There are many commercially available programs, in various price ranges.					
TurboCNC	Up to 8 axis	High	60$	Windows / DOS	https://www.turbocnc.co.uk/
LinuxCNC	Up to 9 axis	High	Free	Linux	https://linuxcnc.org/
MACH 4	Up to 6 axis	High	200$	Windows	http://www.machsupport.com/software/mach4/
CNC Zeus	Up to 4 axis	High	Free	DOS	https://github.com/lumen0/cnczeus
UGS	3 Axis	High	Free	All	https://winder.github.io/ugs_website/

3 - File formats

Neutral Formats	Standards/ Users	File extensions	Geometry type	Parts	BOM	Color
IGES	ANSI, ASME	IGS, IGES	Precise (Brep)	Single	Yes	Yes
JT	Siemens PLM, ISO	JT	Either or Both	Multiple	Yes	Yes
Parasolid	Siemens PLM	X_B, X_T, XMT, XMT_ TXT	Precise (Brep)	Single	Yes	Yes
PRC	Tech Soft	PCR	Precise (Brep)	Single	Yes	Yes
STEP	ISO	STP, STEP	Either or Both	Multiple	Yes	Yes
Stereolithography	3D printing	STL	Tessellated (Mesh)	Single	No	No
Universal 3D	ECMA	U3D	Tessellated (Mesh)	Single	No	Yes
VRML	Web3D, ISO	WRL, VRML	Tessellated (Mesh)	Single	Yes	Yes

(continued)

Proprietary Formats	Vendor	File extensions	Geometry type	Parts	BOM	Color
Inventor	Autodesk	IPT, IAM	Both	Multiple	Yes	Yes
CATIA V5 & V6	Dassault Systems	CATPART, CATPRODUCT	Both	Multiple	Yes	Yes
CATIA V5 & V6	Dassault Systems	3DXML, CGR	Tessellated (Mesh)	Single	Yes	Yes
Pro/ENGINEER/ Creo	PTC	ASM, NEU, PRT, XAS, XPR	Both	Multiple	Yes	Yes
I-DEAS	Siemens PLM	MF1, ARC, UNV, PKG	Both	Multiple	Yes	Yes
NX	Siemens PLM	PRT	Both	Multiple	Yes	Yes
Solid Edge	Siemens PLM	ASM, PAR, PWD, PSM	Both	Multiple	Yes	Yes
Solidworks	DS Solidworks	SLDASM, SLDPART	Both	Multiple	Yes	Yes

4 - Materials for laser cutting

Materials you cannot cut with a laser cutter	
Name	**reason to not cut it**
Any material containing chlorine	*bad for the optics and for you*
Carbon fiber	resin produces bad fumes
Fiberglass	resin produces bad fumes
Glass	can be engraved, not cut
High-density polyethylene (HDPE) thicker than 1.5mm	melts
Polycarbonate (PC, Lexan)	creates a lot of fumes
Printed circuit board (FR4 and other material types)	resin produces bad fumes
PVC	contains chlorine
Vinyl	contains chlorine

Materials you can cut with a lasercutter	
Name	**notes**
ABS (acrylonitrile butadiene styrene)	
Acrylic (also known as Plexiglas, Lucite, PMMA)	
Carbon fiber matswihtout epoxy	cut very slowly
Cork	
Coroplast ('corrugated plastic')	
Cotton	
Polyoxymethylene (POM) (Delrin, acetal)	
Depron foam (polystyrene sheet)	

(*continued*)

Materials you can cut with a lasercutter

Name	**notes**
Gator foam (polystyrene sheet)	foam core can melt
Felt	
Hemp	
High density polyethylene (HDPE)	only <1.5mm! melts if thick
Kapton tape (Polyimide)	
Leather / suede	
Magnetic sheets	
Polyester (Mylar)	
Nylon	melts if thick
Paper / cardboard	
PETG (polyethylene terephthalate glycol)	
Rubbers	if it doesn't contain chloride!!
Solid Styrene	only if thin, lots of smoke
Polytetrafluoroethylene (PTFE, Teflon)	
Thin Polycarbonate Sheeting (<1mm)	only very thin material will work
Wood (plywood, MDF, natural woods...)	

Materials you can engrave with a laser cutter	
Name	**notes**
Glass	will look sandblasted
Ceramic tile	will look sandblasted
Anodized aluminum	Laser ething removes the anodization
Painted/coated metals	Laser etching removes the paint
Stone, Marble, Granite, Soapstone, Onyx.	will look sandblasted

3D printer materials

FDM printers

MATERIAL	FEATURES	APPLICATIONS
ABS (acrylonitrile butadiene styrene)	Tough and durableHeat and impact resistantRequires a heated bed to printRequires ventilation	Functional prototypes
PLA (polylactic acid)	The easiest FDM materials to printRigid, strong, but brittleLess resistant to heat and chemicalsBiodegradableOdorless	Concept modelsLooks-like prototypes
PETG (polyethylene terephthalate glycol)	Compatible with lower printing temperatures for faster productionHumidity and chemical resistantHigh transparencyCan be food safe	Waterproof applicationsSnap-fit components
Nylon	Strong, durable, and lightweightTough and partially flexibleHeat and impact resistantVery complex to print on FDM	Functional prototypesWear resistant parts
TPU (thermoplastic polyurethane)	Flexible and stretchableImpact resistantExcellent vibration dampening	Flexible prototypes
PVA (polyvinyl alcohol)	Soluble support materialDissolves in water	Support material
HIPS (high impact polystyrene)	Soluble support material most commonly used with ABSDissolves in chemical limonene	Support material
Composites (carbon fiber, kevlar, fiberglass)	Rigid, strong, or extremely toughCompatibility limited to some expensive industrial FDM 3D printers	Functional prototypesJigs, fixtures, and tooling

Index

J-m. Molenaar and D. Ingrassia, *Mastering Digitally Controlled Machines*,
Maker Innovations Series, https://doi.org/10.1007/978-1-4842-9849-7

H

I, J

K

L

M

R

S

T

U

V

W, X, Y, Z

Printed in the United States
by Baker & Taylor Publisher Services